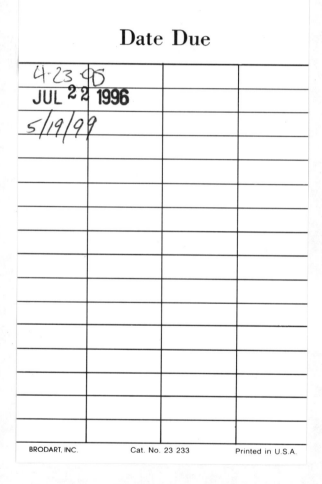

Date Due

4-23 95		
JUL 22 1996		
5/19/99		

BOND MARKETS, ANALYSIS AND STRATEGIES

BOND MARKETS, ANALYSIS AND STRATEGIES

Frank J. Fabozzi
Sloan School of Management
Massachusetts Institute of Technology

&

T. Dessa Fabozzi
Merrill Lynch Capital Markets

Prentice Hall, Englewood Cliffs, NJ 07632

Library of Congress Cataloging-in-Publication Data

Fabozzi, Frank J.
 Bond markets, analysis and strategies / Frank J. Fabozzi & T.
 Dessa Fabozzi.
   p.   cm.
 Includes index.
 ISBN 0-13-079922-X
 1. Bonds   2. Investment analysis.   3. Portfolio management.
 I. Fabozzi, T. Dessa   II. Title
HG4651.F28 1989   88-22446
332.63'23—dc19

Editorial/production supervision and
  interior design: *Susan Fisher*
Cover design: *20/20 Services, Inc.*
Manufacturing buyer: *Ed O'Dougherty*

Printed in the United States of America
10 9 8 7 6 5 4 3 2

ISBN 0-13-079922-X

Prentice-Hall International (UK) Limited, *London*
Prentice-Hall of Australia Pty. Limited, *Sydney*
Prentice-Hall Canada Inc., *Toronto*
Prentice-Hall Hispanoamericana, S.A., *Mexico*
Prentice-Hall of India Private Limited, *New Delhi*
Prentice-Hall of Japan, Inc., *Tokyo*
Simon & Schuster Asia Pte. Ltd., *Singapore*
Editora Prentice-Hall do Brasil, Ltda., *Rio de Janeiro*

To our parents

CONTENTS

PREFACE

Not many years ago, the fixed income market was comprised mainly of "plain vanilla" bonds with simple cash flow structures. Thus, valuation was relatively straightforward. The market has since progressed. Cash flow structures of securities have become increasingly complex as investment banking firms have altered the cash flow streams of bonds to attract investors and enable firms to reduce the cost of raising funds.

Many securities in the fixed income market have options embedded in them. At one time, the idea of decomposing securities into their basic components (a noncallable bond and a call option in the case of callable bonds) was considered innovative. Now this view is commonplace and investment managers focus on alternative models which may be used to price the particular option components.

The fixed income market has received increased attention from many types of investors. Within this market, an array of securities are now available and may be combined with derivative products in order to facilitate portfolio strategies designed to control interest rate risk and/or enhance yields.

Because of the increased importance of this market and the complex structure of the securities, participants must be well informed about the forces that drive the bond market and the fundamental techniques for valuing securities. Once this is mastered, portfolio strategies mentioned in this book, as well as those which develop subsequently, can be employed effectively.

The objective of *Bond Markets, Analysis and Strategies* is to provide an overview of the fixed income market. This includes coverage of the securities available in the market (Treasury securities, agency securities, corporate bonds, municipal bonds, international bonds, mortgages, and mortgage-backed securities), their investment characteristics, the latest techniques for valuing them, and portfolio strategies for using them. The book is by no means exhaustive. However, all relevant topics are covered and each chapter contains references to published books and articles on specific topics for those wishing to extend their study in a particular area.

We are indebted to a number of people who either commented on the manuscript at various stages or provided insightful discussions on some of the topics. These people include: Keith Anderson (Blackstone Financial Management), David Askin (Drexel Burnham Lambert), Anand Bhattacharya (Underwood Neuheus and Co.), John Carlson (Security Pacific), Steve Carlson (Shearson Lehman Hutton), Andrew Carron (The First Boston Corporation), Peter Christensen (Paine-Webber), Jan Dash (Merrill Lynch Capital Markets), Ravi Dattatreya (Prudential-Bache Capital Funding), Mark Dunetz (Kidder, Peabody), Howard Edelstein (Knight-Ridder MoneyCenter), Sylvan Feldstein (Merrill Lynch Capital Markets), Michael Ferri (George Mason University), Laurie Goodman (Goldman Sachs), Gerald Herman (Merrill Lynch Capital Markets), Michael Huebsch (The First Boston Corporation), Judy Hustick (Salomon Brothers), David Jacob (Morgan Stanley), Frank Jones (Barclays deZoete Wedd), Michael Kenny (Federal Home Loan Mortgage Corporation), David Kidwell (Tulane University), Thomas Klaffky (Salomon Brothers), James Kochan (Merrill Lynch Capital Markets), Peter Lambert (Western Asset Management), Linda Lowell (Drexel Burnham Lambert), K.C. Ma (Texas Tech), Robert Maddox (Merrill Lynch Capital Markets), James Mahoney (Kidder, Peabody), Matthew Mancuso (Bear Stearns), William Marshall (Franklin Savings), John McCarthy (Knight-Ridder MoneyCenter), Antonio Mello (MIT), James Meisner (Merrill Lynch Capital Markets), Robert Pari (Merrill Lynch Capital Markets), Fred Price (Bear Stearns), Larry Ng (SpectraSoft), Sharmin Mossavar-Rahmani (Fidelity Management), Chuck Ramsey (Bear Stearns), Ed Rappa (Bear Stearns),

Herman Sandler (Bear Stearns), Paul Sclafani (Nomura Securities), Dexter Senft (The First Boston Corporation), Roy Standfest (Salomon Brothers), Michael Waldman (Salomon Brothers), Richard Wilson (Merrill Lynch Capital Markets), Ben Wolkowitz (Morgan Stanley), and Yu Zhu (Merrill Lynch Capital Markets).

Portions of this manuscript were used in the Fixed Income Seminar at MIT taught by Frank Fabozzi in the Spring 1987 and Spring 1988 semesters. We wish to thank Stewart Myers, Chair of the Department of Applied Economics, Finance, and Accounting, and Richard Schmalensee, Acting Chair for the 1987–88 academic year, for allowing Frank to teach the seminar. Jean Marie DeJordy of MIT skillfully handled the administrative problems associated with this project.

Frank J. Fabozzi
T. Dessa Fabozzi

1

INTRODUCTION

A bond is an instrument in which the issuer (debtor/borrower) promises to repay to the lender/investor the amount borrowed plus interest over some specified period of time. Prior to the 1970s, a typical ("plain vanilla") bond issued in the United States would specify (1) a fixed date at which the amount borrowed (principal) is due and (2) the contractual amount of interest that would be paid every 6 months. The date on which the principal is required to be repaid is called the *maturity date*. The interest rate that the issuer agrees to pay annually on the principal is called the *coupon rate*. Assuming that the issuer does not default or redeem the issue before the maturity date, an investor who holds this bond until the maturity date would be assured of a known cash flow pattern.

The high and volatile interest rates that prevailed in the United States in the late 1970s and the early 1980s brought a wide variety of new types of "bonds" issued by corporations and municipalities designed to make them more attractive to investors. These included: (1) *zero-coupon bonds,* in which there are no periodic coupon payments, but instead the entire principal and interest are paid at the maturity date; (2) *adjustable-rate* or *floating-rate* bonds, in which the coupon payments are indexed to some financial or commodity benchmark; (3) *bonds with embedded options,* such as the option to sell ("put") the bond back to the issuer at predetermined time periods or the option to buy an additional bond; and (4) *bonds issued in the United States* in which the contractual interest payments and/or principal payments are *in a foreign currency* rather than U.S. dollars.

In the residential mortgage market new types of mortgages such as adjustable-rate mortgages and graduated-payment mortgages became commonplace. The pooling of individual mortgages to form mortgage pass-through securities increased dramatically. Using the basic instruments in the mortgage market (mortgages and mortgage pass-through securities), derivative instruments such as collateralized mortgage obligations and stripped mortgage-backed securities were created to meet the specific investment needs of a broadening range of institutional investors.

Exhibit 1.1 shows the composition of the U.S. bond market as of December 31, 1987. Of the $6.636 trillion total bond market, the largest component is by far the mortgage market. Within the mortgage market, the largest sector is the residential mortgage sector. Approximately 32% of residential mortgages have been securitized. That is, they have been pooled to create mortgage pass-through securities. The second-largest sector of the bond market is the market for U.S. government securities, while the smallest sector is the U.S. government agency market (excluding mortgage pass-through securities guaranteed by any agency).

RISKS ASSOCIATED WITH INVESTING IN BONDS

The investor in bonds may be exposed to one or more of the following risks: (1) interest rate risk; (2) reinvestment risk; (3) default risk; (4) call risk (prepayment risk in the case of mortgage-backed securities); (5) inflation risk; (6) foreign-exchange rate risk; and (7) marketability/liquidity risk. All of these risks will be discussed fully in later chapters. Here we provide a brief description of each.

Interest Rate Risk

In Chapter 2 we shall see that a bond's price moves in the opposite direction of the change in interest rates. As interest rates rise (fall), the price of a bond will fall (rise). For an investor who plans to hold a bond

EXHIBIT 1.1   Composition of the U.S. Bond Market as of December 31, 1987 (dollars in billions; based on par value)

U.S. Government Securities			$1,713	(26%)
U.S. Government Agencies (excluding agency pass-through securities)			275	(4%)
Corporate Bonds			1,023	(15%)
State and Local (Municipal) Securities			776	(12%)
Mortgages			2,849	(43%)
Residential mortgages		2,113	(32%)	
Nonsecuritized	1,432	(22%)		
Securitized (mortgage pass-throughs)	681	(10%)		
Commercial mortgages		649	(10%)	
Farm mortgages		87	(1%)	
Total of All Bond Markets			$6,636	

Source: This exhibit was prepared from data supplied by Salomon Brothers Inc.

to maturity, the change in the bond's price prior to maturity is not of concern; however, for an investor who may have to sell the bond before the maturity date, an increase in interest rates after the bond was purchased will mean the realization of a capital loss. This risk is referred to as *interest rate risk*.[1] Not all bonds have the same degree of interest rate risk. In Chapter 4 we shall demonstrate the characteristics of a bond that determine its interest rate risk and explain how to measure this risk.

Reinvestment Risk

As we explain in Chapter 3, the dollar return from investing in a bond comes from three sources: (1) coupon interest payments; (2) any capital gain (or capital loss) when the bond is redeemed, sold, or matures; and (3) interest earned from reinvesting the interim cash flows (coupon payments or principal repayments).[2] As we shall see in

---

[1]Interest rate risk is also referred to as *price risk* or *market risk*.

[2]The importance of interest earned from reinvesting the interim cash flows was first highlighted in a now-classic book by Sidney Homer and Martin L. Leibowitz, *Inside the Yield Book* (Englewood Cliffs, NJ: Prentice Hall; and New York: New York Institute of Finance, 1972).

Chapter 3, in order for an investor to realize a yield equal to the stated yield at the time the bond is purchased, these interim cash flows must be reinvested at an interest rate equal to the stated yield when the bond is purchased. The risk that interim cash flows will have to be reinvested at a lower rate such that the investor will earn a lower yield than the stated yield at the time the bond is purchased is called *reinvestment risk*.

Default Risk

Default risk, also known as *credit risk*, is the risk that the issuer will default on its contractual payments of interest and/or principal. The obligations of the U.S. government are perceived to be free of default risk. For other issuers, the risk of default is gauged by quality ratings assigned by commercial rating companies such as Moody's Investor Service, Standard & Poor's Corporation, Duff & Phelps, and Fitch Investors Service, as well as credit research staffs of dealer firms and institutional investor concerns.

Call Risk

One of the provisions in the contract between the issuer and the bondholder might be that the issuer has the right to retire or "call" all or part of the issue before the maturity date. The issuer wants this right so that if at some time in the future market interest rates decline below the coupon rate on the issue, the issuer can retire the issue and replace it with new bonds issued at a lower interest rate. Early redemption is simply the exercising of an option by the issuer to refinance debt on more favorable terms.

From the investor's perspective, there are three disadvantages of the call provision. First, the cash flow pattern of a callable bond is not known with certainty. Second, because the issuer will call the bonds when interest rates have dropped, the investor is exposed to reinvestment rate risk. That is, the investor will have to reinvest the proceeds received when the bond is called at a lower interest rate than the yield when the bond was purchased. Finally, the capital appreciation potential of a bond will be reduced. For example, when interest rates fall, the price of a bond will rise. However, because the bond may be called, the price of a callable bond may not rise much above the price the issuer will pay if the bond is called. Every callable bond indenture and prospectus specifies a call price schedule. In many instances, the price at which the issuer may call the bond is higher than the bond's face value.

Holding aside default risk, the key characteristic that distinguishes U.S. Treasury obligations, corporate bonds, municipal bonds, and mortgage-backed securities is the degree of certainty of the cash flow pattern. In the case of Treasury securities, with the exception of some outstanding Treasury bonds that are callable, the cash flow is known with certainty. Since almost all long-term corporate and municipal bonds are callable by the issuer prior to maturity, the cash flow pattern of these securities is not known with certainty. Typically, however, the issue has a provision prohibiting the issuer from calling or refunding the issue until a specified number of years after issuance. Moreover, investors generally can expect that the issuer will not call or refund an issue when the current market interest rate is greater than the issue's coupon interest rate.

Mortgage-backed securities also expose the investor to uncertainty about the timing of the cash flow because the investor has effectively granted *each* borrower/homeowner in the pool of mortgages underlying the mortgage-backed security the option to prepay part or all of the mortgage at any time. In fact, the uncertainty of the timing of the cash flow is even greater for mortgage-backed securities than for corporate and municipal bonds because exercising the option to prepay a mortgage does not depend solely on the current market interest rate. It depends also on the unique circumstances facing each homeowner (such as relocations or defaults). These circumstances may cause principal prepayments when the current market interest rate is greater than the mortgage interest rate. Thus a homeowner's decision to prepay a mortgage may be less a purely economic decision than a chief financial officer's decision to refund corporate debt obligations.

Inflation Risk

Inflation risk or *purchasing power risk* is the risk that the return realized from investing in a bond will not be sufficient to offset the loss in purchasing power due to inflation. For example, if an investor purchases a 5-year bond in which he can realize a yield of 7%, but the rate of inflation is 8%, then the purchasing power value of the investment has declined. For all but adjustable- or floating-rate bonds, an investor is exposed to inflation risk because the interest rate that the issuer promises to make is fixed.

Foreign-Exchange Rate Risk

A U.S. investor who purchases a bond in which the issuer promises to make payments in a foreign currency does not know what the resulting cash flow of the bond will be in U.S. dollars. The cash flow will depend on the foreign-exchange rate at the time the cash flow is received. Thus the investor is exposed to *foreign-exchange rate* or *currency risk*.

Marketability Risk

Marketability risk (or *liquidity risk*) involves the ease with which an issue can be sold at or near the prevailing market price. The primary measure of marketability/liquidity is the size of the spread between the bid price (the price at which the issue can be sold) and the ask price (the price at which an issue can be purchased) quoted by a dealer. The greater the dealer spread, the greater the marketability/liquidity risk. The number of active market makers will influence the size of the bid-ask spread; the larger the number of active market makers, the smaller the bid-ask spread." For an investor who plans to hold the bond until the maturity date, marketability/liquidity risk is not important.

OVERVIEW OF FRAMEWORK FOR EVALUATING BONDS

A wide variety of bonds are available in the marketplace. The price that an investor will pay for a bond will depend on market interest rates, the risks associated with the particular issue, and unique features of the particular issue.

In general, the price that an investor will pay for a bond can be expressed as follows (assuming identical maturity and coupon):

Price of a "comparable" Treasury bond

minus

Value of the risk premium for accepting the credit risk associated with the issue

minus

Value of any options the bondholder grants to the issuer

plus

Value of any options the issuer grants to the bondholder

minus

Value of the risk premium required for accepting foreign-exchange rate risk for a nondollar-denominated bond

plus

Value of any tax advantage associated with the issue

minus

Value of the premium required for accepting marketability risk

The key to evaluating bonds is determining the value of each of these components. The starting point is the valuation of a "comparable" Treasury security.

While we have set forth the basic valuation framework in terms of price, the framework can be recast in terms of yield as follows (assuming the same maturity and coupon):

Yield on a "comparable" Treasury bond

plus

Yield premium required for accepting the credit risk associated with the issue

plus

Yield premium required for any options the bondholder grants to the issuer

minus

Yield give-up for any options the issuer grants the bondholder

plus

Yield premium required for accepting foreign exchange rate risk for a nondollar-denominated bond

minus

Yield give-up for any tax advantage associated with the issue

plus

Yield premium required for accepting marketability risk

Notice that there is an inverse relationship between price and yield. A feature of a particular bond issue that increases risk and/or makes the bond less attractive decreases the price of the bond and thus increases its yield.

PORTFOLIO OBJECTIVES AND MANAGEMENT POLICIES FOR BOND INVESTORS

Why do individuals and institutions invest in bonds? The reason is that bonds have cash flow characteristics that make them attractive to investors who have certain portfolio objectives to satisfy.[3]

The traditional reason for investing in bonds is that they provide the investor with a steady income stream (unless callable), where income is equated with coupon payments. Thus by monitoring credit and call risk and adequately diversifying a portfolio by type of issuer, an investor can expect the promised cash flow with a high degree of certainty.

For institutional investors such as pension funds, life insurance companies, trusts, banks, and thrifts, funds must be invested to satisfy contractual obligations. These liabilities may be a single sum at a future date (called a *bullet liability*) or a stream of liabilities. If properly constructed, the cash flow from a portfolio of bonds can be used to satisfy either a bullet liability or a stream of liabilities.

There are investment advisors whose portfolio objective is to maximize the total return over some holding period for a given level of risk. The total return over some holding period is simply the ending value of the portfolio plus any cash received during the holding period minus the beginning value of the portfolio, all divided by the beginning value of the portfolio. An institution that seeks to maximize the holding-period return can follow one or both of the following strategies: (1) timely shifting of funds between bonds and stocks; and (2) changing the composition of a bond portfolio to capitalize on expected changes in market interest rates and/or changes in spreads between different sectors of the bond market.

Unfortunately, there are some investment advisors who attempt to maximize some accounting "yield" measure rather than total return.

OVERVIEW OF THE BOOK

The next three chapters of this book set forth the analytical framework necessary to understand the pricing of bonds and their investment characteristics. Chapter 2 explains how the price of a bond is deter-

---

[3]For a more detailed discussion, see Richard W. McEnally, "Portfolio Objectives and Management Policies for Fixed Income Investors," in Frank J. Fabozzi and T. Dessa Garlicki, (eds.), *Advances in Bond Analysis and Portfolio Strategies* (Chicago, IL: Probus Publishing, 1987).

mined. The various measures of a bond's return are illustrated and critically evaluated in Chapter 3, which is followed by an explanation of the price volatility characteristics of bonds in Chapter 4.

As we explained earlier in this chapter when describing the framework for valuing bonds, Treasury securities provide the benchmark against which all other bonds are valued. Thus it is imperative to have a thorough understanding of the Treasury market. Chapter 5 discusses Treasury securities, Treasury-derivative securities (zero-coupon Treasury securities or "stripped" Treasury securities), and federally sponsored credit agency securities. In Chapter 6 we analyze the Treasury market and illustrate several portfolio strategies used in this market.

In Chapter 7 we review corporate bonds, municipal bonds, and international bonds, looking at their investment characteristics and special features. Common swap strategies and techniques for analyzing callable and convertible bonds are discussed in Chapter 8. Chapter 9 focuses on mortgages, and Chapter 10 deals with mortgage-backed securities (pass-throughs, collateralized mortgage obligations, and stripped mortgage-backed securities).

Chapter 11 discusses interest rate futures contracts, how they are priced, and the role they play in bond portfolio management. Interest rate option contracts, their investment characteristics, the factors that determine their price, and basic investment strategies using options are covered in Chapter 12. Structured portfolio strategies are strategies designed to achieve the performance of some predetermined benchmark. These strategies include indexing, the subject of Chapter 13, and liability funding strategies (immunization and cash flow matching), the subject of Chapter 14.

2

PRICING OF BONDS

In this chapter we explain how the price of a bond is determined, and in the next we discuss how the yield on a bond is measured. To understand pricing models and yield measures it is necessary to understand the time value of money. Therefore we begin this chapter with a review of the time value of money.

REVIEW OF TIME VALUE OF MONEY

The notion that money has a time value is one of the basic concepts in the analysis of any financial instrument. Money has time value because of the opportunity to invest it at some interest rate.

Future Value

To determine the future value of any sum of money invested today, equation (2.1) can be used:

(2.1) $P_n = P_0 (1 + r)^n$

where n = number of periods
P_n = future value n periods from now (in \$)
P_0 = original principal (in \$)
r = interest rate per period (in decimal form)

The expression $(1 +r)^n$ represents the future value of $1 invested today for n periods at a compounding rate of r.

For example, suppose a pension fund manager invests $10 million in a financial instrument that promises to pay 9.2% per year for 6 years. The future value of the $10 million investment is $16,956,500, that is:

$$P_6 = \$10,000,000 \ (1.092)^6$$
$$= \$10,000,000 \ (1.69565)$$
$$= \$16,956,500$$

In our previous example we showed how to compute the future value when interest is paid once per year (that is, the period is equal to the number of years). When interest is paid more than one time per year, both the interest rate and the number of periods used to compute the future value must be adjusted as follows:

$$r = \frac{\text{Annual interest rate}}{\text{Number of times interest is paid per year}}$$

n = Number of times interest is paid per year × number of years

For example, suppose that the portfolio manager in the previous example invests $10 million in a financial instrument that promises to pay an annual interest rate of 9.2% for 6 years, but the interest is paid semiannually (that is, twice per year). Then:

$$r = \frac{.092}{2} = .046$$

$$n = 2 \times 6 = 12$$

and

$$P_{12} = \$10,000,000 \ (1.046)^{12}$$
$$= \$10,000,000 \ (1.71546)$$
$$= \$17,154,600$$

Notice that the future value of $10 million when interest is paid semiannually ($17,154,600) is greater than when interest is paid annually ($16,956,500), even though the same annual rate is applied to both investments. The higher future value when interest is paid semiannually reflects the greater opportunity for reinvesting the interest paid.

Future Value of an Ordinary Annuity

When the same amount of money is invested periodically, it is referred to as an *annuity*. When the first investment occurs 1 period from now, it is referred to as an *ordinary annuity*. The future value of an ordinary annuity can be found by finding the future value of each investment at the end of the investment horizon and then adding the future values. However, it is easier to compute the future value of an ordinary annuity using equation (2.2).

$$(2.2) \quad P_n = A\left[\frac{(1 + r)^n - 1}{r}\right]$$

where A = amount of the annuity (in $)

The term in the *square* brackets is the *future value of an ordinary annuity of $1* at the end of n periods.

To see how this formula can be applied, suppose that a portfolio manager purchases $20 million par value of a 15-year bond that promises to pay 10% interest per year. The payment is made once a year by the issuer, with the first annual interest payment occurring 1 year from now. How much will the portfolio manager have if he (1) holds the bond until it matures 15 years from now and (2) invests the annual interest payments at an annual interest rate of 8%?

The amount that the portfolio manager will have at the end of 15 years will be equal to:

1. The $20 million when the bond matures
2. 15 annual interest payments of $2,000,000 (.10 x $20 million)
3. The interest earned by investing the annual interest payments at 8% per year.

We can determine the sum of the second and third items by applying equation (2.2). In this illustration the annuity is $2,000,000 per year. Therefore:

A = $2,000,000
r = .08
n = 15

Turning to the coupon rate, for a given maturity and a given yield to maturity, the higher the coupon rate, the more dependent the bond's total dollar return will be on the reinvestment of the coupon payments in order to produce the yield to maturity at the time of purchase. This means that when maturity and yield to maturity are held constant, premium bonds are more dependent on the interest-on-interest component than bonds selling at par. Discount bonds are less dependent on the interest-on-interest component than bonds selling at par. For zero-coupon bonds, none of the bond's total dollar return is dependent on the interest-on-interest component. So a zero-coupon bond has zero reinvestment risk if held to maturity. Thus the yield earned on a zero-coupon bond held to maturity is equal to the promised yield to maturity.

REALIZED COMPOUND YIELD

In the previous section we explained that the yield to maturity is a *promised* yield. At the time of purchase an investor is promised a yield, as measured by the yield to maturity, if both of the following conditions are satisfied:

1. The bond is held to maturity.
2. All coupon interest payments are reinvested at the yield to maturity.

We focused on the second assumption, and we showed that the interest-on-interest component for a bond may constitute a substantial portion of the bond's total dollar return. Therefore reinvesting the coupon interest payments at a rate of interest less than the yield to maturity will produce a lower yield than the yield to maturity.

Rather than assume that the coupon interest payments are reinvested at the yield to maturity, an investor can make an explicit assumption about the reinvestment rate based on his expectations. The *realized compound yield* is a measure of yield that incorporates an explicit assumption about the reinvestment rate.[8]

Let's take a careful look at the first assumption—that a bond will be held to maturity. Suppose, for example, that an investor who has a 5-year investment horizon is considering the following four bonds:

---

[8]The realized compound yield is also referred to as *total return total, horizon return, realized compound yield, effective yield,* and *holding period yield.*

Bond	Coupon	Maturity	Yield to Maturity
A	5%	3 years	9.0%
B	6%	20 years	8.6%
C	11%	15 years	9.2%
D	8%	5 years	8.0%

Assuming that all four bonds are of the same credit quality, which one is the most attractive to this investor? An investor who selects Bond C because it offers the highest yield to maturity is failing to recognize that his investment horizon calls for selling the bond after 5 years, at a price that depends on the yield required in the market for 10-year, 11% coupon bonds at the time. Hence there could be a capital gain or capital loss that will make the return higher or lower than the yield to maturity promised now. Moreover, the higher coupon on Bond C relative to the other three bonds means that more of this bond's return will be dependent on the reinvestment of coupon interest payments.

Bond A offers the second highest yield to maturity. On the surface, it seems to be particularly attractive because it eliminates the problem of realizing a possible capital loss when the bond must be sold prior to the maturity date. In addition, the reinvestment risk seems to be less than for the other three bonds because the coupon rate is the lowest. However, the investor would not be eliminating the reinvestment risk since after 3 years he must reinvest the proceeds received at maturity for 2 more years. The yield that the investor will realize will depend on interest rates 3 years from now on 2-year bonds when the proceeds must be rolled over.

The yield to maturity doesn't seem to be helping us to identify the best bond. How, then, do we find out which is the best bond? The answer depends on the investor's expectations. Specifically, it depends on the interest rate at which the coupon interest payments can be reinvested until the end of the investor's planned investment horizon. Also, for bonds with a maturity longer than the investment horizon, it depends on the investor's expectations about required yields in the market at the end of the planned investment horizon. Consequently, any of these bonds can be the best alternative, depending on some reinvestment rate and some future required yield at the end of the planned investment horizon. The realized compound yield measure takes these expectations into account and will determine the best investment for the investor based on his expectations.

The yield-to-call measure is subject to the same problems as the yield to maturity. First, it assumes that the bond will be held until the first call date. Second, it assumes that the coupon interest payments will be reinvested at the yield to call. If an investor's planned investment horizon is shorter than the time to the first call date, the bond may have to be sold for less than its acquisition cost. If, on the other hand, the investment horizon is longer than the time to the first call date, there is the problem of reinvesting the proceeds from the time the bond is called until the end of the planned investment horizon. Consequently, the yield to call doesn't tell us very much. The realized compound yield, however, can accommodate the analysis of callable bonds.

Computing the Realized Compound Yield for a Bond

The idea underlying the realized compound yield is simple. The objective is first to compute the total future dollars that will result from investing in a bond assuming a reinvestment rate. The realized compound yield is then computed as the interest rate that will make the initial investment in the bond grow to the computed total future dollars.

The procedure for computing the realized compound yield for a bond held over some investment horizon can be summarized as follows. For an assumed reinvestment rate, the dollar return that will be available at the end of the investment horizon can be computed for both the coupon interest payments and the interest-on-interest component. In addition, at the end of the planned investment horizon the investor will receive either the par value or some other value (based on the market yield on the bond when it is sold). The realized compound yield is then the interest rate that will make the amount invested in the bond (that is, the current market price plus accrued interest) grow to the total future dollars available at the end of the planned investment horizon.

More formally, the steps for computing the realized compound yield for a bond held over some investment horizon are as follows:

Step 1.   Compute the total coupon payments plus the interest-on-interest based on the assumed reinvestment rate. The coupon payments plus the interest-on-interest can be computed using equation (3.7). In using this formula, the reinvestment rate is one-half the annual interest rate that the investor assumes can be earned on the reinvestment of coupon interest payments.

Step 2.   Determine the projected sale price at the end of the planned investment horizon. The projected sale price will depend on the projected required yield at the end of the planned investment horizon. The projected sale price will be equal to the present value of the remaining cash flows of the bond discounted at the projected required yield.

Step 3.   Sum the values computed in Steps 1 and 2. The sum is the total future dollars that will be received from the investment given the assumed reinvestment rate and the projected required yield at the end of the investment horizon.[9]

Step 4.   To obtain the semiannual realized compound yield, use the following formula:

$$(3.9) \quad \left(\frac{\text{Total future dollars}}{\text{Purchase price of bond}} \right)^{1/n} - 1$$

Notice that this formula is simply the application of equation (3.3), the yield for an investment with just one future cash flow.

Step 5.   Since interest is assumed to be paid semiannually, double the interest rate found in Step 4. The resulting interest rate is the realized compound yield.

To illustrate the computation of the realized compound yield, suppose that an investor with a 3-year investment horizon is considering purchasing a 20-year, 8% coupon bond for $828.40. The yield to maturity for this bond is 10%. The investor expects that he will be able to reinvest the coupon interest payments at an annual interest rate of 6% and that at the end of the planned investment horizon the 17-year

---

[9]The total future dollars computed here is different from the total dollar return that we used in showing the importance of the interest-on-interest component in the previous section. The total dollar return included only the capital gain (or capital loss if there was one), not the purchase price, which is included in calculating the total future dollars. That is:

Total dollar return = Total future dollars - Purchase price of bond

bond will be selling to offer a yield to maturity of 7%. The realized compound yield for this bond is found as follows.

Step 1.   Compute the total coupon payments plus the interest-on-interest, assuming an annual reinvestment rate of 6%, or 3% every 6 months. The coupon payments are $40 every 6 months for 3 years or 6 periods (the planned investment horizon). Applying equation (3.7), the total coupon interest plus interest-on-interest is:

$$
\begin{aligned}
\text{Coupon interest} \\
+ \\
\text{Interest-on-interest}
\end{aligned}
\quad
\begin{aligned}
&= \$40 \left[\frac{(1.03)^6 - 1}{.03} \right] \\[2ex]
&= \$40 \left[\frac{1.1941 - 1}{.03} \right] \\[2ex]
&= \$40 \ (6.4684) \\[1ex]
&= \$258.74
\end{aligned}
$$

Step 2.   The projected sale price at the end of 3 years, assuming that the required yield to maturity for 17-year bonds is 7%, is found by determining the present value of 34 coupon payments of $40 plus the present value of the maturity value of $1,000, discounted at 3.5%. The price is $1,098.51.[10]

Step 3.   Adding the amount in Steps 1 and 2 gives total future dollars of $1,357.25.

---

[10]The present value of the 34 coupon payments discounted at 3.5% is:

$$
= \$40 \left[\frac{1 - \dfrac{1}{(1.035)^{34}}}{.035} \right] = \$788.03
$$

The present value of the maturity value discounted at 3.5% is:

$$
\frac{\$1,000}{(1.035)^{34}} = \$310.48
$$

The projected sale price is $788.03 plus $310.48, or $1,098.51.

Step 4. Compute the following:

$$\left(\frac{\$1,357.25}{\$828.40} \right)^{1/6} - 1$$

$$= (1.63840)^{.16667} - 1$$

$$= 1.0858 - 1$$

$$= .0858 \text{ or } 8.58\%$$

Step 5. Doubling 8.58% gives a realized compound yield of 17.16%.

There is no need to assume that the reinvestment rate will be constant for the entire investment horizon. The following example demonstrates how the realized compound yield measure can accommodate multiple reinvestment rates.

Suppose that an investor has a 6-year investment horizon. The investor is considering a 13-year, 9% coupon bond selling at par. The investor's expectations are as follows:

1. The first four semiannual coupon payments can be reinvested from the time of receipt to the end of the investment horizon at a simple annual interest rate of 8%.

2. The last eight semiannual coupon payments can be reinvested from the time of receipt to the end of the investment horizon at a 10% simple annual interest rate.

3. The required yield to maturity on 7-year bonds at the end of the investment horizon will be 10.6%.

Using these three assumptions, the realized compound yield is computed as follows.

Step 1. Coupon payments of $45 every 6 months for 6 years (the investment horizon) will be received. The coupon interest plus interest-on-interest for the first four coupon payments, assuming a semiannual reinvestment of 4%, is:

$$\text{Coupon interest} + \text{Interest-on-interest} = \$45 \left[\frac{(1.04)^4 - 1}{.04} \right]$$

$$= \$191.09$$

This gives the coupon plus interest-on-interest as of the end of the second year (4 periods). Reinvested at 4% until the end of the planned investment horizon, 4 years or 8 periods later, $191.09 will grow to:

$191.09 (1.04)^8 = $261.52

The coupon interest plus interest-on-interest for the last eight coupon payments, assuming a semiannual reinvestment rate of 5%, is:

$$\begin{array}{c}\text{Coupon interest}\\ +\\ \text{Interest-on-interest}\end{array} \quad \begin{aligned} &= \$45\left[\dfrac{(1.05)^8 - 1}{.05}\right]\\[6pt] &= \$429.71 \end{aligned}$$

The coupon interest plus interest-on-interest from all 12 coupon interest payments is $691.23 ($261.52 + $429.71).

Step 2.   The projected sale price of the bond, assuming that the required yield is 10.6%, is $922.31.[11]

Step 3.   The total future dollars are $1,613.54 ($691.23 + $922.31).

Step 4.   Compute the following:

---

[11]The present value of coupon payments discounted at 5.3% is:

$$= \$45\left[\dfrac{1 - \dfrac{1}{(1.053)^{14}}}{.053}\right] = \$437.02$$

The present value of the maturity value discounted at 5.3% is:

$$\dfrac{\$1,000}{(1.053)^{14}} = \$485.29$$

The projected sale price is $437.02 plus $485.29, or $922.31.

$$= \left(\frac{\$1,613.54}{\$1000.00} \right)^{1/12} - 1$$

$$= (1.61354)^{.08333} - 1$$

$$= 1.0407 - 1$$

$$= .0407 \text{ or } 4.07\%$$

Step 5. Doubling 4.07% gives a realized compound yield of 8.14%.

Applications of the Realized Compound Yield (Horizon Analysis)

The realized compound yield allows a portfolio manager to project the performance of a bond on the basis of his planned investment horizon and expectations concerning reinvestment rates and future market yields. This permits the portfolio manager to evaluate which of several potential bonds being considered for acquisition will perform the best over the planned investment horizon. As we have emphasized, this cannot be done using the yield to maturity as a measure of relative value. Using realized compound yield to assess performance over some investment horizon is called *horizon analysis.*

Horizon analysis is also used to evaluate bond swaps. In a bond swap the portfolio manager considers exchanging a bond held in the portfolio for another bond. When the objective of the bond swap is to enhance the return of the portfolio over the planned investment horizon, the realized compound yield for the bond being considered for purchase can be computed and compared with the realized compound yield for the bond held in the portfolio to determine if the bond being held should be replaced. We shall discuss several bond swap strategies throughout the book.

An often-cited objection to the realized compound yield is that it requires the portfolio manager to formulate assumptions about reinvestment rates and future yields, as well as to think in terms of an investment horizon. Unfortunately, some portfolio managers find comfort in measures such as the yield to maturity and yield to call simply because they do not require incorporating any expectations. The horizon analysis framework enables the portfolio manager to analyze the performance of a bond under different interest rate scenarios for reinvestment rates and future market yields. Only by investigating multiple scenarios can the portfolio manager see how sensitive the bond's performance will be to each scenario.

SUMMARY

In this chapter we explained the conventional yield measures commonly used by bond market participants: current yield, yield to maturity, and yield to call. We then reviewed the three potential sources of dollar return from investing in a bond—coupon interest, interest-on-interest, and, capital gain (or loss)—and showed that none of the three conventional yield measures deals satisfactorily with all of these sources. The current yield fails to consider both interest-on-interest and capital gain (or loss). The yield to maturity considers all three sources, but assumes that all coupon interest can be reinvested at the yield to maturity. The risk that the coupon payments will be reinvested at a rate less than the yield to maturity is called reinvestment risk. The yield to call has the same shortcoming; it assumes that the coupon interest can be reinvested at the yield to call. We then presented a yield measure, the realized compound yield, that is more meaningful than either yield to maturity or yield to call for assessing the relative attractiveness of a bond given the portfolio manager's expectations and planned investment horizon.

4

BOND PRICE VOLATILITY

The purpose of this chapter is to explain the characteristics of a bond that affect its price volatility and to present three measures of price volatility: (1) price value of a basis point; (2) yield value of a price change; and (3) duration. We then take a closer look at duration and discuss another investment characteristic of a bond, convexity.

A REVIEW OF THE PRICE/YIELD RELATIONSHIP FOR OPTION-FREE BONDS

As we explained in Chapter 2, a fundamental principle of an option-free bond (that is, a bond that does not have an embedded option) is that the price of the bond changes in the opposite direction of the change in the required yield for the bond. This principle follows from the fact that the price of a bond is equal to the present value of its expected cash flows. An increase (decrease) in the required yield decreases (increases) the present value of its expected cash flows, and therefore the bond's price. Exhibit 4.1 illustrates this property for the following six hypothetical bonds, where the bond prices are shown assuming a par value of $100:

1. A 9% coupon bond with 5 years to maturity
2. A 9% coupon bond with 25 years to maturity
3. A 6% coupon bond with 5 years to maturity
4. A 6% coupon bond with 25 years to maturity
5. A zero coupon bond with 5 years to maturity
6. A zero coupon bond with 25 years to maturity

When the price/yield relationship for any option-free bond is graphed, it exhibits the shape shown in Exhibit 4.2. Notice that as the required yield rises, the price of the option-free bond declines. However, the relationship is not linear (that is, it is not a straight line). The shape of the price/yield relationship for any option-free bond is referred to as *convex*.

The price/yield relationship that we have discussed refers to an instananeous change in the required yield. As we explained in Chapter 2, the price of a bond will change over time as a result of (1) a change in the perceived credit risk of the issuer, (2) a discount or premium bond moving toward par as it approaches the maturity date, and (3) a change in market interest rates.

EXHIBIT 4.1   Price/Yield Relationship for Six Hypothetical Bonds

Required Yield	Price at Required Yield Coupon/Maturity in Years					
	9%/5	9%/25	6%/5	6%/25	0%/5	0%/25
6.00%	112.7953	138.5946	100.0000	100.0000	74.4094	22.8107
7.00	108.3166	123.4556	95.8417	88.2722	70.8919	17.9053
8.00	104.0554	110.7410	91.8891	78.5178	67.5564	14.0713
8.50	102.0027	105.1482	89.9864	74.2587	65.9537	12.4795
8.90	100.3966	100.9961	88.4983	71.1105	64.7017	11.3391
8.99	100.0395	100.0988	88.1676	70.4318	64.4236	11.0975
9.00	100.0000	100.0000	88.1309	70.3570	64.3928	11.0710
9.01	99.9604	99.9013	88.0943	70.2824	64.3620	11.0445
9.10	99.6053	99.0199	87.7654	69.6164	64.0855	10.8093
9.50	98.0459	95.2539	86.3214	66.7773	62.8723	9.8242
10.00	96.1391	90.8720	84.5565	63.4881	61.3913	8.7204
11.00	92.4624	83.0685	81.1559	57.6712	58.5431	6.8767
12.00	88.9599	76.3572	77.9197	52.7144	55.8395	5.4288

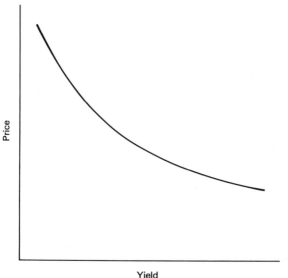

**EXHIBIT 4.2
Shape of Price/Yield
Relationship for an
Option-Free Bond**

THE PRICE VOLATILITY CHARACTERISTICS
OF OPTION-FREE BONDS

Exhibit 4.3 shows for the six hypothetical bonds in Exhibit 4.1 the percentage change in the bond's price for various changes in the required yield, assuming that the initial yield for all six bonds is 9%. An examination of Exhibit 4.3 reveals the following properties concerning the price volatility of an option-free bond.

Property 1. Although the prices of all option-free bonds move in the opposite direction of the change in required yield, the percentage price change is not the same for all bonds.

Property 2. For very small changes in the required yield, the percentage price change for a given bond is roughly the same regardless of whether the required yield increases or decreases.

Property 3. For large changes in the required yield, the percentage price change is not the same for an increase in the required yield as it is for a decrease in the required yield.

Property 4. For a given change in basis points, the percentage price increase is greater than the percentage price decrease. The implication of this property is that if an investor owns a bond (that is, is long a bond), the price appreciation that will be realized if the required yield decreases is greater than the capital loss that will be realized if the required yield rises by the same number of basis points. For an investor who is short a bond, the reverse is true: the potential capital loss is greater than the potential capital gain if the required yield changes by a given number of basis points.

An explanation for these four properties of bond price volatility lies in the convex shape of the price/yield relationship. We will investigate this in more detail later in the chapter.

EXHIBIT 4.3   Instantaneous Percentage Price Change for Six Hypothetical Bonds

Six hypothetical bonds, priced initially to yield 9%:

9% coupon, 5 years to maturity, price	= 100.0000
9% coupon, 25 years to maturity, price	= 100.0000
6% coupon, 5 years to maturity, price	= 88.1309
6% coupon, 25 years to maturity, price	= 70.3570
0% coupon, 5 years to maturity, price	= 64.3928
0% coupon, 25 years to maturity, price	= 11.0710

Yield Changes to	Change in Basis Points	Percentage Price Change in Yield Changes Coupon/Maturity in Years					
		9%/5	9%/25	6%/5	6%/25	0%/5	0%/25
6.00%	-300	12.80%	38.59%	13.47%	42.13%	15.56%	106.04%
7.00	-200	8.32	23.46	8.75	25.46	10.09	61.73
8.00	-100	4.06	10.74	4.26	11.60	4.91	27.10
8.50	-50	2.00	5.15	2.11	5.55	2.42	12.72
8.90	-10	0.40	1.00	0.42	1.07	0.48	2.42
8.99	-1	0.04	0.10	0.04	0.11	0.05	0.24
9.01	1	-0.04	-0.10	-0.04	-0.11	-0.05	-0.24
9.10	10	-0.39	-0.98	-0.41	-1.05	-0.48	-2.36
9.50	50	-1.95	-4.75	-2.05	-5.09	-2.36	-11.26
10.00	100	-3.86	-9.13	-4.06	-9.76	-4.66	-21.23
11.00	200	-7.54	-16.93	-7.91	-18.03	-9.08	-37.89
12.00	300	-11.04	-23.64	-11.59	-25.08	-13.28	-50.96

CHARACTERISTICS OF A BOND THAT AFFECT ITS PRICE VOLATILITY

There are two characteristics of an option-free bond that determine its price volatility: coupon and term to maturity.

Characteristic 1.   For a given term to maturity and initial yield, the price volatility of a bond is greater the lower the coupon rate. This characteristic can be seen by comparing the 9%, 6%, and zero-coupon bonds with the same maturity.

Characteristic 2.   For a given coupon rate and initial yield, the longer the term to maturity, the greater the price volatility. This can be seen in Exhibit 4.3 by comparing the 5-year bonds to the 25-year bonds with the same coupon.

An implication of this characteristic is that if an investor wants to increase a portfolio's price volatility because he expects interest rates to fall, all other factors being constant, bonds with long maturities should be held in the portfolio. To reduce a portfolio's price volatility in anticipation of a rise in interest rates, bonds with shorter-term maturities should be held in the portfolio.

PRICE VALUE OF A BASIS POINT AS A MEASURE OF PRICE VOLATILITY

The *price value of a basis point*, also referred to as the *dollar value of a basis point*, is the change in the price of the bond if the required yield changes by 1 basis point. Note that this measure of price volatility indicates *dollar price volatility* as opposed to percentage price volatility (price change as a percent of the initial price). Typically, the price value of a basis point is expressed as the absolute value of the change in price. Owing to property 2 of the price/yield relationship, price volatility is the same for an increase or a decrease of 1 basis point in required yield.

We will illustrate how to calculate the price value of a basis point by using the six bonds in Exhibit 4.1. For each bond, the initial price, the price after increasing the required yield by 1 basis point (from 9% to 9.01%), and the price value of a basis point (the difference between the two prices) are as follows:

Bond	Initial Price (9% yield)	Price at 9.01% Yield	Price Value of a Basis Point*
5-year, 9% coupon	100.0000	99.9604	0.0396
25-year, 9% coupon	100.0000	99.9013	0.0987
5-year, 6% coupon	88.1309	88.0945	0.0364
25-year, 6% coupon	70.3570	70.2824	0.0746
5-year, zero coupon	64.3928	64.3620	0.0308
25-year zero coupon	11.0710	11.0445	0.0265

*Absolute value per $100 of par value.

Since this measure of price volatility is in terms of dollar price change, dividing the price value of a basis point by the initial price gives the percentage price change for a 1-basis-point change in yield.

YIELD VALUE OF A PRICE CHANGE AS A MEASURE OF PRICE VOLATIITY

Another measure of the price volatility of a bond used by investors is the change in the yield for a specified price change. This is estimated by first calculating the bond's yield to maturity if the bond's price is decreased by, say, X dollars.[1] Then the difference between the initial yield and the new yield is the yield value of an X dollar price change. The smaller this value, the greater is the dollar price volatility because it would take a smaller change in yield to produce a price change of X dollars.

As we will explain in Chapter 5, Treasury notes and bonds are quoted in 32nds of a percentage point of par. Consequently, in the Treasury market investors compute the yield value of 1/32. The yield value of 1/32 for our two hypothetical 9% coupon bonds is computed as follows, assuming that the price is decreased by 1/32.

Bond	Initial Price Minus 32nd*	Yield at New Price	Initial Yield	Yield Value of a 32nd
5-year, 9% coupon	99.96875	9.008	9.000	0.008
25-year, 9% coupon	99.96875	9.003	9.000	0.003

*Initial price of 100 minus 1/32 of 1%.

[1]Recall from the previous chapter that the yield to maturity is the interest rate that will make the present value of the cash flow from the bond if held to maturity equal to the bond's price (plus accrued interest).

Corporate bonds and municipal bonds, the subject of Chapter 7, are traded in 8ths of a point. Consequently, investors in these markets compute the yield value of an 8th. The calculation of the yield value of 1/8 for our six hypothetical 9% coupon bonds is as follows, assuming that price is decreased by 1/8:

Bond	Initial Price Minus 8th*	Yield at New Price	Initial Yield	Yield Value of an 8th
5-year, 9% coupon	99.8750	9.032	9.000	0.032
25-year, 9% coupon	99.8750	9.013	9.000	0.013

*Initial price of 100 minus 1/8 of 1%.

DURATION AS A MEASURE OF PRICE VOLATILITY

In Chapter 2 we explained that the price of an option-free bond can be expressed mathematically as follows:[2]

$$(4.1) \quad P = \frac{C}{(1+y)^1} + \frac{C}{(1+y)^2} + \ldots + \frac{C}{(1+y)^n} + \frac{M}{(1+y)^n}$$

where P = price of the bond

C = *semiannual* coupon interest (in $)

M = maturity value (in $)

n = number of semiannual periods (number of years × 2)

y = one-half the yield to maturity or required yield

To determine the approximate change in price for a small change in yield, the first derivative of equation (4.1) with respect to the required yield can be computed:

$$(4.2) \quad \frac{dP}{dy} = \frac{(-1) C}{(1+y)^2} + \frac{(-2) C}{(1+y)^3} + \ldots + \frac{(-n) C}{(1+y)^{n+1}} + \frac{(-n) M}{(1+y)^{n+1}}$$

Rearranging equation (4.2) we obtain:

[2]Equation (4.1) assumes that the next coupon payment is exactly 6 months from now and there is no accrued interest. As we explained at the end of Chapter 2, it is not difficult to extend the model to account for the first coupon payment occurring less than 6 months from the valuation date and to adjust the price to include accrued interest.

$$(4.3) \quad \frac{dP}{dy} = -\frac{1}{(1+y)}\left[\frac{1\,C}{(1+y)^1} + \frac{2\,C}{(1+y)^2} + \ldots + \frac{n\,C}{(1+y)^n} + \frac{n\,M}{(1+y)^n}\right]$$

The term in square brackets is the weighted average term to maturity of the cash flows from the bond, where the weights are the present value of the cash flow.

Equation (4.3) indicates the approximate dollar price change for a small change in the required yield. Dividing both sides of equation (4.3) by P gives the approximate percentage price change:

$$(4.4) \quad \frac{dP}{dy}\frac{1}{P} = -\frac{1}{(1+y)}\left[\frac{1\,C}{(1+y)^1} + \frac{2\,C}{(1+y)^2} + \ldots + \frac{n\,C}{(1+y)^n}\right.$$
$$\left. + \frac{n\,M}{(1+y)^n}\right]\frac{1}{P}$$

The expression in the brackets divided by the price (or multiplied by the reciprocal of the price), is commonly referred to as *Macaulay duration*.[3] That is:

$$\text{Macaulay duration} = \frac{\dfrac{1\,C}{(1+y)^1} + \dfrac{2\,C}{(1+y)^2} + \ldots + \dfrac{n\,C}{(1+y)^n} + \dfrac{n\,M}{(1+y)^n}}{P}$$

which can be rewritten as:

[3]In a 1938 National Bureau of Economic Research study on bond yields, Frederick Macaulay coined this term and used this measure rather than maturity as a proxy for the average length of time that a bond investment is outstanding. (See Frederick Macaulay, *Some Theoretical Problems Suggested by the Movement of Interest Rates, Bond Yields, and Stock Prices in the U.S. Since 1856,* [New York: National Bureau of Economic Research, 1938].) In examining the interest rate sensitivity of financial institutions, Redington and Samuelson independently developed the duration concept. (See F.M. Redington, "Review of the Principle of Life Office Valuation," *Journal of the Institute of Actuaries,* 1952, pp. 286–340; and Paul A. Samuelson, "The Effect of Interest Rate Increases on the Banking System," *American Economic Review,* March 1945, pp. 16–27.) For a more recent development and extension of the duration concept, see Michael Hopewell and George G. Kaufman, "Bond Price Volatility and Years to Maturity," *American Economic Review,* September 1973, pp. 749–753. An excellent book on duration is Gerald O. Bierwag, *Duration Analysis,* (Cambridge, MA: Ballinger Publishing, 1987).

$$\text{(4.5) Macaulay   duration} = \frac{\displaystyle\sum_{t=1}^{n} \frac{t\,C}{(1+y)^{t}} + \frac{n\,M}{(1+y)^{n}}}{P}$$

Substituting Macaulay duration into equation (4.4) for the approximate percentage price change gives:

$$\text{(4.6)} \quad \frac{dP}{dy}\,\frac{1}{P} = -\frac{1}{(1+y)}\ \text{Macaulay   duration}$$

Investors commonly refer to the ratio of Macaulay duration to $(1 + y)$ as modified duration; that is:

$$\text{(4.7) Modified duration} = \frac{\text{Macaulay   duration}}{(1+y)}$$

Substituting equation (4.7) into equation (4.6) gives:

$$\text{(4.8)} \quad \frac{dP}{dy}\,\frac{1}{P} = -\text{Modified duration}$$

Equation (4.8) states that modified duration is related to the approximate percentage change in price for a given change in yield. Since for all option-free bonds modified duration is positive, equation (4.8) states that there is an inverse relationship between modified duration and the approximate percentage change in price for a given yield change. This is expected from our fundamental principle that bond prices move in the opposite direction of interest rates.

Exhibits 4.4 and 4.5 show the computation of the Macaulay duration and modified duration of two 5-year coupon bonds. The durations computed in these exhibits are in terms of duration per period. Consequently, the durations are in half-years because the cash flows of the bonds occur every 6 months. To adjust the durations to an annual figure, the durations must be divided by 2, as shown at the bottom of Exhibit 4.4 and 4.5. In general, if the cash flows occur m times per year, the durations are adjusted by dividing by m. That is:

$$\text{Duration in years} = \frac{\text{Duration in } m \text{ periods per year}}{m}$$

The Macaulay duration and modified duration in years for the six hypothetical bonds is as follows:

Bond	Macaulay Duration (in years)	Modified Duration (in years)
9%/5-year	4.13	3.96
9%/25-year	10.33	9.88
6%/5-year	4.35	4.16
6%/25-year	11.10	10.62
0%/5-year	5.00	4.78
0%/25-year	25.00	23.92

EXHIBIT 4.4   Calculation of Macaulay Duration and Modified Duration for 9%, 5-Year Bond Selling to Yield 9%

Coupon rate = 9.00%
Term (years) = 5
Initial yield = 9.00%

Period (t)	Cash Flow*	PV of $1 0.045	PV of CF	t x PVCF
1	$ 4.50	0.956937	4.306220	4.30622
2	4.50	0.915729	4.120785	8.24156
3	4.50	0.876296	3.943335	11.83000
4	4.50	0.838561	3.773526	15.09410
5	4.50	0.802451	3.611030	18.05514
6	4.50	0.767895	3.455531	20.73318
7	4.50	0.734828	3.306728	23.14709
8	4.50	0.703185	3.164333	25.31466
9	4.50	0.672904	3.028070	27.25262
10	104.50	0.643927	67.290443	672.90442
Total			100.000000	826.87899

*Cash flow per $100 of par value.

$$\text{Macaulay duration (in half-years)} = \frac{826.87899}{100.000000} = 8.27$$

$$\text{Macaulay duration (in years)} = \frac{8.27}{2} = 4.13$$

$$\text{Modified duration (in years)} = \frac{4.13}{1.0450} = 3.96$$

EXHIBIT 4.5   Calculation of Macaulay Duration and Modified Duration for 6%, 5-Year Bond Selling to Yield 9%

Coupon rate = 6.00%
Term (years) = 5
Initial yield   = 9.00%

Period (t)	Cash Flow*	PV of $1 0.045	PV of CF	t x PVCF
1	$ 3.00	0.956937	2.870813	2.87081
2	3.00	0.915729	2.747190	5.49437
3	3.00	0.876296	2.628890	7.88666
4	3.00	0.838561	2.515684	10.06273
5	3.00	0.802451	2.407353	12.03676
6	3.00	0.767895	2.303687	13.82212
7	3.00	0.734828	2.204485	15.43139
8	3.00	0.703185	2.109555	16.87644
9	3.00	0.672904	2.018713	18.16841
10	103.00	0.643927	66.324551	663.24551
Total			88.130923	765.89520

*Cash flow per $100 of par value.

$$\text{Macaulay duration (in half-years)} = \frac{765.89520}{88.130923} = 8.69$$

$$\text{Macaulay duration (in years)} = \frac{8.69}{2} = 4.35$$

$$\text{Modified duration (in years)} = \frac{4.35}{1.0450} = 4.16$$

Dollar Duration

Modified duration is a proxy for the percentage change in price. Investors also like to know the dollar price volatility of a bond. Of course, equation (4.2) can be used to compute the dollar price volatility. Alternatively, multiplying both sides of equation (4.8) by P gives:

$$(4.9)\quad \frac{dP}{dy} = -(\text{Modified duration})\, P$$

The expression on the right-hand side is called *dollar duration*. That is:

(4.10) Dollar duration = –(Modified duration) P

For our six hypothetical bonds, the dollar duration per $100 of par value is as follows:

Bond	Modified Duration	Price	Dollar Duration
9%/5 year	3.96	100.0000	396.0000
9%/25 year	9.88	100.0000	988.0000
6%/5 year	4.16	88.1309	366.6245
6%/25 year	10.62	70.3579	747.2009
0%/5 year	4.78	64.3928	307.7976
0%/25 year	23.92	11.0710	264.8183

Properties of Duration

As can be seen from the various durations computed for the six hypothetical bonds, the modified duration and Macaulay duration of a coupon bond are less than the maturity. It should be obvious from the formula that the Macaulay duration of a zero-coupon bond is equal to its maturity; however, a zero-coupon bond's modified duration is less than its maturity. Also, as can be seen from our hypothetical bonds, the lower the coupon, generally the greater the modified and Macaulay duration of the bond.[4]

Notice the consistency between the properties of bond price volatility we discussed earlier and the properties of modified duration. We showed that when all other factors are constant, the greater the maturity, the greater the price volatility. A property of modified duration is that when all other factors are constant, the greater the maturity, the greater the modified duration. We also showed that the lower the coupon rate, all other factors being constant, the greater the bond price volatility. As we just noted, generally the lower the coupon rate, the greater the modified duration. Thus the greater the modified duration, the greater the price volatility.

What is not so obvious is what happens to the modified duration of option-free bonds as the required yield changes. A property of modified duration is that as the required yield increases (decreases), modified duration decreases (increases). For example, for the 25-year, 9% coupon bond, modified duration is 9.88 when the required yield is 9%; should the required yield increase instantaneously to 9.8%, modified duration would fall to 9.39. If, instead, the required yield decreased from 9% to 8.20%, the modified duration would rise to 10.40. The same property holds for dollar duration. The dollar duration of

---

[4]This property does not hold for long-maturity deep-discount bonds.

$988 at a 9% required yield would fall to $869.36 at a 9.8% required yield, but rise to $1,127.86 at an 8.2% required yield.

Approximating the Percentage Price Change Using Modified Duration

If we multiply both sides of equation (4.8) by the change in the required yield (dy), we have the following relationship:

$$(4.11) \quad \frac{dP}{P} = - \text{Modified duration} \times dy$$

Equation (4.11) can be used to approximate the percentage price change for a given change in required yield.

To illustrate the relationship, consider the 6%, 25-year bond selling at 70.3570 to yield 9%. The modified duration for this bond is 10.62. If yields increase instantaneously from 9% to 9.10%, a yield change of +0.0010 (10 basis points), the *approximate* percentage change in price using equation (4.11) is:

$$- 10.62 \, (+.0010) = -.0106 \text{ or } 1.06\%$$

Notice from Exhibit 4.3 that the actual percentage change in price is −1.05%. Similarly, if yields decrease instantaneously from 9% to 8.90% (a 10-basis-point decrease), the approximate percentage change in price using equation (4.11) would be +1.06%. From Exhibit 4.3, the actual percentage price change would be +1.07%. This example illustrates that for small changes in the required yield, modified duration gives a good approximation of the percentage change in price.

Instead of a small change in required yield, let's assume that yields increase by 200 basis points, from 9% to 11% (a yield change of +0.02). The approximate percentage change in price using equation (4.11) is:

$$-10.62 \, (+0.02) = -21.24\%$$

How good is this approximation? As can be seen from Exhibit 4.3, the actual percentage change in price is only −18.03%. Moreover, if the required yield decreased by 200 basis points, from 9% to 7%, the approximate percentage change in price based on duration would be

+21.24%, compared to an actual percentage change in price of +25.46%. Thus we can see that not only is the approximation off, but also that modified duration estimates a symmetric percentage price change that, as we pointed out earlier in this chapter, is not a property of the price/yield relationship for bonds for large changes in yield.

Approximating the Dollar Price Change Using Dollar Duration

Once we know the percentage price change, and the initial price, the estimated dollar price change using modified duration can be determined. Alternatively, the estimated dollar price change can be obtained by multiplying both sides of equation (4.11) by P, giving

$$dP = - (\text{Modified duration}) \, P \, (dy)$$

From equation (4.10), we can substitute dollar duration for the product of modified duration and P. Thus:

(4.12) $dP = - (\text{Dollar duration}) \, (dy)$

For small changes in the required yield, equation (4.12) does a good job in estimating the change in price. For example, consider the 6%, 25-year bond selling at 70.3570 to yield 9%. The dollar duration is 747.2009. For a 1-basis-point (.0001) increase in the required yield, the estimated price change per $100 of face value is:

$$dP = - (\$747.2009) \, (.0001)$$
$$= -\$0.747$$

From Exhibit 4.1, we see that the actual price is 70.2824. The actual price change would therefore be 0.746 (70.2824 − 70.3750). Notice that the dollar duration for a 1-basis-point change is the same as the price value of a basis point.

Now let's see what happens when there is a large change in the required yield for the same bond. If the required yield increases from 9% to 11% (or 200 basis points), the approximate dollar price change per $100 face value is:

$$dP = - (\$747.2009)\ (.02)$$

$$= -\$14.94$$

From Exhibit 4.1, we see that the actual price for this bond if the required yield is 11% is 57.6712. Thus the actual price decline is 12.6858 (57.6712 – 70.3570). The estimated dollar price change is more than the actual price change. The reverse is true for a decrease in the required yield. This result is consistent with what we illustrated earlier. When there are large movements in the required yield, using dollar duration or modified duration will not adequately approximate the price reaction. Duration will overestimate the price change when the required yield rises, thereby underestimating the new price. When the required yield falls, duration will underestimate the price change and thereby underestimate the new price.

Graphical Presentation of Duration and Price Change

Exhibit 4.6 shows the price/yield relationship for any option-free bond. The difference between Exhibit 4.2 and Exhibit 4.6 is that the latter includes a tangent line to the price/yield relationship at y^*.

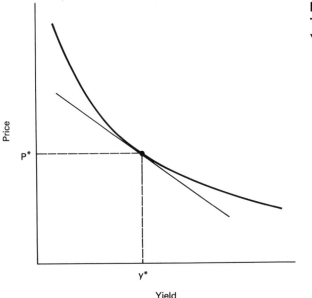

**EXHIBIT 4.6
Tangent to Price/
Yield Relationship**

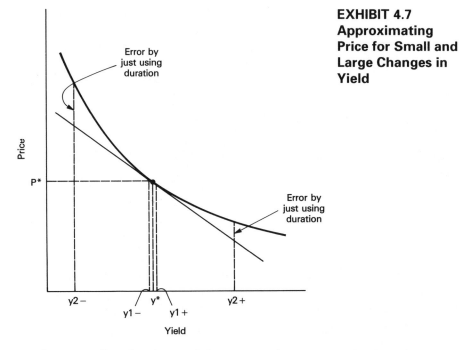

EXHIBIT 4.7
Approximating Price for Small and Large Changes in Yield

Mathematically, the slope of the tangent line at y^* is the first derivative of the formula for the price (equation (4.1)), evaluated at the point y^*. The equation for the tangent line is simply the dollar duration.

It is the tangent line that is used to approximate the price change of a bond if the required yield changes. The estimated price is always below the actual price, which is consistent with our earlier observation that duration underestimates the new price. From Exhibit 4.7 we can see how good the approximation is. For small changes in the required yield, $y1+$ and $y1-$, the tangent line (dollar duration) does a good job estimating the change in price. However, as we move further away from y^*—say to $y2+$ or $y2-$ —the approximation becomes poorer.

The tangent line does not do a good job approximating the actual price for large changes in yield because of the convex shape of the price/yield relationship. The greater the convexity of the bond's price/yield relationship, the poorer the approximation.

CONVEXITY

By using duration (modified or dollar), we attempted to estimate a convex relationship with a straight line (the tangent line). Is it possible to obtain a mathematical relationship that provides a better approximation to the price of the bond if the required yield changes?

Using the first two terms of a Taylor expansion series, the price change can be approximated as follows:[5]

$$(4.13) \quad dP = \frac{dP}{dy} \, dy + \frac{1}{2} \frac{d^2 P}{dy^2} \, (dy)^2 + \text{Error}$$

Dividing both sides of equation (4.13) by P to get the percentage price change gives us:

$$(4.14) \quad \frac{dP}{P} = \frac{dP}{dy} \frac{1}{P} \, dy + \frac{1}{2} \frac{d^2 P}{dy^2} \frac{1}{P} \, (dy)^2 + \frac{\text{Error}}{P}$$

The first term on the right-hand side of equation (4.13) is equation (4.12); that is, it is the dollar price change based on dollar duration. Thus the first term in equation (4.13) is our approximation of the price change based on duration. In equation (4.14), the first term on the right hand side is the approximate percentage change in price based on modified duration.

The second term in equations (4.13) and (4.14) include the second derivative of the price function (equation (4.1)). It is the second derivative that measures the convexity of the price/yield relationship. Some market participants refer to the second derivative of price (equation (4.1)) as the *dollar convexity* of the bond. Others refer to the product of 1/2 and the second derivative shown in equation (4.13) as the *dollar convexity*. It is this convention that we shall use. That is:

$$(4.15) \quad \text{Dollar convexity} = \frac{1}{2} \frac{d^2 P}{dy^2}$$

The product of the dollar convexity and the square of the change in the required yield indicates the estimated price change due to convexity. That is, the approximate change in price due to convexity is:[6]

---

[5]A Taylor expansion series is discussed in calculus textbooks. A Taylor expansion series can be used to approximate a mathematical function. Here, the mathematical function to be approximated is the price function.

[6]If dollar convexity is measured as simply the second derivative, then equation (4.16) would be multiplied by 1/2.

(4.16) $dP = (\text{Dollar convexity}) \, (dy)^2$

The second derivative divided by price is a measure of the percentage change in the price of the bond due to convexity, and is referred to as simply *convexity*. Once again, some market participants measure convexity by multiplying the second derivative by $1/2$, which is the convention we shall adopt. Thus convexity is computed as follows:

(4.17) Convexity $= \dfrac{1}{2} \dfrac{d^2 P}{dy^2} \dfrac{1}{P}$

and the percentage price change due to convexity is:

(4.18) $\dfrac{dP}{P} = (\text{Convexity}) \, (dy)^2$

To compute the dollar convexity and convexity, the second derivative of the price equation (4.1) must be determined. The second derivative is:

(4.19) $\dfrac{d^2 P}{dy^2} = \displaystyle\sum_{t=1}^{n} \dfrac{t \, (t+1) \, C}{(1+y)^{t+2}} + \dfrac{n \, (n+1) \, M}{(1+y)^{n+2}}$

Exhibits 4.8 and 4.9 demonstrate how to calculate the second derivative (equation (4.19)), dollar convexity, and convexity for the two 5-year coupon bonds. As in the case of duration, the convexity measure is in terms of periods squared. To convert the convexity measures to an annual figure, equations (4.15) and (4.17) must be divided by 4 (which is 2 squared). In general, if the cash flows occur m times per year, convexity is adjusted to an annual figure as follows:

$$\text{Convexity in years} = \dfrac{\text{Convexity in } m \text{ periods per year}}{m^2}$$

The second derivative, annualized convexity, and annualized dollar convexity for our six hypothetical bonds can be summarized as follows:

Bond (per $100 par)	Second Derivative	Convexity (per $100 par)	Dollar Convexity
9%/5-year	7,781.02	9.73	$ 973.00
9%/25-year	64,288.42	80.36	8,036.00
6%/5-year	7,349.45	10.42	918.32
6%/25-year	51,476.26	91.46	6,434.85
0%/5-year	6,486.30	12.59	810.71
0%/25-year	25,851.93	291.89	3,231.51

EXHIBIT 4.8   Calculation of Convexity and Dollar Convexity for 9%, 5-Year Bond Selling to Yield 9%

Coupon rate   =   9.00%
Term (years) =   5
Initial yield   =   9.00%
Price   =   100

Period (t)	Cash Flow*	$\dfrac{1}{(1.045)^{t+2}}$	$t(t+1)\,CF$	$\dfrac{t(t+1)CF}{(1.045)^{t+2}}$
1	$ 4.50	0.876296	9	7.886
2	4.50	0.838561	27	22.641
3	4.50	0.802451	54	43.332
4	4.50	0.767895	90	69.110
5	3.40	0.734828	135	99.201
6	4.50	0.703185	189	132.901
7	4.50	0.672904	252	169.571
8	4.50	0.643927	324	208.632
9	4.50	0.616198	405	249.560
10	104.50	0.589663	11495	6778.186
Total			12980	7781.020

*Cash flow per $100 of par value.

Second derivative = 7,781.02

$$\text{Convexity (half-years)} = \frac{7781.020}{100.0000} \times \frac{1}{2} = 38.9051$$

$$\text{Convexity (years)} = \frac{38.9051}{4} = 9.73$$

$$\text{Dollar convexity} = 100 \times 9.73 = 973$$

EXHIBIT 4.9   Calculation of Convexity and Dollar Convexity for 6%, 5-Year Bond Selling to Yield 9%

Coupon rate   =   6.00%
Term (years) =   5
Initial yield   =   9.00%
Price   =   88.1309

Period (t)	Cash Flow*	$\dfrac{1}{(1.045)^{t+2}}$	$t(t+1)\,CF$	$\dfrac{t(t+1)\,CF}{(1.045)^{t+2}}$
1	$ 3.00	0.876296	6	5.257
2	3.00	0.838561	18	15.094
3	3.00	0.802451	36	28.888
4	3.00	0.767895	60	46.073
5	3.00	0.734828	90	66.134
6	3.00	0.703185	126	88.601
7	3.00	0.672904	168	113.047
8	3.00	0.643927	216	139.088
9	3.00	0.616198	270	166.373
10	103.00	0.589663	11330	6680.891
Total			12320	7349.446

*Cash flow per $100 of par value.

Second derivative = 7,349.45

$$\text{Convexity (half-years)} = \frac{7349.45}{88.1309} \times \frac{1}{2} = 41.6962$$

$$\text{Convexity (years)} = \frac{41.6962}{4} = 10.42$$

$$\text{Dollar convexity} = 88.1309 \times 10.42 = 918.32$$

Approximating Percentage Price Change Using Duration and Convexity

Equation (4.14) tells us that the percentage price change of a bond can be estimated using both duration and convexity. To illustrate how this is done, consider the 6%, 25-year bond selling to yield 9%. The modified duration and the convexity for this bond are 10.62 and 91.46, respectively. If the required yield increases by 200 basis points, from 9% to 11%, the approximate percentage change in the price of the bond is:

Percentage change in price due to duration from equation (4.11)

= – (Modified duration) (*dy*)

= – (10.62) (.02) = –.2124 = –21.24%

    plus

Percentage change in price due to convexity from equation (4.17)

= (Convexity) (*dy*)^2

= (91.46) (.02)^2 = .0366 = 3.66%

The estimated percentage price change due to duration and convexity is:

–21.24% + 3.66% = –17.58

From Exhibit 4.3 we see that the actual change is -18.03%. Using both duration and convexity provides a better approximation of the actual price change for a large movement in the required yield. Suppose, instead, that the required yield *decreases* by 200 basis points. Then the approximate percentage change in the price of the bond using modified duration and convexity is:

Percentage change in price due to duration from equation (4.11)

= – (Modified duration) (*dy*)

= – (10.62) (–.02) = +.2124 = +21.24%

    plus

Percentage change in price due to convexity from equation (4.17)

= (Convexity) (*dy*)^2

= (91.46) (–.02)^2 = .0366 = 3.66%

The estimated percentage price change due to duration and convexity is:

+21.24% + 3.66% = 24.90%

From Exhibit 4.3 we see that the actual change is +25.46%. Once again, using both duration and convexity provides a good approximation of the actual price change for a large movement in the required yield.

The Value of Convexity

Up to this point, we have focused on how taking convexity into account can improve the approximation of a bond's price change for a given yield change. The convexity of a bond, however, has another important investment implication, which is illustrated in Exhibit 4.10. The exhibit has two bonds, A and B. The two bonds have the same duration and are offering the same yield; however, they have different convexities. Bond B is more convex (bowed) than Bond A.

What is the implication of the greater convexity for B? Regardless of whether the market yield rises or falls, B will have a higher price. That is, if the required yield rises, the capital loss on Bond B will be less than it will be on Bond A. A fall in the required yield will generate greater price appreciation for B than for A.

Generally, the market will take the greater convexity of B compared to A into account in pricing the two bonds. That is, the market will price convexity. Consequently, while there may be times when a situation such as that depicted in Exhibit 4.10 will exist, generally the market will require investors to "pay up" (accept a lower yield) for the greater convexity offered by Bond B.

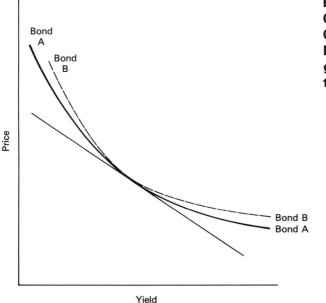

**EXHIBIT 4.10
Comparison of
Convexity of Two
Bonds: Bond B has
greater convexity
than Bond A.**

The question is: How much should the market want investors to pay up for convexity? Look again at Exhibit 4.10. Notice that if investors expect that market yields will change by very little—that is, they expect low interest rate volatility—the advantage of owning Bond B over Bond A is insignificant because both bonds will offer approximately the same price for small changes in yields. Thus investors should not be willing to pay much for convexity. In fact, if the market is pricing convexity high, which means that A will be offering a higher yield than B, then investors with expectations of low interest rate volatility would probably be willing to "sell convexity"—that is, to sell B if they own it and buy A. In contrast, if investors expect substantial interest rate volatility, Bond B would probably sell at a much lower yield than A.

Properties of Convexity

All option-free bonds have the following convexity properties.

Property 1.   As the required yield increases (decreases), the convexity of a bond decreases (increases). This property is referred to as *positive convexity.* An implication of positive convexity is that the duration of an option-free bond moves in the right direction as market yields change. That is, if market yields rise, the price of a bond will fall. The price decline is slowed down by a decline in the duration of the bond as market yields rise. In contrast, should market yields fall, duration increases so that percentage price change accelerates. With an option-free bond, both these changes in duration occur.

This is graphically portrayed in Exhibit 4.11. The slope of the tangent line in the exhibit gets flatter as the required yield increases. A flatter tangent line means a smaller modified duration as the required yield rises. In contrast, the tangent line gets steeper as the required yield decreases, implying that the modified duration gets larger. This property will hold for all option-free bonds. Also, from this graphical presentation we can see that the convexity is actually measuring the rate of change of the dollar duration as market yields change.

Property 2.   For a given yield and maturity, the lower the coupon, the greater the convexity of a bond. This can be seen from the computed convexity for our hypothetical bonds. Of the three 5-year bonds, the zero-coupon bond has the highest convexity and the 9%

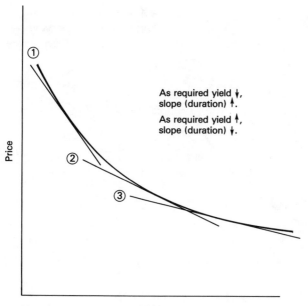

**EXHIBIT 4.11
Change in Duration
as the Required Yield
Changes**

coupon bond has the lowest convexity. The same is true of the 25-year bonds depicted.

Property 3.   For a given yield and modified duration, the lower the coupon, the smaller the convexity. The investment implication of this property is that zero-coupon bonds have the lowest convexity for a given modified duration.

Property 4.   The convexity of a bond increases at an increasing rate as duration increases. This is depicted in Exhibit 4.12. An investment implication is that if an investor swaps one bond for another with double the duration of the bond sold, the convexity of the bond will more than double.

ADDITIONAL CONCERNS WHEN USING DURATION

Our illustrations have demonstrated that relying on duration as the sole measure of the price volatility of a bond may mislead investors. There are two other concerns about using duration that we should point out.

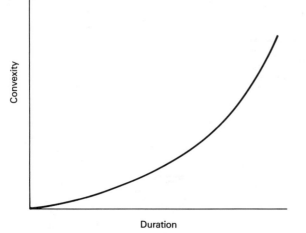

EXHIBIT 4.12
Relationship Between
Duration and Convexity

First, in the derivation of the relationship between modified duration and bond price volatility, we started with the price equation (4.1). This price equation assumes that all cash flows for the bond are discounted at the same discount rate. The appropriateness of this assumption is examined in Chapter 6, where we analyze the yield curve. Essentially, the derivation of equation (4.3) assumes that the yield curve is flat and all shifts are parallel.

To overcome this restrictive assumption, several researchers have developed more refined models to allow for the possibility of yield curve changes that are not parallel.[7] While these duration measures are of theoretical interest, their applications in portfolio and trading strategies have been limited. Moreover, studies have found that the results from using Macaulay duration (and modified duration by extension) differed little from those obtained using the more complex duration formulations in a certain bond strategy. This is discussed further in Chapter 14.

Our second concern is the misapplication of duration to bonds with embedded options. We have stressed throughout this chapter

---

[7]For a discussion of various duration formulations based on alternative interest rate processes, see Gerald O. Bierwag, George G. Kaufman, and Alden Toevs, "Recent Developments in Bond Portfolio Immunization Strategies," in George G. Kaufman, Gerald O. Bierwag, and Alden Toevs, eds. *Innovations in Bond Portfolio Management*, (Greenwich, CT: JAI Press, 1983).

that the principles explained apply to option-free bonds. We will focus on the price volatility of bonds with embedded options in Chapter 8.

SUMMARY

In this chapter we discussed the price volatility characteristics of option-free bonds and reviewed three measures of bond price volatility (price value of a basis point, yield value of a price change, and duration). We then focused on the various duration measures— Macaulay duration, modified duration, and dollar duration—showing the relationship between bond price volatility and each of these measures. Finally, we looked at the convexity of a bond, showing how convexity can be used to improve our understanding of the price volatility of a security and the investment implications of convexity. Having read this chapter, you should now understand that, holding aside credit risk, there are three components to evaluating the attractiveness of an option-free bond: yield, duration, and convexity.

5

TREASURY AND FEDERALLY SPONSORED CREDIT AGENCY SECURITIES

In the previous three chapters we provided the analytical framework for evaluating bonds. In this chapter we begin our review of fixed-income securities and derivative contracts. This chapter will cover the securities of the U.S. Treasury (including zero coupon Treasury securities) and federally sponsored credit agency securities. In the next chapter we will analyze the Treasury market and discuss various portfolio strategies that use these securities.

TREASURY SECURITIES

U.S. Treasury securities are backed by the full faith and credit of the United States government. Consequently, they are viewed by market participants as having no *credit* risk. Interest rates on Treasury securities are the benchmark interest rates throughout the U.S. economy as well as in international capital markets. Market participants talk of yields on non-Treasury securities as trading above (or below) a particular Treasury security.

Two factors account for the prominent role of Treasury securities: volume (in terms of dollars outstanding) and liquidity. The U.S. Department of the Treasury is the largest single issuer of debt in the world, with Treasury securities accounting for $1.7 trillion (consisting of over 180 Treasury note and bond issues and 30 Treasury bill issues). In contrast, the entire U.S. corporate bond market accounts for about $1 trillion and over 10,000 issues; the U.S. municipal bond market accounts for about $776 billion, with more than 70,000 separate issuers generating millions of individual issues. The large volume of its total debt and the large size of any one of its issues have contributed to making the Treasury market the most active, and hence the most liquid, market in the world. The spread between bid and ask prices is considerably narrower than in other sectors of the fixed-income market, and more issues can be readily purchased. In contrast, many issues in the corporate and municipal markets are illiquid and cannot be readily located.

Treasury Securities Issued

There are two categories of government securities—discount and coupon securities. The fundamental difference between these two types of securities is the form in which the holder receives interest and, as a result, the prices at which they are issued. Coupon securities pay interest every 6 months.[1] Discount securities do not make periodic interest payments. Instead, the security holder receives interest at the maturity date, the interest being the difference between the face value received at maturity and the purchase price.

The current practice of the Treasury is to issue all securities with maturities of 1 year or less as discount securities. These securities are called Treasury *bills*. All securities with maturities longer than 1 year are issued as coupon securities. Treasury coupon securities issued with original maturities between 2 and 10 years are called *notes*; those with original maturities greater than 10 years are called *bonds*.

Although Treasury notes are not callable, many outstanding Treasury bond issues are callable within 5 years of maturity. Treasury bonds issued since February 1985 are not callable.

Treasury securities are available in book-entry form at the Federal Reserve Bank. This means that the investor receives only a receipt as evidence of ownership instead of an engraved certificate. An advantage of book entry is ease in transferring ownership of the security.

---

[1]The Treasury has issued securities targeted to foreign investors that pay interest annually rather than semiannually. For an explanation of these issues, see Kenneth D. Garbade, "Foreign-Targeted Treasury Securities," Chap. 5 in Frank J. Fabozzi, ed., *The Handbook of Treasury Securities* (Chicago, IL: Probus Publishing, 1987).

Treasury bills come only in book-entry form. Treasury coupon securities issued after January 1, 1983, are required to be in book-entry form.

Interest income from Treasury securities is subject to federal income taxes but is exempt from state and local income taxes. However, capital gains from the sale of Treasury securities may be taxed at the state and local level.

The Primary Market

Treasury securities are typically issued on an auction basis. There are regular cycles in which the Treasury auctions and issues securities of specific maturities. A description of these cycles is provided in Exhibit 5.1.

The auction for Treasury bills and Treasury coupon securities is conducted on a yield basis.[2] Competitive bids for Treasury bills must be submitted on a bank-discount basis (to be explained shortly). For Treasury coupon securities, the bidder submits a bid based on the yield to maturity that he is willing to accept. Noncompetitive tenders may also be submitted for up to $1 million face amount. Such tenders include no bid yield, only a quantity. The price awarded to noncompetitive bidders is the average price determined by the competitive bidders.

The auction results are determined by first deducting the total noncompetitive tenders from the total securities being auctioned. The remainder represents the par amount of bonds to be awarded to the competitive bidders. The lowest-yield bidders are awarded their bonds at their bid price. Successively higher-yielding bidders are awarded bonds at their bid price until the total amount offered (less noncompetitive tenders) is awarded to competitive bidders. The highest yield at which bonds are awarded is known as the "stop-out" yield, and bidders at that price are awarded a percentage of their total tender. The difference between the average yield of all the bids accepted by the Treasury and the stop-out yield is called the *tail*.

To illustrate, auction results for a $9 billion issue might be determined as follows:

Total issue	= $9.0 billion
Less noncompetitive bids	= 0.5 billion
Left for competitive bidders	= $8.5 billion

[2]Before 1974 the Treasury conducted auctions for coupon securities on the basis of price rather than yield.

EXHIBIT 5.1 Treasury Auction Cycles

Discount Securities:

3-month (91-day) Treasury bills

Auctioned every Monday; issued on the following Thursday.

6-month (182-day) Treasury bills

Same auction and issue cycle as for 3-month Treasury bills (auctioned on Monday; issued on Thursday). Thus 182-day Treasury bills eventually trade in consonance with 91-day Treasury bills.

52-week (364 day) Treasury bills

Auctioned every fourth Thursday; issued on the following Thursday. Thus 364-day Treasury bills eventually trade in consonance with 182-day and then 91-day Treasury bills.

Coupon Securities:

2-year

2-year Treasury notes are auctioned every month, normally near the end of the month, for settlement on the last business day of the month. They mature on the last business day of the month 2 years after their settlement date.

5-year

5-year Treasury notes are auctioned on a quarterly cycle near the end of February, May, August, and November for settlement at the beginning of March, June, September, and December. These issues mature on the 15th of February, May, August, and November approximately 5 years and 2 months after their settlement date. (These notes are thus 5-year, 2-month notes and their first coupon is a long coupon, that is, the first coupon represents approximately 8 months' interest.)

Mini-refunding (4-year/7-year)

The mini-refunding is a quarterly cycle issue of, typically, a 4-year note and a 7-year note. These issues are anounced at the same time, typically during the middle of the auction month. They are then typically auctioned on consecutive business days late in March, June, September, and December for settlement at the beginning of January, April, July, and October. The 4-year note matures on the last business day of March, June, September, and December 4 years after settlement; the 7-year note matures on the 15th day of January, April, July, and October 7 years after settlement.

EXHIBIT 5.1 *(Continued)*

Refunding (3-year/10-year/ 30-year)	The refunding cycle is a quarterly-cycle issue of notes and bonds that are issued on the 15th of February, May, August, and November and are typically auctioned on the Tuesday, Wednesday, and Thursday of the second week prior to the issue. Each refunding typically contains three issues: (1) a 3-year note; (2) a 10-year note; and (3) a 30-year bond. These issues mature on the 15th of February, May, August, or November, the appropriate number of years (3, 10, or 30) after their issue. However, the issues in the refunding cycle have been subject to some variations.
Summary of *Maturity Schedule:*	February 15, May 15, August 15, and November 15: 3-year, 5-year, 10-year, and 30-year securities.
	January 15, April 15, July 15, and October 15: 7-year security.
	End of month: 2-year (monthly) and 4-year (March, June, September, and December) securities.

Total competitive bids might have been received as follows:

$ Amount (billions)	Bid
$ 0.9	8.21
2.1	8.22
3.5	8.23
4.0	8.24
7.0	8.25
Etc.	

The Treasury would allocate the issue to competitive bidders from the low-yield bid to the high-yield bid until $8.5 billion were distributed. Those who bid 8.21, 8.22, and 8.23 would be awarded the entire amount for which they bid. The total awarded to these bidders would be $6.5 billion, leaving $2 billion still to be awarded. Each of the bidders at 8.24 would be awarded one-half his or her bid. The results of the auction would show 8.21 high, 8.23 average, and 8.24 the stop, with 50% of the securities awarded at the stop. Those who bid higher in yield than 8.24 would have "missed" or been "shut out." This auction would have a tail of .01 (8.24 minus 8.23).

Role of Primary Dealers.   The auction process relies on the participation of primary government securities dealers. The primary dealers are expected to participate in every auction and typically bid for about 3% of every issue that is auctioned. The primary dealers subsequently redistribute the issue, at a profit or a loss, to both nonprimary dealers and institutional investors. The primary dealers are also expected to maintain a certain level of trading activity in the secondary market. Primary dealers must report their financial status to the Federal Reserve Bank of New York every day; hence they are also known as "reporting Fed dealers."

Secondary Market

The secondary market for Treasury securities is an over-the-counter market in which a group of U.S. government securities dealers continually provide bids and offers on outstanding Treasuries.[3] The secondary market is the most liquid financial market in the world. In the secondary market the most recently auctioned Treasury issues for each maturity are referred to as "on-the-run" or "current-coupon" issues. Issues auctioned prior to the current-coupon issues are typically referred to as "off-the-run" issues and are not as liquid as on-the-run issues.

Bid and Offer Quotes on Treasury Bills.   Bids and offers in the dealer market for Treasury bills are on a bank-discount basis (in basis points), not on a price basis.

The yield on a bank-discount basis is computed as follows:

$$(5.1) \quad Y_D = \frac{D}{F} \times \frac{360}{t}$$

where Y_D = yield on a bank-discount basis
  D = dollar discount, which is equal to the difference between the face value and the price
  F = face value
  t = number of days remaining to maturity

---

[3]Actually, some trading of Treasury coupon securities occurs on the New York Stock Exchange. However, the volume of these exchange-traded transactions is very small when compared to the over-the-counter transactions.

For example, a Treasury bill with 100 days to maturity, a face value of $100,000, and selling for $97,569 would be quoted as 8.75% on a bank-discount basis:

$$D = \$100,000 - \$97,569$$
$$= \$2,431$$

Therefore:

$$Y_D = \frac{\$2,431}{\$100,000} \times \frac{360}{100}$$
$$Y_D = 8.75\%$$

Given the yield on a bank-discount basis, it is simple to find the price of a Treasury bill. The price is found by first solving equation (5.1) for the dollar discount (D) as follows:

$$(5.2) \quad D = Y_D \times F \times \frac{t}{360}$$

The price is then:

$$(5.3) \quad \text{Price} = F - D.$$

For our 100-day Treasury bill with a face value of $100,000, if the yield on a bank-discount basis is quoted as 8.75%, D is equal to:

$$D = .0875 \times \$100,000 \times \frac{100}{360}$$
$$D = \$2,431$$

Therefore:

$$\text{Price} = \$100,000 - \$2,431$$
$$= \$97,569$$

The quoted yield on a bank-discount basis is not a meaningful measure of the return from holding a Treasury bill for two reasons. First, the measure is based on a face-value investment rather than on the actual dollar amount invested. Second, the yield is annualized on the basis of a 360- rather than a 365-day year, making it difficult to compare the yield with coupon securities that pay interest on a 365-day basis (such as Treasury notes or bonds).

Despite its shortcomings as a measure of return, this is the way that dealers in the market quote Treasury bills. However, many dealer quote sheets and some reporting services show two other yield measures that attempt to make the yield comparable to a coupon bond and other money market instruments.

The measure that seeks to make the Treasury bill quote comparable to a coupon bond is called the *bond-equivalent yield* (also called the *coupon-equivalent yield*).[4] This yield measure takes into consideration (1) the price rather than the face value in computing yield, (2) a 365-day year rather than a 360-day year, and (3) the reinvestment opportunities available on a coupon security with more than 182 days (6 months) to maturity. The formula for the bond-equivalent yield for a Treasury bill depends on whether there are 6 months (182 days) or less to maturity, or more than 6 months to maturity. The reason for this is that in order to compare a Treasury bill with a coupon security, it is necessary to take into consideration the fact that on a coupon security with more than 6 months to maturity there is an opportunity to reinvest the coupon payment. The formula for computing the bond-equivalent yield for a Treasury bill with 182 days (6 months) or less to maturity is:

(5.4) Bond-equivalent yield
(for $t \leq 182$)
$$= \frac{365\,(Y_D)}{360 - t\,(Y_D)}$$

The formula for computing the bond-equivalent yield for a Treasury bill with more than 182 days to maturity is :[5]

(5.5) Bond-equivalent yield =
(for $t > 182$)
$$\frac{-\dfrac{2t}{365} + 2\sqrt{\left(\dfrac{t}{365}\right)^2 - \left(\dfrac{2t}{365} - 1\right)\left(1 - \dfrac{1}{P}\right)}}{\dfrac{2t}{365} - 1}$$

[4]As explained in Chapter 3, the bond-equivalent yield is found by doubling the semiannual interest rate that equates the present value of the cash flow to the price of the bond.

[5]Marcia Stigum, *Money Market Calculations* (Homewood, IL: Dow Jones Irwin, 1981), pp. 33–34.

where *P* is the price of the Treasury bill that will produce $1 of face value at maturity.

The *CD-equivalent yield* (also called the *money market–equivalent yield*) makes the yield on a Treasury bill more comparable to the quoted yields on money market instruments that pay interest on a 360-day basis, taking into consideration the price of the Treasury bill rather than its face value. The formula for the CD-equivalent yield is:

$$(5.6) \quad \text{CD-equivalent yield} = \frac{360 \, Y_D}{360 - t \, (Y_D)}$$

The top part of Exhibit 5.2 shows quotes on three Treasury bills on April 5, 1988, as reported by the Knight-Ridder MoneyCenter. The first quote is the yield on a bank-discount basis, the second is the bond-equivalent yield, and the third is the CD-equivalent yield.

Bids and Offers on Treasury Coupon Securities.   Prior to being auctioned, a new Treasury coupon issue is quoted on a yield-to-maturity basis (e.g., 8.52 or 11.23). The auction process determines the coupon rate, and thereafter the issue trades on dollar price in price units of 1/32 of 1% of par (par is taken to be $100). For example, a quote of 92-14 refers to a price of 92 and 14/32. Thus, on the basis of $100,000 par value, a change in price of 1% equates to $1,000 and 1/32 equates to $31.25. A *plus* sign following the number of 32nds means that a 64th is added to the price. For example, 92-14+ refers to a price of 92 and 29/64 or 92.453125% of par value.

On quote sheets and screens the price quote is followed by some "yield-to-maturity" measure. The yield quotes shown may be based on the Street or Treasury method. The difference between the two yield measures is the procedure used to discount the first coupon payment when it is not exactly 6 months away. The first coupon payment may not occur in exactly 6 months for two reasons. First, when the Treasury issues certain securities, the first coupon payment may be more or less than 6 months away—a situation referred to as an "odd" or "irregular" first coupon payment. When the first coupon payment is *more* than 6 months away, the security is said to have a *long first coupon*. The 5-year Treasury note is an example of a Treasury security usually issued as a long first coupon security (see Exhibit 5.1). The first coupon payment for the 5-year Treasury note occurs approximately 8 months after the issuance date. When the first coupon payment is *less* than 6 months

EXHIBIT 5.2   Treasury Bill and Bond Notes from Knight-Ridder

TREASURY BILL AND COUPON YIELDS   -- 4/05   04:19P

BILLS	BID	ASK	BOND EQUIVALENT		C.D. EQUIVALENT		EFFECTIVE	
3Mo 7/07/88	6.00	-98+	6.178-	6.162	6.093-	6.078		
6Mo 10/06/88	6.20	-18+	6.490-	6.474	6.402-	6.386		
1Yr 3/16/89	6.55+	-54	6.976-	6.959	6.993-	6.976		

COUPONS	BID	ASK	FED		SIA		EFFECTIVE	
7 3/8 3/90	99.20	-21+	7.582-	7.556	7.581-	7.555	7.581-	7.555
7 3/8 2/91	98.31	-00+	7.784-	7.765	7.779-	7.760	7.779-	7.760
7 7/8 3/92	99.16+	-18	8.019-	8.005	8.019-	8.005	8.019-	8.005
7 5/8 5/93	97.23	-25	8.180-	8.165	8.177-	8.162	8.167-	8.152
8 5/8 1/95	100.24+	-26	8.474-	8.465	8.470-	8.461	8.470-	8.461
8 1/8 2/98	96.17+	-19	8.653-	8.645	8.650-	8.643	8.650-	8.643
9 3/8 2/06	103.28+	-30	8.935-	8.930	8.933-	8.928	8.916-	8.911
8 7/8 8/17	100.07	-08+	8.854-	8.849	8.852-	8.848	8.846-	8.841

89

from the date of issuance, the Treasury security is said to have a *short first coupon*. This happens with a security whose scheduled auction date (the 15th or end of the month) falls on a weekend or a holiday. In such cases, the Treasury issues the security on the next business day but pays the first coupon on the 15th or the end of month 6 months later. Thus the first coupon payment is less than 6 months away. The second reason for a short first coupon is when the security is purchased between coupon dates.

The difference between Street and Treasury practices in computing yield is the procedure for discounting over a long-first-coupon period and over a fractional 6-month period.[6] The Treasury method (also called the "Fed" method) assumes simple interest over the period from the valuation date to the next coupon payment. The Street method (also called the Securities Industry Association or SIA method) assumes compound interest over the period from the valuation date to the next coupon payment.[7] Once a security is issued and traded in the secondary market, investors and traders use the Street method.

Exhibit 5.2 shows the bid-ask price, Fed (Treasury) yield, and SIA (Street) yield for the current (on-the-run) Treasury coupon issues on April 5, 1988.

The invoice price that the buyer pays is equal to the agreed-upon price plus accrued interest. Accrued interest is based on the actual number of days that the security is held. (This is referred to as "actual over actual" basis.) The accrued interest is determined as follows:

$$\frac{C}{2} \times \frac{\text{Actual number of days held}}{\text{Actual number of days in coupon period}}$$

[6]For a further discussion of the Fed yield and the effective or Street yield, see Sharmin Mossavar-Rahmani, "Measuring Risk and Reward in the Treasury Market," Chap. 4 in *The Handbook of Treasury Securities: Trading and Portfolio Strategies*.

[7]For example, suppose that the next coupon payment is X days from the valuation date (or previous coupon date) and W is the number of days between the issuance date (or previous coupon date) and the first coupon date (or next coupon date). Letting K denote the ratio of X to W, the discounting of a coupon payment, C, for both methods for a semiannual yield to maturity, y, is:

Simple interest over period (Treasury method):

$$\frac{C}{(1 + Ky)}$$

Compound interest over period (Street method):

$$\frac{C}{(1 + y)^K}$$

Financing Dealer Positions

Suppose a government dealer has purchased $10 million of a particular Treasury security. Where does he obtain the funds to finance that position? Of course, the dealer can finance the position with his own funds. Typically, however, the dealer will use the repurchase agreement or "repo" market to obtain financing. In the repo market the dealer can use the $10 million of the Treasury security as collateral for a loan. The term of the loan and the interest rate that the dealer agrees to pay (called the *repo rate*) are specified. When the term of the loan is 1 day, it is called an *overnight repo*; a loan for more than 1 day is called a *term repo*.

The transaction is referred to as a repurchase agreement because it calls for the sale of the security and its repurchase at a future date. Both the sale and the purchase price are specified in the agreement. The difference between the purchase (repurchase) price and the sale price is the dollar interest cost of the loan.[8]

Let's illustrate the repurchase agreement with our dealer who needs to finance $10 million of a Treasury bond that he purchased and plans to hold overnight. Suppose that a customer of the dealer has excess funds of $10 million. The dealer would agree to deliver ("sell") $10 million of the Treasury bond to the customer for an amount determined by the repo rate and buy ("repurchase") the same Treasury security from the customer for $10 million. Suppose that the overnight repo rate is 6.5%. Then, as will be explained below, the dealer would agree to deliver the Treasury bonds for $9,998,194 and repurchase the same bonds for $10 million the next day. The $1,806 difference between the "sale" price of $9,998,194 and the repurchase price of $10 million is the dollar interest on the financing. From the customer's perspective, the same agreement is called a *reverse repo*.

The following formula is used to calculate the dollar interest on a repo transaction:

$$\text{Dollar interest} = (\text{Dollar principal}) \times (\text{Repo rate}) \times \left(\frac{\text{Repo term}}{360} \right)$$

[8]For a more detailed description of the mechanics of repurchase agreements, see Andrea J. Trachtenberg, "Repurchase Agreements," Chap. 7 in *The Handbook of Treasury Securities: Trading and Portfolio Strategies*. The proper structuring of a repo cannot be overemphasized. In the 1980s the failure of several securities firms (for example, Drysdale Securities Corporation and Lombard-Wall, Inc.), and the resulting losses for their customers because of improperly structured repo agreements, attest to the importance of understanding the mechanics of the repo market.

Notice that the interest is computed on a 360-day basis. In our example, for a repo rate of 6.5% and a repo term of 1 day (overnight), the dollar interest is $1,806:

$$= \$10,000,000 \times .065 \times \frac{1}{360}$$

$$= \$1,806$$

What are the advantages of using the repo market for the dealer borrowing on a short-term basis and for the customer lending funds on a short-term basis? For the dealer, the repo rate is less than the cost of bank financing. From the customer's perspective, the repo market offers an attractive yield on a short-term secured transaction that is highly liquid.

Thus far we have focused on financing a government dealer's long position in the repo market. The repo market can also be used by government dealers to cover a short position. For example, suppose that a government dealer sold short $10 million of Treasury securities 2 weeks ago and must now cover the position. The dealer can do a reverse repo (agree to buy the securities and sell them back).

Trading and arbitrage strategies involving cash market Treasury securities and Treasury futures rely on dealer financing in the repo market. For example, suppose that a dealer can purchase Treasury bonds with funds financed with a 30-day term repo. Suppose also that the dealer can enter into an agreement at the same time to sell the Treasury bonds for a specified price 30 days from now. If the cost of financing the position (the repo rate) is less than the rate that the dealer would earn holding the Treasury bonds and selling them 30 days from now, then an arbitrage profit will be realized. How can the dealer obtain a price now for the sale (or delivery) of the Treasury bonds 30 days from now? As we shall see in Chapter 11, this can be done in the Treasury bond futures market. Thus there is a relationship between the repo rate, the Treasury bond price, and the futures price. If the repo rate is such that the dealer can finance the Treasury bond and sell it in the futures market so as to earn a return higher than the repo rate, arbitrage profits are available. The actions of dealers and other market partici-pants will assure that these arbitrage profits are short-lived, however. In fact, dealers regularly calculate the break-even rate that will elimi-nate any arbitrage profits; this is called the *implied repo rate*. When the implied repo rate and the repo rate differ, arbitrage opportunities may be available.[9]

STRIPPED TREASURY SECURITIES

Merrill Lynch and Salomon Brothers created zero-coupon Treasury securities in August 1982. Merrill Lynch marketed these Treasury securities as "Treasury Income Growth Receipts" (TIGRs), while Salomon Brothers marketed them as "Certificates of Accrual on Treasury Securities" (CATS). The two investment banking firms created these instruments by purchasing long-term Treasury bonds and depositing them in a bank custody account. They then issued receipts representing an ownership interest in each coupon payment on the underlying Treasury bond in the account and a receipt on the underlying Treasury bond's maturity value. This process of separating each coupon payment, as well as the principal (called the *corpus*), and selling securities against them is referred to as *coupon stripping*.[10] Although the receipts created from the coupon-stripping process were not issued by the U.S. Treasury, the underlying bond deposited in the bank custody account is a debt obligation of the U.S. Treasury; thus the cash flow from the underlying security is certain.

To illustrate the process, suppose $100 million of a Treasury bond with a 20-year maturity and a coupon rate of 10% is purchased to create zero-coupon Treasury securities. The cash flow from this Treasury bond is 40 semiannual payments of $5 million each ($100 million times .10 divided by 2) *and* the repayment of principal (corpus) of $100 million 20 years from now. This Treasury bond is deposited in a bank custody account. Receipts are then issued, each with a different single-payment claim on the bank custody account. Since in our example there are 41 different payments that will be made by the Treasury, each receipt representing a single-payment claim on each Treasury payment is effectively a zero-coupon bond. The amount of the maturity value for a receipt on a particular Treasury payment, coupon or corpus, depends on the amount of the payment to be made by the Treasury on

---

[9]In this chapter we are focusing on repo transactions involving Treasury securities. Dealers in the mortgage-backed securities also finance their position in the repo market. In the repo market for mortgage-backed securities, it is common for the securities that are delivered to be similar, but not identical, to the securities sold.

[10]The profits that can be obtained from coupon stripping are explained in the next chapter.

the underlying Treasury bond. In our example, 40 coupon receipts each have a maturity value of $5 million, and one receipt, the corpus, has a maturity value of $100 million. The maturity dates for the receipts will coincide with the corresponding payment dates by the Treasury.

Before long, other investment banking firms joined Merrill Lynch and Salomon Brothers in creating zero-coupon receipts.[11] These receipts are referred to as *trademark* zero-coupon Treasury securities since they are associated with a particular firm. Because receipts of one firm were rarely traded by competing dealers, the secondary market was not liquid for any one trademark. To broaden the market and improve the liquidity of these receipts, a group of primary dealers in the government market agreed to issue generic receipts that would not be directly associated with any of the participating dealers. These generic receipts are referred to as "Treasury Receipts" (TRs).

The problem with both the trademark and the generic receipts was that they cleared by physical delivery, which proved cumbersome and inefficient. In August 1985 the Treasury announced its Separate Trading of Registered Interest and Principal of Securities (STRIPS) program. This program allows the stripping of designated Treasury issues for the purpose of creating zero-coupon Treasury securities. The zero-coupon Treasury securities created under the STRIPS program are direct obligations of the U.S. government. Moreover, the securities clear through the Federal Reserve's book-entry system.

The STRIPS program put an end to the origination of trademarks and generic receipts. By September 1986, $100 billion of securities had been issued under this program. Because of the greater marketability of the STRIPS compared to trademarks and generic receipts, these securities now dominate the zero-coupon Treasury market.

FEDERALLY SPONSORED CREDIT AGENCY SECURITIES

The market for securities of federally sponsored credit agencies, while smaller than that for Treasury securities, has in recent years become an active and important sector of the bond market. Federally sponsored credit agencies were created by Congress as *privately* owned financial

---

[11]For example, Lehman Brothers offered "Lehman Investment Opportunities Notes" (LIONs), E. F. Hutton offered "Treasury Bond Receipts" (TBRs), and Dean Witter Reynolds offered "Easy Growth Treasury Receipts" (ETRs).

intermediaries whose purpose is to channel funds to particular sectors of the economy that Congress believes requires special assistance.

There are five federally sponsored credit agencies. The *Farm Credit System* is responsible for the credit market in the agricultural sector of the economy. Three federally sponsored credit agencies— *Federal Home Loan Bank, Federal Home Loan Mortgage Corporation,* and *Federal National Mortgage Association*—are responsible for providing credit to the mortgage and housing sectors.[12] The *Student Loan Marketing Association* provides funds to support higher education.

The federally sponsored credit agencies obtain their funds by issuing securities. Credit agencies issue two types of securities: discount notes and bonds. Discount notes are short-term obligations, with maturities ranging from overnight to 360 days. Bonds are sold with maturities greater than 2 years. Agencies have issued securities using some of the recent innovative bond structures that we will discuss in this book.

These securities are not backed by the full faith and credit of the U.S. government, as is the case with Treasury securities. Consequently, an investor who purchases a federally sponsored credit agency security is exposed to credit risk. The yield spread between these securities and Treasury securities of comparable maturity reflects differences in perceived credit risk and liquidity. The spread due to credit risk reflects the financial problems faced by the credit agency and the likelihood that the federal government will allow the credit agency to default on its outstanding obligations.

Two examples will illustrate this point. In late 1981/early 1982 the net income of the Federal National Mortgage Association weakened and analysts reported that the securities of this credit agency carried greater risk than previously perceived. As a result, the yield spread on the debt of this credit agency over Treasuries rose from 91 basis points (on average) in 1981 to as high as 150 basis points.[13] In subsequent years the Federal National Mortgage Association's net income improved and its yield spread to Treasuries narrowed. As another example, in

---

[12]One federal entity that facilitates credit in the housing sector that we shall discuss in Chapter 10 is the Government National Mortgage Association. While this federal entity, popularly known as Ginnie Mae, is often referred to as an "agency," it is not a privately owned entity. Instead, it is part of the Department of Housing and Urban Development. Ginnie Mae does not issue securities. However, it does guarantee issues that are backed by the full faith and credit of the U.S. government.

[13]Michael J. Moran, "The Federally Sponsored Credit Agencies: An Overview," *Federal Reserve Bulletin,* June 1986, p. 380.

1985 the yield on securities of the Farm Credit System rose substantially above those on comparable-maturity Treasuries because of the agency's financial difficulties. Between 1985 and 1986 the spread varied according to the prospects of congressional approval of a bailout measure for the system.

The price-quotation convention for federally sponsored credit agency securities is the same as that for Treasury securities. That is, the bid and asked price quotations are expressed as a percentage of par plus fractional 32nds of a point.

The remainder of this chapter is given over to brief descriptions of three of the five federally sponsored credit agencies. The two agencies not included here—the Federal Home Loan Mortgage Corporation and the Federal National Mortgage Association—will be discussed in Chapter 10.

Farm Credit System

The purpose of the Farm Credit System is to facilitate adequate, dependable credit and related services to the agricultural sector of the economy. The Farm Credit System consists of three entities: the Federal Land Banks, Federal Intermediate Credit Banks, and Banks for Cooperatives. The regulatory agency that oversees the Farm Credit System is the Farm Credit Administration.

All financing for the Federal Credit System is arranged through the Federal Farm Credit Banks Funding Corporation, which issues consolidated obligations through a selling group consisting of approximately 150 members. For discount notes, the selling group consists of only four dealers.[14]

Federal Home Loan Bank System

The Federal Home Loan Bank System consists of the 12 district Federal Home Loan Banks (which are instrumentalities of the U.S. government) and their member banks. An independent federal agency, the Federal Home Loan Bank Board, regulates all federally chartered savings and loan associations and savings banks, as well as state-chartered institutions insured by the Federal Savings and Loan Insurance Corporation.

[14]William C. Oliva and David M. Head, *Structure and Operations of Selected Federal Agencies and International Organizations* (New York: Salomon Brothers, Inc, December 1985), p. 3.

The major source of debt funding for the Federal Home Loan Banks is obtained from the issuance of consolidated debt obligations. These obligations are joint and several obligations of the 12 Federal Home Loan Banks. They are generally issued through a nationwide selling group consisting of numerous securities dealers. Discount notes are sold through a few dealers located in the New York and Boston Federal Reserve Bank Districts.

Student Loan Marketing Association

Popularly known as "Sallie Mae," the Student Loan Marketing Association provides liquidity for private lenders participating in the Federal Guaranteed Student Loan Program, the Health Education Assistance Loan Program, and the PLUS loan program (a program that provides loans for the parents of undergraduate students). Sallie Mae is permitted to purchase and offer investors participation in student loans.

Sallie Mae issues unsecured debt obligations in the form of discount notes. In January 1982 Sallie Mae began issuing notes whose coupon rate, which was paid every 6 months, changed on the basis of the bond-equivalent yield on 91-day Treasury bills. These notes are called floating-rate notes and will be discussed in Chapter 7. Sallie Mae also has long-term fixed-rate securities and zero-coupon bonds outstanding.

SUMMARY

In this chapter we discussed Treasury securities, zero-coupon Treasury securities, and federally sponsored credit agency securities. The Treasury market plays a prominent role in all financial markets because yields on Treasuries, which are perceived as having no credit risk, are the benchmark for yields on comparable non-Treasury securities. Unlike Treasuries, securities issued by federally sponsored credit agencies expose the investor to credit risk as well as less liquidity.

6

ANALYSIS
OF THE TREASURY MARKET

The yield on Treasury securities is a benchmark for determining the yield on non-Treasury securities. Consequently, all financial market participants are interested in the relationship between yield and maturity for Treasury securities. In this chapter we examine this relationship and its implications for coupon stripping. Toward the end of the chapter we discuss various strategies to enhance portfolio performance in the Treasury market.

ANALYSIS OF THE YIELD CURVE

The graphical depiction of the relationship between the yield on Treasury securities for different maturities is known as the *yield curve*. Exhibit 6.1 shows four hypothetical yield curves.

While a yield curve is typically constructed on the basis of observed yields and maturities, the term structure of interest rates is the relationship between the yield on zero-coupon Treasury securities and their maturities. Any noncallable security can be considered a package of zero-coupon instruments. That is, each zero-coupon instrument in the package has a maturity equal to its coupon payment date

EXHIBIT 6.1   Four Hypothetical Yield Curves

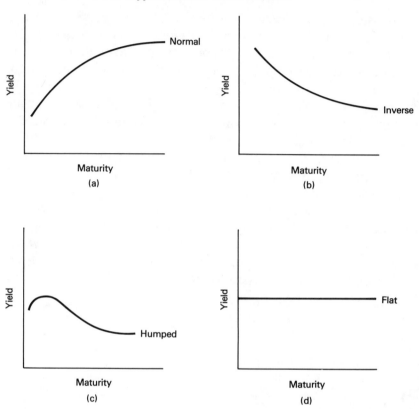

and, in the case of the principal, the maturity date. The value of the security should equal the value of all the component zero-coupon instruments. If this does not hold, it is possible to create arbitrage profits. To determine the value of each zero-coupon instrument, it is necessary to know the yield on the zero-coupon Treasury corresponding to that maturity. This yield is called the *spot rate,* and the graphical depiction of the relationship between the spot rate and its maturity is called the *spot rate curve.*

In this section we explain how the theoretical spot rate curve is constructed and the implications for arbitrage opportunities if the actual yield curve departs from the theoretical spot rate curve. More specifically, if the yields for the two curves are different, the process of coupon stripping described in the previous chapter may be profitable. In turn, this process will drive market yields toward the theoretical spot rates.

Constructing the Theoretical Spot Rate Curve

It is possible to construct a theoretical spot rate curve from the observed yields on Treasury bills and Treasury coupon securities. To see how this is done, we'll use the hypothetical price, yield (yield to maturity), and maturity for the 20 Treasury securities shown in Exhibit 6.2.[1]

The basic principle is that the value of a Treasury coupon security should be equal to the value of a package of zero-coupon Treasury securities. Consider first the 6-month Treasury bill in Exhibit 6.2. Since a Treasury bill is a zero-coupon instrument, its yield of 8% is equal to the spot rate. Similarly, for the 1-year Treasury, the yield of 8.3% is the 1-year spot rate. Given these two spot rates, we can compute the spot rate for a 1.5-year zero-coupon Treasury. The value or price of a 1.5-year zero-coupon Treasury should equal the present value of three cash flows from the 1.5-year coupon Treasury, where the yield used for discounting is the spot rate corresponding to the cash flow. Using $100 as par, the cash flow for the 1.5-year coupon Treasury is:

0.5 years	.085 × $100 × .5	=	$ 4.25
1.0 year	.085 × $100 × .5	=	$ 4.25
1.5 years	.085 × $100 × .5 + 100	=	$ 104.25

The present value of the cash flow is then:

$$\frac{4.25}{(1+y_1)^1} + \frac{4.25}{(1+y_2)^2} + \frac{104.25}{(1+y_3)^3}$$

where y_1 = one-half the 6-month theoretical spot rate
y_2 = one-half the 1-year theoretical spot rate
y_3 = one-half the 1.5-year theoretical spot rate

Since the 6-month spot rate and 1-year spot rate are 8.0% and 8.3%, respectively:

$$y_1 = .04 \text{ and } y_2 = .0415$$

Therefore the present value of the 1.5-year coupon Treasury security is:

---

[1]In practice, when the yield curve is constructed using the methodology described here, only the observed yields of bonds selling at par (current coupon issues) are used. The resulting yield curve is called the *par yield curve*.

EXHIBIT 6.2   Maturity and Yield to Maturity for 20 Hypothetical Treasury Securities

Maturity	Coupon	Yield to Maturity	Price
0.50	0.0000	0.0800	96.15
1.00	0.0000	0.0830	92.19
1.50	0.0850	0.0890	99.45
2.00	0.0900	0.0920	99.64
2.50	0.1100	0.0940	103.49
3.00	0.0950	0.0970	99.49
3.50	0.1000	0.1000	100.00
4.00	0.1000	0.1040	98.72
4.50	0.1150	0.1060	103.16
5.00	0.0875	0.1080	92.24
5.50	0.1050	0.1090	98.38
6.00	0.1100	0.1120	99.14
6.50	0.0850	0.1140	86.94
7.00	0.0825	0.1160	84.24
7.50	0.1100	0.1180	96.09
8.00	0.0650	0.1190	72.62
8.50	0.0875	0.1200	82.97
9.00	0.1300	0.1220	104.30
9.50	0.1150	0.1240	95.06
10.00	0.1250	0.1250	100.00

$$\frac{4.25}{(1.0400)^1} + \frac{4.25}{(1.0415)^2} + \frac{104.25}{(1+y_3)^3}$$

Since the price of the 1.5-year coupon Treasury security is $99.45, the following relationship must hold:

$$99.45 = \frac{4.25}{(1.0400)^1} + \frac{4.25}{(1.0415)^2} + \frac{104.25}{(1+y_3)^3}$$

We can now solve for the theoretical 1.5-year spot rate as follows:

$$99.45 = 4.08654 + 3.91805 + \frac{104.25}{(1+y_3)^3}$$

$$91.44541 = \frac{104.25}{(1+y_3)^3}$$

$$(1+y_3)^3 = 1.140024$$

$$y_3 = .04465$$

Doubling this yield, we obtain the bond-equivalent yield of .0893 or 8.93%, which is the theoretical 1.5-year spot rate.

Given the theoretical 1.5-year spot rate, we can obtain the theoretical 2-year spot rate. The cash flow for the 2-year coupon Treasury in Exhibit 6.2 is:

0.5 years	.090 × $100 × .5	=	$ 4.50
1.0 year	.090 × $100 × .5	=	$ 4.50
1.5 years	.090 × $100 × .5	=	$ 4.50
2.0 years	.090 × $100 × .5 + 100	=	$104.50

The present value of the cash flow is then:

$$\frac{4.50}{(1+y_1)^1} + \frac{4.50}{(1+y_2)^2} + \frac{4.50}{(1+y_3)^3} + \frac{104.50}{(1+y_4)^4}$$

where y_4 = one-half the 2-year theoretical spot rate

Since the 6-month spot rate, 1-year spot rate, and 1.5-year spot rate are 8.0%, 8.3%, and 8.93%, respectively:

$$y_1 = .04 \qquad y_2 = .0415 \qquad \text{and } y_3 = .04465$$

Therefore the present value of the 2-year coupon Treasury security is:

$$\frac{4.50}{(1.0400)^1} + \frac{4.50}{(1.0415)^2} + \frac{4.50}{(1.04465)^3} + \frac{104.50}{(1+y_4)^4}$$

Since the price of the 2-year coupon Treasury security is $99.64, the following relationship must hold:

$$99.64 = \frac{4.50}{(1.0400)^1} + \frac{4.50}{(1.0415)^2} + \frac{4.50}{(1.04464)^3} + \frac{104.50}{(1+y_4)^4}$$

We can now solve for the theoretical 2-year spot rate as follows:

$$99.64 = 4.32692 + 4.14853 + 3.94730 + \frac{104.50}{(1+y_4)^4}$$

$$87.21725 = \frac{104.50}{(1+y_4)^4}$$

$$(1+y_4)^4 = 1.198158$$

$$y_4 = .046235$$

Doubling this yield, we obtain the theoretical 2-year spot rate bond-equivalent yield of 9.247%.

We can then use the theoretical 2-year spot rate and the 2.5-year coupon Treasury in Exhibit 6.2 to compute the 2.5-year theoretical spot rate. In general, to compute the theoretical spot rate for the nth 6-month period, the following equation must be solved:

$$P_n = \frac{C^*}{(1+y_1)^1} + \frac{C^*}{(1+y_2)^2} + \frac{C^*}{(1+y_3)^3} + \dots + \frac{C^*+100}{(1+y_n)^n}$$

where P_n = price of the coupon Treasury with n periods to maturity
(per \$100 of par value)

C^* = coupon interest for the coupon Treasury with n periods
to maturity per \$100 of par value

y_t for $t = 1, 2, \dots, n-1$ are the theoretical spot rates that are known

The above expression can be rewritten as follows:

$$P_n = C^* \sum_{t=1}^{n-1} \frac{1}{(1+y_t)^t} + \frac{C^*+100}{(1+y_n)^n}$$

Solving for y_n, we get:

$$y_n = \left[\frac{C^* + 100}{P_n - C^* \sum_{t=1}^{n-1} \frac{1}{(1 + y_t)^t}} \right]^{1/n} - 1$$

Doubling y gives the theoretical spot rate on a bond-equivalent basis.

The above equation was used to determine the theoretical spot rates for each hypothetical Treasury security shown in Exhibit 6.2. The theoretical spot rates are presented in Exhibit 6.3. *It is this yield/maturity structure that would be used to construct the theoretical spot rate curve that is referred to as the term structure of interest rates.*

Creating a Spot Rate Curve
from Zero-Coupon Treasury Securities

In Chapter 5 we discussed zero-coupon Treasury securities. It would seem logical that the observed yield on zero-coupon Treasury

EXHIBIT 6.3   Theoretical Spot Yields and Implied Forward Rates

Maturity	Yield to Maturity	Theoretical Spot Yield	Implied Forward Rate
0.50	0.0800	0.08000	—
1.00	0.0830	0.08300	0.08600
1.50	0.0890	0.08930	0.10196
2.00	0.0920	0.09247	0.10201
2.50	0.0940	0.09468	0.10354
3.00	0.0970	0.09787	0.11389
3.50	0.1000	0.10129	0.12193
4.00	0.1040	0.10592	0.13862
4.50	0.1060	0.10850	0.12925
5.00	0.1080	0.11021	0.12566
5.50	0.1090	0.11175	0.12721
6.00	0.1120	0.11584	0.16136
6.50	0.1140	0.11744	0.13673
7.00	0.1160	0.11991	0.15228
7.50	0.1180	0.12405	0.18287
8.00	0.1190	0.12278	0.10382
8.50	0.1200	0.12546	0.16880
9.00	0.1220	0.13152	0.23722
9.50	0.1240	0.13377	0.17468
10.00	0.1250	0.13623	0.18351

securities can be used to construct an actual spot rate curve. There are problems with this approach, however.

First, the liquidity of the zero-coupon market is not as great as that of the coupon Treasury market. Second, there are maturity sectors of the zero-coupon Treasury market that attract specific investors who may be willing to trade off yield for an attractive feature associated with that particular maturity sector, thereby distorting the term structure relationship. For example, unlike domestic taxable entities, the Japanese tax code grants Japanese investors preferential tax treatment on zero-coupon Treasuries.[2] As a result, there is often considerable participation by Japanese investors in long-maturity zero-coupon Treasury bonds, which has the effect of driving down yields in that maturity sector.

Term Structure Modeling

The methodology demonstrating how the theoretical spot rate curve can be constructed from observed yields, although useful, is in practice quite complex for several reasons. First, there may be more than one Treasury issue with the same maturity selling at different yields.[3] Second, there is not a current Treasury issue for every possible maturity, so a continuous yield curve cannot be drawn using the procedure we just illustrated. Third, some Treasury securities sell above or below par, which may result in different tax treatments. Finally, there are some outstanding Treasury bonds that are callable.

The objective in empirical estimation of the term structure is to construct a spot rate curve that (1) fits the data sufficiently well and (2) is a sufficiently smooth function.[4] Several methodologies have been

---

[2]More specifically, the Japanese government grants a favorable capital gains tax treatment on those zero-coupon Treasuries where the corpus is the underlying collateral. This is why Treasury receipts for the last coupon payment and the corpus are issued separately, and are identified in dealer quotes and on screens as "coupon" or "corpus." The Treasury receipt representing payment from the underlying "coupon" will sell at a higher yield than the receipt from the underlying corpus.

[3]A procedure for computing the theoretical spot rate curve by using Treasuries with different coupons but the same maturity is explained in John Caks, "The Coupon Effect on Yield to Maturity," *The Journal of Finance*, March 1977, pp. 103–115. For a mathematically simpler version of this approach, see Alden L. Toevs and Lawrence Dyer, *The Term Structure of Interest Rates and Its Use in Asset and Liability Management* (New York: Morgan Stanley, October 1986), p. 47.

[4]For a further discussion of the desirable properties of models for estimating the term structure, see Terence C. Langetieg and Stephen J. Smoot, "An Appraisal of Alternative Spline Methodologies for Estimating the Term Structure of Interest Rates," working paper, University of Southern California, December 1981.

suggested to estimate the term structure.[5] Recently, Vasicek and Fong proposed an approach that has been applied to historical price data on Treasury securities with satisfactory results.[6] The approach produces forward rates (discussed below) that are a smooth, continuous function of maturity. The model has desirable asymptotic properties for long maturities, and exhibits both sufficient flexibility to fit a wide variety of shapes of the term structure and sufficient robustness to produce stable forward rates. An adjustment for any possible tax effect and for call features is included in the Vasicek-Fong model.

Implied Forward Rates

Suppose that an investor has a 1-year investment horizon and is faced with the following two alternatives:

Alternative 1: Buy a 1-year Treasury bill.

Alternative 2: Buy a 6-month Treasury bill, and when it matures, buy another 6-month Treasury bill.

The investor will be indifferent between the two alternatives if they produce the same yield over the 1-year investment horizon. The investor knows the spot rate on the 6-month Treasury bill and that on the 1-year Treasury bill. However, he does not know what yield will be available on a 6-month Treasury bill purchased 6 months from now. The yield on a 6-month Treasury bill 6 months from now is called the *forward rate*. Given the spot rate for the 6-month Treasury bill and that for the 1-year bill, the forward rate on a 6-month Treasury bill that will make the investor indifferent to the two alternatives can be determined as follows.

By investing in the 1-year Treasury bill, the investor will receive $100 at the end of 1 year. The price (cost) of the 1-year Treasury bill would be:

[5]See, for example, Willard R. Carleton and Ian Cooper, "Estimation and Uses of the Term Structure of Interest Rates," *Journal of Finance*, September 1976, pp. 1067–1083; J. Huston McCulloch, "Measuring the Term Structure of Interest Rates," *Journal of Business*, January 1971, pp. 19–31, and J. Huston McCulloch, "The Tax Adjusted Yield Curve," *Journal of Finance*, June 1975, pp. 811–830.

[6]Earlier approaches have attempted to estimate the term structure of interest rates by fitting polynomial splines of the second or third order. Splines, being piecewise polynomials, are inherently ill-suited to fit an exponential-type curve that would represent the term structure. (See Langetieg and Smoot, "An Appraisal of Alternative Spline Methodologies for Estimating the Term Structure of Interest Rates.") Vasicek and Fong propose an approach, which can be termed *exponential spline fitting*, that overwhelms the drawbacks of using piecewise splines. See Oldrich A. Vasicek and H. Gifford Fong, "Term Structure Modeling Using Exponential Splines," *Journal of Finance*, May 1982, pp. 339–348.

$$\frac{100}{(1+y_2)^2}$$

where y_2 = one-half the bond-equivalent yield of the theoretical 1-year spot rate

Suppose that the investor purchased a 6-month Treasury bill for $X. At the end of 6 months, the value of this investment would be:

$$X(1+y_1)$$

where y_1 = one-half the bond-equivalent yield of the theoretical 6-month spot rate

Let f_2 be one-half the forward rate on a 6-month Treasury bill available 6 months from now. Then the future dollars available at the end of 1 year from the $X investment is:

$$X(1+y_1)(1+f_2)$$

Suppose that we want to know how many $X the investor must invest today in order to get $100 1 year from now. This can be found as follows:

$$X(1+y_1)(1+f_2)=100$$

Solving, we get:

$$X=\frac{100}{(1+y_1)(1+f_2)}$$

The investor will be indifferent between the two alternatives confronting him if he makes the same dollar investment and receives $100 at the end of 1-year from both alternatives. That is, the investor will be indifferent if:

$$\frac{100}{(1+y_2)^2}=\frac{100}{(1+y_1)(1+f_2)}$$

Solving for f_2, we get:

$$f_2 = \frac{(1 + y_2)^2}{(1 + y_1)} - 1$$

Doubling f_2 gives the bond-equivalent yield for the 6-month forward rate.

For a concrete illustration, we will use the theoretical spot rates shown in Exhibit 6.3. We know that:

6-month bill spot rate = .080; therefore y_1 = .0400.
1-year bill spot rate   = .083; therefore y_2 = .0415.

Substituting into the equation, we have:

$$f_2 = \frac{(1.0415)^2}{1.0400} - 1$$
$$= .043$$

The forward yield on a 6-month security, quoted on a bond-equivalent basis, is 8.60% (.043 x 2). Let's confirm our results. The price of a 1-year Treasury bill with a $100 maturity value is:

$$\frac{100}{(1.0415)^2} = 92.19$$

If 92.19 is invested for 6 months at the 6-month spot rate of 8%, the amount at the end of 6 months will be:

92.19 (1.0400) = 95.8776

If 95.8776 is reinvested for another 6 months in a 6-month Treasury offering 4.3% for 6 months (8.6% annually), the amount at the end of 1 year will be:

95.8876 (1.043) = 100

Both alternatives will have the same $100 payoff if the 6-month Treasury bill yield 6 months from now is 4.3% (8.6% on a bond-equivalent basis). This means that if an investor is guaranteed a 4.3%

yield on a 6-month Treasury bill 6 months from now, he will be indifferent between the two alternatives.

We used the theoretical spot rates to compute the forward rate. The resulting forward rate is called the *implied forward rate*. Although we demonstrated only how to get the 6-month implied forward rate 6 months from now, it is a simple exercise to compute the 6-month implied forward rate any number of periods from now. In general, the formula for the 6-month implied forward rate n periods from now is:

$$f_n = \frac{(1 + y_n)^n}{(1 + y_{n-1})^{n-1}} - 1$$

where y_n is a semiannual spot rate

Doubling f_n gives the 6-month implied forward rate on a bond-equivalent basis.

The last column in Exhibit 6.3 shows the 6-month implied forward rate on a bond-equivalent basis for the theoretical spot rates shown in the same exhibit.

Overview of Theories of the Term Structure of Interest Rates

In Exhibit 6.1 we presented four hypothetical yield curves. Panel A shows an upward-sloping yield curve; that is, yields rise as maturity increases. This shape is commonly referred to as a "normal" or "positive" yield curve. Panel B shows a downward-sloping or "inverted" yield curve in which yields decline as maturity increases. Panel C shows a "humped" yield curve. Finally, Panel D shows a "flat" yield curve. Historically, all four yield curves have been observed at different points in the business cycle.

Two theories have evolved to explain the observed shapes of the yield curve: the expectations theory and the preferred habitat or market segmentation theory.[7]

According to the *expectations theory*, the shape of the yield curve is determined by market participants' (borrowers' and lenders') expectations of future interest rates. That is, the shape is determined by

---

[7]For a detailed discussion of these theories, see Richard W. McEnally, "The Term Structure of Interest Rates," Chap. 53 in Frank J. Fabozzi and Irving M. Pollack, eds., *The Handbook of Fixed Income Securities* (Homewood, IL: Dow Jones-Irwin, 1987).

expected forward interest rates. There are two forms of the expectations theory: the pure expectations theory and the liquidity premium theory.

Proponents of the *pure expectations theory,* also called the *unbiased expectations theory,* argue that the shape of the yield curve is determined *only* by expected forward interest rates. When interest rates are expected to rise, the yield curve will be normal or positively sloped; when they are expected to fall, the yield curve will be inverted or negatively sloped. If the pure expectations theory holds, the implied forward rates that we discussed earlier will be the market's unbiased estimate of the yields expected in the future.

The *liquidity premium theory,* also called the *biased expectations theory,* asserts that the shape of the yield curve is determined by *both* expectations of future interest rates and a premium demanded (in terms of higher yield) for extending maturity. As explained in Chapter 4, the longer the maturity, the greater the bond price volatility. Investors want to be compensated for accepting this risk associated with longer-term securities. Consequently, the forward rates embody both interest rate expectations and a liquidity premium. According to this theory, the implied forward rates will not be an unbiased estimate of the market's expectations of future interest rates because they embody a liquidity premium.

The *preferred habitat* or *market segmentation theory* postulates that the major reason for the shape of the yield curve is because asset/liability management constraints (either regulatory or self-imposed), cause creditors (borrowers) to restrict their lending (financing) to specific maturity sectors. Thus the shape of the yield curve is determined by supply and demand for securities within the specific maturity sector.

The preferred habitat theory basically assumes that, when lending or financing, creditors and borrowers will not freely substitute securities from one maturity sector to another on the basis of interest rate expectations. The expectations theory, in contrast, assumes that market participants (creditors and borrowers) will move from one maturity sector to another according to their interest rate expectations.

COUPON STRIPPING AND THE YIELD CURVE

In Chapter 5 we explained the process of stripping Treasury securities to create zero-coupon Treasury securities. The potential profitability of such a venture depends on the actual yields on Treasury securities and the theoretical spot rate curve.

To see how a government dealer can realize a profit from coupon stripping (creating zero-coupon Treasury securities), consider a 10-year, 12.5% coupon Treasury selling at par (offering a yield to maturity of 12.5%). Suppose that a government dealer buys the issue at par and strips it, expecting to sell the zero-coupon Treasury securities at the yields indicated for the corresponding maturity shown in Exhibit 6.2.

Exhibit 6.4 shows the price that would be received for each zero-coupon Treasury security created. The price for each zero-coupon Treasury is just the present value of the cash flow from the stripped Treasury discounted at the yield corresponding to the maturity of the security (from Exhibit 6.2). The total proceeds received from selling the zero-coupon Treasury securities would be $104.1880 per $100 of par

EXHIBIT 6.4 **Profit Opportunity from Coupon Stripping Using Observed Yield for the Maturity**

Maturity	Cash Flow	Present Value at 12.5%	Yield to Maturity	Present Value at Yield to Maturity
0.50	6.25	5.8824	0.0800	6.0096
1.00	6.25	5.5363	0.0830	5.7618
1.50	6.25	5.2107	0.0890	5.4847
2.00	6.25	4.0942	0.0920	5.2210
2.50	6.25	4.6157	0.0940	4.9676
3.00	6.25	4.3442	0.0970	4.7040
3.50	6.25	4.0886	0.1000	4.4418
4.00	6.25	3.8481	0.1040	4.1663
4.50	6.25	3.6218	0.1060	3.9267
5.00	6.25	3.4087	0.1080	3.6938
5.50	6.25	3.2082	0.1090	3.4863
6.00	6.25	3.0195	0.1120	3.2502
6.50	6.25	2.8419	0.1140	3.0402
7.00	6.25	2.6747	0.1160	2.8384
7.50	6.25	2.5174	0.1180	2.6451
8.00	6.25	2.3693	0.1190	2.4789
8.50	6.25	2.2299	0.1200	2.3210
9.00	6.25	2.0987	0.1220	2.1528
9.50	6.25	1.9753	0.1240	1.9930
10.00	106.25	31.6046	0.1250	31.6046
Total		100.0000		104.1880

EXHIBIT 6.5 Profit Opportunity from Coupon Stripping Using Theoretical Spot Yield Curve

Maturity	Cash Flow	Present Value at 12.5%	Theoretical Spot Yield	Present Value at Spot Yield
0.50	6.25	5.8824	0.08000	6.0096
1.00	6.25	5.5363	0.08300	5.7618
1.50	6.25	5.2107	0.08930	5.4824
2.00	6.25	4.9042	0.09247	5.2163
2.50	6.25	4.6157	0.09468	4.9595
3.00	6.25	4.3442	0.09787	4.6923
3.50	6.25	4.0886	0.10129	4.4227
4.00	6.25	3.8481	0.10592	4.1360
4.50	6.25	3.6218	0.10850	3.8850
5.00	6.25	3.4087	0.11021	3.6553
5.50	6.25	3.2082	0.11175	3.4367
6.00	5.25	3.0195	0.11584	3.1801
6.50	6.25	2.8419	0.11744	2.9766
7.00	6.25	2.6747	0.11991	2.7660
7.50	6.25	2.5174	0.12405	2.5343
8.00	6.25	2.3693	0.12278	2.4092
8.50	6.25	2.2299	0.12546	2.2217
9.00	6.25	2.0987	0.13152	1.9861
9.50	6.25	1.9753	0.13377	1.8266
10.00	106.25	31.6046	0.13623	28.4426
Total		100.0000		100.0010

value of the Treasury issue purchased by the dealer. This would result in a profit of $4.1880 per $100 purchased.

To understand why the government dealer has the opportunity to realize this profit, look at the third column of Exhibit 6.4. That column shows how much the government dealer paid for each of the cash flows by buying the entire package of cash flows (i.e., by buying the bond). For example, consider the $6.25 coupon payment in 4 years. By buying the 10-year Treasury bond priced to yield 12.5%, the dealer pays a price based on 12.5% (6.25% semiannual) for that coupon payment, or equivalently, $3.8481. However, under the assumptions of this illustration, investors were willing to accept a lower yield, 10.4% (5.2% semiannual), to purchase a zero-coupon Treasury security with 4 years to maturity. Thus investors were willing to pay $4.1663. On this one coupon payment, the government dealer realizes a profit equal to the difference between $4.1663 and $3.8481 (or .3182). From all the cash

EXHIBIT 6.6 Profit Opportunity from Coupon Stripping for an Assumed Spot Yield Curve

Maturity	Cash Flow	Theoretical Spot Yield	Assumed Spot Yield	Present Value at Spot Yield
0.50	6.25	0.08000	0.08000	6.0096
1.00	6.25	0.08300	0.08300	5.7618
1.50	6.25	0.08930	0.08930	5.4824
2.00	6.25	0.09247	0.09210	5.2200
2.50	6.25	0.09468	0.09450	4.9617
3.00	6.25	0.09787	0.09740	4.6986
3.50	6.25	0.10129	0.10100	4.4270
4.00	6.25	0.10592	0.10430	4.1616
4.50	6.25	0.10850	0.10700	3.9099
5.00	6.25	0.11021	0.10900	3.6763
5.50	6.25	0.11175	0.11000	3.4682
6.00	6.25	0.11584	0.11300	3.2318
6.50	6.25	0.11744	0.11400	3.0402
7.00	6.25	0.11991	0.11700	2.8197
7.50	6.25	0.12405	0.12000	2.6079
8.00	6.25	0.12278	0.12278	2.4092
8.50	6.25	0.12546	0.12400	2.2478
9.00	6.25	0.13152	0.12600	2.0810
9.50	6.25	0.13377	0.12700	1.9403
10.00	106.25	0.13623	0.12900	30.4380
Total				102.5931

flows, the total profit is $4.1880. In this instance, coupon stripping shows that "the sum of the parts is greater than the whole."

Suppose that instead of the observed yield to maturity from Exhibit 6.2, the yields that investors want is the same as the theoretical spot rates shown in Exhibit 6.3. Exhibit 6.5 demonstrates that in this case the total proceeds from the sale of the zero-coupon Treasury securities would be approximately equal to $100, making coupon stripping uneconomic. If the actual spot rate curve is different from the theoretical spot rate curve, coupon stripping may be profitable, as shown in Exhibit 6.6, which assumes a spot rate curve in which the spot rate for each maturity is between the observed yield to maturity and the theoretical spot rate.

It is the process of coupon stripping that will prevent the actual spot rate curve observed on zero-coupon Treasuries from departing significantly from the theoretical spot rate curve. As more stripping is done, forces of demand and supply will cause rates to return to their theoretical spot rate levels. This is, in fact, what has happened in the Treasury market.

Creating Synthetic Treasury Coupon Securities Using Zero-Coupon Treasuries

So far we've explained how a government dealer can profit from coupon stripping. There may be times where the shape of the zero-coupon Treasury yield curve makes it profitable for a dealer to create a synthetic Treasury security by repackaging zero-coupon Treasury securities and selling the repackaged security at a lower yield (higher price). This is done by buying zero-coupon Treasury securities so as to produce a cash flow identical to that for an outstanding Treasury coupon security.

EXHIBIT 6.7   Profit Opportunity from Creating a Synthetic Treasury Coupon Security for an Observed Spot Yield Curve

Maturity	Cash Flow	Theoretical Spot Yield	Assumed Spot Yield	Present Value at Spot Yield
0.50	6.25	0.08000	0.08000	6.0096
1.00	6.25	0.08300	0.08300	5.7618
1.50	6.25	0.08930	0.09000	5.4769
2.00	6.25	0.09247	0.09400	5.2011
2.50	6.25	0.09468	0.09500	4.9558
3.00	6.25	0.09787	0.09800	4.6906
3.50	6.25	0.10129	0.10350	4.3903
4.00	6.25	0.10592	0.10700	4.1191
4.50	6.25	0.10850	0.11000	3.8602
5.00	6.25	0.11021	0.11400	3.5903
5.50	6.25	0.11175	0.11750	3.3354
6.00	6.25	0.11584	0.11900	3.1237
6.50	6.25	0.11744	0.12000	2.9302
7.00	6.25	0.11991	0.12600	2.6571
7.50	6.25	0.12405	0.12900	2.4473
8.00	6.25	0.12278	0.13000	2.2818
8.50	6.25	0.12546	0.13600	2.0425
9.00	6.25	0.13152	0.13900	1.8648
9.50	6.25	0.13377	0.14000	1.7282
10.00	106.25	0.13623	0.14200	26.9488
Total				97.4155

Once again, let's consider a 10-year, 12.5% coupon bond selling at par to yield 12.5%. Suppose that the spot rates are those shown in the fourth column of Exhibit 6.7. The total proceeds that would be received from stripping the bond and selling it as zero-coupon Treasuries would then be $97.4155. Obviously, the venture would be unprofitable, since the cost of the issue is $100.

Suppose, however, that instead of doing the coupon stripping, the government dealer purchased 19 zero-coupon Treasury securities with maturities from 0.5 to 9.5 years that had a maturity value of $6.25 each and a 10-year zero-coupon Treasury security with a maturity value of $106.25. This package of zero-coupon Treasuries would produce the same cash flow as the 10-year, 12.5% Treasury security. The cost is only $97.4155, not the $100 price for the coupon Treasury. By creating the synthetic Treasury coupon security, the government dealer can realize a profit by buying the zeros while selling the repackaged Treasury (assuming the sale price is $100).

As in the case of coupon stripping, it is the process of creating a synthetic coupon Treasury security that will drive the spot rates toward the theoretical spot rates.

PORTFOLIO STRATEGIES WITH CASH MARKET TREASURY SECURITIES

In this section we describe three strategies that can be used by money managers to enhance portfolio performance in the Treasury cash market. In later chapters strategies involving both Treasury securities and futures and options on Treasury securities will be discussed.

Comparing Coupon Treasuries and Zero-Coupon Treasuries with the Same Maturity

As we explained in Chapter 3, assessing the relative value of two securities on the basis of yield to maturity may provide misleading conclusions. For managers of tax-exempt portfolios who intend to hold a Treasury security until maturity, there is an analytical technique for assessing the relative value of a zero-coupon Treasury and a coupon Treasury. The technique is best presented by means of an illustration.

Suppose that an investor is considering the following two Treasury securities:

Coupon	Yield to maturity	Price	Maturity
12.6%	12.60%	100.00	12 years
0	11.90%	24.98	12 years

The yield to maturity for the zero-coupon Treasury is 11.90%, which, since it requires no reinvestment of coupon payments, means that the realized compound yield will be 11.90%. The realized compound yield that will result from holding the 12.6% Treasury security will depend on the rate at which the coupon payments can be reinvested. We can determine the reinvestment rate that will produce the same total future dollars from both investments. This rate is called the *break-even reinvestment rate.*

Suppose that instead of investing $100 in the 12.6% coupon Treasury an investor decides to invest in the zero-coupon Treasury. The semiannual yield to maturity is 5.95%; therefore $100 invested in the zero-coupon Treasury will grow to $400 at the end of 24 periods (12 years), that is:

$$\$100 \ (1.0595)^{24} = \$400$$

If the investor places $100 in the 12.6% Treasury, he will be indifferent between the zero-coupon Treasury and the 12.6% Treasury if the latter produces total future dollars of $400. As we explained in Chapter 3, the total future dollars from holding an investment to maturity will be equal to the sum of (1) the coupon payments, (2) the maturity value, and (3) the interest-on-interest from reinvesting the coupon payments. For our 12.6% Treasury bond, the investor knows for certain that for each $100 invested, the following future dollars will be received:

Coupon payments (24 x $6.30)	=	$151.20
Maturity value	=	100.00

Therefore $251.20 will be received with certainty. For the 12.6% Treasury to generate $400, interest-on-interest must equal $148.80 ($400 − $251.20). Alternatively, the coupon interest plus the interest-on-interest must equal $300.

From equation (3.7), the formula for the coupon plus interest-on-interest is equal to:

$$C\left[\frac{(1+r)^n - 1}{r}\right]$$

where C = semiannual coupon payment
  r = semiannual reinvestment rate
  n = number of semiannual coupon payments

In our illustration the investor knows that the semiannual coupon interest is \$6.30 and that the resulting figure should be equal to \$300. Substituting, we have:

$$300 = 6.30\left[\frac{(1+r)^{24} - 1}{r}\right]$$

Solving the above equation for r gives a semiannual break-even reinvestment rate of 5.53%. Therefore, if the investor believes he can realize at least an 11.06% (2 x 5.53%) reinvestment rate, the 12.6% Treasury will provide more future dollars than the zero-coupon Treasury. If he expects to earn a reinvestment rate less than 11.06%, the zero-coupon Treasury is a better investment since it will provide a higher realized compound yield.

Our analysis has assumed that the money manager could invest all of the coupon payments at a tax-free rate. When coupon payments are taxable, the analysis must take this into consideration.

The break-even reinvestment rate concept is equally applicable for comparing both zero-coupon corporate and municipal bonds with their coupon counterparts.

Improving Portfolio Performance Based on Duration-Equivalent Portfolio Swaps

In the Treasury market a portfolio manager has a wide range of coupon Treasury securities and zero-coupon Treasury securities to choose from. In constructing portfolios, money managers are interested in the three parameters that we have been discussing in this book: yield, duration, and convexity. Constant monitoring of the Treasury markets may identify opportunities for replacing a Treasury security held in a portfolio with two or more other Treasury securities so as to improve the investment characteristics of the portfolio while keeping the interest rate sensitivity, as measured by duration, constant. That is, it may be possible to create a synthetic security that will outperform a single Treasury security held in a portfolio. This can be done if the convexity of the synthetic security is greater than that of the single Treasury security held, and the cost of purchasing the better convexity is not so high that it will adversely affect the synthetic's market performance.

A Treasury security held in a portfolio can be replaced by a synthetic Treasury security comprised of two actual Treasury securities: one with a maturity less than that of the bond held in the portfolio and another with a maturity greater than that of the bond held in the portfolio. The single security currently held is called the *bullet security.* The synthetic security consisting of the two securities to replace the bullet security is called the *barbell.*

To illustrate this strategy, consider an actual market situation.[8] On November 20, 1987, the three parameters of the 2-year, 5-year, and 10-year on-the-run Treasuries were as follows:

Issue	Yield to Maturity	Modified Duration	Convexity
2-year	7.71%	1.78	0.041
5-year	8.35	3.96	0.195
10-year	8.84	6.54	0.568

Suppose that a money manager held $10 million of the 5-year Treasury in her portfolio. She could synthetically create a Treasury security with a modified duration of the 5-year Treasury (3.96) by buying $5.4 million of the 2-year Treasury and $4.6 million of the 10-year security. The modified duration for the barbell (2-year Treasury/ 10-year Treasury) is the weighted average of the modified duration of each bond:

$$\frac{(\$5.4 \times 1.78 + \$4.6 \times 6.54)}{\$10} = 3.96$$

The convexity of the barbell is:

$$\frac{(\$5.4 \times 0.041 + \$4.6 \times 0.568)}{\$10} = 0.283$$

Since the convexity of the 5-year Treasury is 0.195, the convexity gain from the barbell is 0.088 (0.283 − 0.195). The yield to maturity

[8]This illustration is adapted from N. R. Vijayaraghavan and Monte H. Shapiro, "Duration-Equivalent Butterfly Swaps," in Frank J. Fabozzi, ed., *Fixed Income Portfolio Strategies* (Chicago, IL: Probus Publishing, 1989).

of the barbell is 8.57%,[9] which is 22 basis points less than the yield to maturity of the 5-year Treasury. Thus, to pick-up convexity, there was a yield-to-maturity give-up of 22 basis points. But this is not the proper yield measure to focus on.

The realized compound yield for a 1-month investment horizon can be computed for a range of interest rate changes. Assuming a parallel shift in the yield curve, the difference between the 1-month realized compound yield of the barbell and that of the bullet (5-year Treasury) would be:

Interest Rate Change (basis points)	Difference in Realized Compound Yield Barbell Minus Bullet (in basis points)
+ 100	13.0
+ 50	2.6
0	−1.1
− 50	5.3
− 100	26.6

As can be seen, the barbell will outperform the bullet under every interest rate scenario except when interest rates are unchanged. This result is due to the better convexity of the barbell and the cost of acquiring the improved convexity.

There are other risks associated with this strategy in addition to the probability that interest rates will remain stable. In particular, if the yield curve shift is not parallel, the outcome may not be favorable even if interest rates move substantially. For example, consider a steepening of the yield curve as follows:

2-year Treasury	−100 basis-point change
5-year Treasury	− 75 basis-point change
10-year Treasury	− 50 basis-point change

The barbell will underperform the bullet by 62 basis points.

In contrast, suppose the yield curve flattens as follows:

2-year Treasury	100 basis-point change
5-year Treasury	75 basis-point change
10-year Treasury	50 basis-point change

---

[9]The yield to maturity is the portfolio yield computed as explained in Chapter 3.

The barbell will outperform the bullet by 46 basis points.

Thus to properly analyze a duration-equivalent swap it is important to investigate what will happen if the yield curve does not change in a parallel fashion.

Swapping Within the Treasury Market to Improve a Portfolio's Cash Flow

Suppose that a money manager owns $100 million of the following on-the-run Treasury issue: 8% coupon, 7 years to maturity, selling at par to yield 8%. If the money manager has no need for liquidity and plans to hold this security until maturity, the following cash flow will be received:

Every 6 months for the next 7 years	=	$ 4,000,000
At the end of year 7	=	$100,000,000

Let's also suppose that the following 7-year off-the-run coupon Treasury and 7-year zero-coupon Treasury are available: 11.75% coupon selling at 119.88 to yield 8.4% and zero-coupon Treasury selling at 56.9757 to yield 8.20%.

Now consider what would happen if the portfolio comprised the following combination: $68,085,106 par value of the 11.75% Treasury and $31,914,894 maturity value of the zero-coupon bond. The cash flow from holding these two securities would be:

Every 6 months for the next 7 years =		
From the 11.75% Treasury:		
$68,085,106 x 0.1175 x 0.5	= $	4,000,000
At the end of year 7:		
From the 11.75% Treasury	= $	68,085,106
From the zero-coupon Treasury	= $	31,914,894
Total	=	$ 100,000,000

Therefore the portfolio of the off-the-run 11.75% Treasury and the zero-coupon Treasury would generate a cash flow identical to the cash flow of the on-the-run 8% Treasury. The cost of the portfolio consisting of these two securities would be:

1.198800 x $68,085,106	=	$ 81,620,425
0.569757 x $31,914,894	=	$ 18,183,734
Total cost	=	$ 99,804,160

The cost of the portfolio is less than the market value of the on-the-run issue. Therefore, if the money manager sells the 8% Treasury for $100 million and uses $99,804,160 of the proceeds to purchase the 11.75% Treasury and the zero-coupon Treasury, the money manager will have the same cash flow at a reduced cost. This assumes that no tax liability will result from selling the bond held in the portfolio if a capital gain is realized. Opportunities such as this do arise in the Treasury market. The portfolio to replace a single Treasury issue may consist of more than two securities.

In Chapter 14 we shall discuss strategies that can be used to ensure that a future liability stream will be satisfied. Often Treasury securities are used in portfolios for this purpose. If the money manager in our previous example was managing funds for a pension sponsor and was holding the 8% Treasury until maturity to satisfy projected pension liabilities, the off-the-run coupon Treasury and the zero-coupon Treasury could be purchased and the on-the-run Treasury sold, producing a take-out of dollars equal to $195,841 ($100,000,000 − $99,804,159) at zero risk if the portfolio is held until maturity.

SUMMARY

The yield on Treasury securities provides the base rate off of which non-Treasury securities are priced. More specifically, we saw in this chapter that it is the term structure of interest rates, which is represented by the theoretical spot rate curve for zero-coupon Treasuries, that is used for pricing securities. While the yield curve for actual zero-coupon Treasuries can be used to construct the spot rate curve, we explained the limitations of this approach in estimating the term structure. A simplified approach for estimating the term structure was presented in this chapter; more sophisticated econometric techniques have been developed. We also demonstrated that the profitability of stripping coupon Treasury securities to create zero-coupon Treasury securities and of creating synthetic coupon Treasury securities from zero-coupon Treasury securities depends on the shape and level of the actual yield curve. Finally, three strategies for enhancing portfolio performance in the Treasury market were explained.

7

CORPORATE, MUNICIPAL, AND INTERNATIONAL BONDS

This chapter discusses the various types of corporate, municipal, and international bonds and their investment characteristics.

CORPORATE BONDS

As their name indicates, corporate bonds are issued by corporations. They are classified by type of issuer. The four general classifications used by bond information services are: (1) utilities; (2) transportations; (3) industrials; and (4) banks and finance companies. Finer breakdowns are often used to create more homogeneous groupings. For example, utilities are subdivided into electric power companies, gas distribution companies, water companies, and comunication companies. Transportations are further divided into airlines, railroads, and trucking companies. Industrials are the catchall class, and the most heterogeneous of the groupings with respect to investment characteristics. Industrial bonds are issued by all kinds of manufacturing, merchandising, and service companies.

Either real property (using a mortgage) or personal property may be pledged to offer security beyond that of the general credit standing of the issuer. With a *mortgage bond*, the issuer has granted the bondholders a lien against the pledged assets. (A lien is a legal right to sell mortgaged property to satisfy unpaid obligations to bondholders.) *Debenture bonds* are not secured by a specific pledge of property, but that does not mean that they have no claim on the property of issuers or on their earnings. Debenture bondholders have the claim of general creditors on all assets of the issuer not pledged specifically to secure other debt. And they even have a claim on pledged assets to the extent that these assets have value greater than necessary to satisfy secured creditors. *Subordinated debenture bonds* are issues that rank in seniority after secured debt, after debenture bonds, and often after some general creditors in their claim on assets and earnings. When a corporation issues a bond, the type of security will determine the cost to the issuer. For a given corporation, mortgage bonds will cost less than debenture bonds, and debenture bonds will cost less than subordinated debenture bonds. *Guaranteed bonds* are obligations guaranteed by another entity. The value of the guarantee is as good as the financial ability of the guarantor to satisfy the obligation.

Most corporate bonds are *term bonds;* that is, they run for a term of years, then become due and payable.[1] The term may be long or short. Generally, obligations due less than 10 years from the date of issue are called *notes.* Most corporate borrowings take the form of *bonds* due in 20 to 30 years. Term bonds may be retired by payment at final maturity or retired prior to maturity if provided for in the indenture. The indenture states in great detail the promises of the the corporate bond issuer and the rights of bondholders.

Credit Risk

Unlike Treasury securities, corporate bonds expose the investor to credit risk. This is the risk that the issuer will default on its obligations. At any one time the yield offered in the market for a corporate bond varies according to how market participants estimate the uncertainty of future payment of dollar amounts of interest and principal. Professional money managers use various techniques to analyze information on companies and bond issues in order to estimate the ability of the issuer to live up to its future contractual obligations.[2] This

---

[1]Some corporate bond issues are so arranged that specified principal amounts become due on specified dates. Such issues are called *serial bonds*. Equipment trust certificates are structured as serial bonds.

[2]For an indepth discussion of credit analysis, see Jane Tripp Howe, "Credit Analysis for Corporate Bonds," Chapter 22 in Frank J. Fabozzi and Irving M. Pollack (eds.), *The Handbook of Fixed Income Securities* (Homewood, IL: Dow Jones-Irwin, 1987).

activity of the investment management process is known as *credit analysis*. Most large institutional investors and investment banking firms have their own credit analysis departments. However, most individual investors and some institutional bond investors make no such analytical studies. Instead, they rely primarily on bond ratings published by commercial rating companies that perform bond analysis and express their conclusions through a system of ratings. Four commercial rating companies are: (1) Moody's Investors Service; (2) Standard & Poor's; (3) Duff and Phelps; and (4) Fitch Investors Service.

The two most widely used systems of bond ratings are those of Moody's and Standard & Poor's. In both systems the term *high grade* means low credit risk or, conversely, high probability of future payments. The highest-grade bonds are designated by Moody's by the letters *Aaa*, and by Standard & Poor's by *AAA*. The next-highest grade is *Aa* or *AA;* then for the third grade both agencies use *A*. The next three grades are designated *Baa* or *BBB*, *Ba* or *BB*, and *B*, respectively. There are also *C* grades. In addition, Standard & Poor's uses a plus or minus sign to provide a narrower credit-quality breakdown within each class, while Moody's uses 1, 2, or 3 to provide this breakdown. Bonds rated triple A (AAA or Aaa) are said to be *prime*, double-A bonds (AA or Aa) are of *high quality*, single-A issues are classified as *upper medium grade*, and triple B issues as *medium grade*. These four categories are referred to as *investment grades*. Lower-rated bonds are said to have speculative elements or to be *distinctly speculative*. They are also known as junk bonds.

Quality Spreads.   The yields offered on corporate bonds depend on their perceived quality or credit rating. To compensate for their greater credit risk, lower-quality-rated issues must offer higher yields than issues with higher ratings. The yield spread between two issues that are identical in all respects except for quality is referred to as the *quality yield spread.*

The quality yield spread between corporate bond issues of different quality ratings and between corporate bonds and Treasury securities generally varies over the interest rate cycle. Specifically, quality yield spreads between lower- and higher-quality securities tend to widen when interest rates are high but narrow when interest rates are low. During periods of low interest rates investors tend to increase their holdings of lower-credit quality issues in order to obtain additional yield, and this narrows the spread between high-grade and lower-grade credit issues. Conversely, during periods in which investors anticipate a poor economic climate and interest rates are high, there is often a "flight to quality" as investors pursue more conservative credit-risk exposure by selling lower-quality and purchasing higher-quality issues. This widens the spread between high-grade and lower-grade credit issues.

Call Risk

Most long-term corporate issues have a call provision whereby the issuer has an option to buy back all or part of the issue prior to maturity. Some issues specify that the issuer must retire a predetermined amount of the issue periodically. Either way, the bondholder is exposed to the risk that the issue will be called at a disadvantageous time. This risk is referred to as *call risk*.

Specifically, there are two adverse consequences if an issue is called when interest rates have declined. First, the proceeds received must be reinvested at a lower interest rate. Second, the appreciation potential for this issue is limited by the price that the issuer specifies in the indenture that it will redeem the issue for (the call price). This price performance characteristic is referred to as *price compression*. Investors expect to be compensated for accepting call risk.

In the case where call risk exists because the issuer is given the choice of calling the bonds prior to maturity, this choice is nothing more than a call option that bondholders grant the issuer. This call option can be valued using an options-pricing framework. In order to evaluate the option, it is important to understand exactly what option the bondholder has granted (sold) the issuer. Various types of corporate call provisions are discussed in this chapter.[3] In the next chapter a framework for the analysis of callable bonds will be presented.

Call and Refund Provisions.   An important question in negotiating the terms of a new bond issue is whether the issuer shall have the right to redeem the *entire amount* of bonds outstanding on a date before maturity. Issuers generally want this right because they recognize that at some time in the future the general level of interest rates may fall sufficiently below the issue's coupon rate so that redeeming the issue and replacing it with another issue with a lower coupon rate would be

---

[3]For the most comprehensive coverage available on corporate call provisions, see Richard W. Wilson, *Corporate Senior Securities* (Chicago, IL: Probus Publishing, 1987).

attractive. For the reasons just discussed, the bondholder does not want the issuer to have that right.

The usual practice is a provision that denies the issuer the right to redeem bonds during the first 5 to 10 years after the date of issue with proceeds received from issuing lower-cost debt obligations ranking equal to or superior to the debt to be redeemed. This type of redemption is called *refunding*. While most long-term issues have these refunding restrictions, they are usually immediately callable, in whole or in part, if the source of funds comes from other than lower-interest-cost money. Cash flow from operations, proceeds from a common stock sale, or funds from the sale of property are examples of such sources. While the redemption price is often at a premium over par, in many cases the call price equals the par value.

Many bonds have some call protection—for example, they may not be called for the first 3 to 7 years, but thereafter may be called *for any reason*. Investors often confuse refunding protection with call protection. Call protection is much more absolute in that the bonds cannot be redeemed for any reason. Refunding restrictions only provide protection against the one type of redemption mentioned above. Failure to recognize this difference has resulted in unnecessary losses for some investors.[4]

As a rule, corporate bonds are callable at a premium above par. Generally, the amount of the premium declines as the bond approaches maturity, and often reaches par a number of years after issuance. The initial amount of the premium may be as much as 1 year's coupon interest or as little as coupon interest for half a year or less.

Sinking-Fund Provision.   Corporate bond indentures may require the issuer to retire a specified portion of an issue each year. This is referred to as a *sinking-fund requirement*. Generally, the issuer may satisfy the sinking-fund requirement by either (1) making a cash payment of the face amount of the bonds to be retired to the corporate trustee, who then calls the bonds for redemption using a lottery; or (2) delivering to the trustee bonds with a total face value equal to the amount that must be retired from purchases in the open market.[5]

---

[4]Electric utilities most often issue bonds with 5 years of refunding protection, although in high-interest-rate environments issues with 10 years of refunding protection have been sold. Long-term industrial bonds generally have 10 years of refunding protection but are immediately callable.

[5]A third method of satisfying the sinking-fund requirement is usually available to electric utility bond issuers. Instead of actually retiring bonds, the company may certify to the trustee that it has utilized unfunded property credits in lieu of the sinking fund—that is, it has made property and plant investments that have not been pledged as security for issuing debt.

Usually, the sinking-fund call price is the par value if the bonds were originally sold at par. When issued at a price in excess of par, the call price generally starts at the issuance price and scales down to par as the issue approaches maturity.

Many corporate bond indentures include a provision that grants the issuer the option to retire double or another multiple of the amount stipulated for sinking-fund retirement. This doubling option effectively reduces the bondholder's call protection since when interest rates decline, the issuer may find it advantageous to exercise this option at the special sinking-fund call price in order to retire a substantial portion of the high cost outstanding issue.

While the purpose of the sinking-fund provision is to reduce credit risk by paying off the majority of the issue prior to maturity, this mandatory call provision also increases call risk.

Options Granted to Bondholders

The call option granted to an issuer represents an option sold by the bondholder. In some issues there are options that the issuer grants to the bondholder; that is, options that the bondholder purchases from the issuer when acquiring the bonds. Three examples of bonds with embedded options that are sold to bondholders are: (1) convertible or exchangeable bonds; (2) units of debt with warrants to buy common stock or bonds; and (3) putable bonds. Convertible bonds, exchangeable bonds, and units of debt with warrants to buy common stock are referred to as *equity-linked debt*.[6]

Convertible and Exchangeable Bonds.   The conversion provision in a corporate bond issue grants the bondholder the right to convert the bond to a predetermined number of shares of common stock of the issuer. A convertible bond is therefore a corporate bond with a call option to buy the common stock of the issuer. Exchangeable bonds grant the bondholder the right to exchange the bonds for the common stock of a firm *other* than the issuer of the bond. For example, Dart & Kraft has an exchangeable bond issue outstanding that is exchangeable for the common stock of Minnesota Minning and Manufacturing.[7]

---

[6]For an explanation of the tax advantages of units of debt with warrants over convertible and exchangeable bonds from the issuer's perspective, see E. Phillip Jones and Scott P. Mason, "Equity-Linked Debt," *Midland Journal of Finance*, Winter 1986, pp. 47–58.

[7]Dart & Kraft obtained the 3M common stock in exchange for the sale of one of its subsidiaries, Riker Laboratories.

Ford Motor Credit exchangeable bonds are exchangeable for the common stock of the parent company, Ford Motor Company. There are a few issues that are exchangeable into more than one security. General Cinema, for example, has an outstanding issue that is convertible into the common stock of R. J. Reynolds and Sea-Land Corporation.

The number of shares of common stock that the bondholder will receive from exercising the call option of a convertible bond or exchangeable bond is called the *conversion ratio*. At the time of issuance the issuer has effectively granted the bondholder the right to purchase the common stock at a price equal to:

$$\frac{\text{Par value of convertible bond}}{\text{Conversion ratio}}$$

This price is referred to as the *par conversion price* and often in the indenture as simply *conversion price*.

The conversion privilege may be permitted for all or only some portion of the bond's life. The conversion ratio may decline over time. It is always adjusted proportionately for stock splits and stock dividends. Convertible issues are callable by the issuer. This permits the issuer to force conversion of the issue. There are some convertible bonds that do have call protection. This protection can be in one of two forms: either the issuer is not allowed to redeem the issue prior to a specified date; or the issuer is not permitted to call the issue until the stock price has increased by a predetermined percentage price above the par conversion price.[8] Thus, in addition to having purchased a call option on the common stock, a convertible bondholder has sold a call option on the bond.

The analysis of convertible bonds is illustrated in the next chapter.

Units of Debt with Warrants.   When a bond is issued, warrants may be attached as part of the offering unit. A warrant grants the holder the right to purchase a designated security at a specified price. Therefore a warrant is simply a call option. The warrant may permit the holder to purchase the common stock of the issuer of the debt or the

---

[8]For example, a convertible issue of National City Corp. could not be called prior to January 1, 1988, unless the common stock trades at a premium of 50% above the par conversion price.

common stock of a firm other than the issuer. Alternatively, the warrant may grant the holder the right to purchase a debt obligation of the issuer or another firm. Most warrants can be detached from the bond and sold separately. The warrant can generally be exercised with cash or by using the debt that was part of the unit offering. In the case of convertible and exchangeable bonds, only the bond may be used to exercise the option.

The warrant may permit the bondholder to buy common stock of the issuer, as does a convertible bond. However, the embedded call option in the convertible bond cannot be sold separately from the bond, while a warrant can be. Thus the holder of a bond and a warrant is in a long position in the corporate bond of the issuer and a long position in a call option on the common stock of the issuer. The same is true of a unit of debt with warrants to buy common stock of a firm other than the issuer: the holder of a bond and a warrant in this case is in a long position in the corporate bond of the issuer and a long position in a call option on the common stock of some other firm.

Warrants to purchase additional bonds of the same issuer are sometimes called *contingent take-down options.*[9] The exercise price is usually par value, and the issue that is deliverable to the bondholder may or may not be identical to the bond to which the warrant is attached.

Putable Bonds.   A putable bond grants the bondholder the right to sell the issue back to the issuer at par value on designated dates. The advantage to the bondholder is that if interest rates rise after the issue date, thereby reducing the value of the bond, the bondholder can put the bond to the issuer for par. Thus a putable corporate bond is composed of a nonputable corporate bond plus a long put option on that bond.

Marketability Risk

There are really two secondary corporate bond markets. One is the *exchange market,* where certain exchange members make a market in listed issues. The other is the *over-the-counter market.* Most of the trading takes place in the over-the-counter market.

---

[9]For a further discussion, see Robert W. Kopprasch, "Contingent Take-Down Options," Chap. 23 in Frank J. Fabozzi and Irving M. Pollack, eds., *The Handbook of Fixed Income Securities,* 1st ed. (Homewood, IL: Dow Jones-Irwin, 1983).

Any bond that is quoted continually by a dealer is a marketable bond; there is obviously a market for it. But investors who seek to implement trading and portfolio strategies want to know much more than that; they want to know how good the market is for that particular bond. It is useful to recognize differences in the quality of markets for different corporate bond issues.

The principal basis for grading the marketability of securities is the size of the spread between dealers' bid and offer prices. A narrow spread—say, one-quarter to one-half of 1%—indicates a very marketable issue. A wide spread—such as 2% or 3%—means low marketability. The principal determinant of the size of the spread is usually the volume of trading activity in an issue. The number of dealers is more or less proportionate to the trading activity. If there is a lot of activity in a bond issue, there will be a lot of dealers seeking the trade. A large volume of trading activity and a large number of dealers make a highly competitive market in which spreads are pressed downward.

An investor who plans to hold a bond until its maturity date should be willing to accept the premium for bearing marketability risk and, in fact, if the likelihood of having to sell the security prior to maturity is remote, should seek securities with high marketability risk (assuming that the credit risk associated with the security is acceptable). On the other hand, a portfolio manager who frequently rebalances a portfolio must weigh the trade-off between marketability risk and increased potential yield.

Other Features of Corporate Bonds

In addition to those already discussed, there are other features that impact the risk/return characteristics of a corporate bond. These are discussed in the following paragraphs.

Zero-Coupon Corporate Bonds. The yield to maturity of a corporate bond when it is purchased indicates the yield the investor will realize if the coupon payment is reinvested at a rate equal to the yield to maturity. The investor's actual return if the corporate bond is held to maturity depends on the rate at which the coupon payments can be reinvested. The risk that the coupon payments will be reinvested at a rate less than the yield to maturity at purchase, resulting in a realized compound yield less than the yield to maturity at purchase, is called *reinvestment risk*. With a zero-coupon corporate bond, there are no coupon payments to reinvest, so there is no reinvestment risk. Therefore, holding a corporate zero-coupon bond to maturity results in a realized compound yield equal to the yield to maturity at the time of purchase. The first public offering of zero-coupon corporate bonds was by J. C. Penney Company, Inc., in April 1982.

Floating-Rate Securities.   The coupon interest on floating-rate securities is reset periodically on the basis of some predetermined benchmark. For example, the coupon rate may be reset every 6 months at a rate equal to 50 basis points above the 6-month Treasury bill rate. Although the coupons on most issues are reset on the basis of some financial index, some issues use a nonfinancial index, such as the price of a commodity, as the benchmark for the coupon rate. For example, there are three outstanding issues of the Sunshine Mining Company whose coupon rate is based on the value of 50 ounces of silver.

Floating-rate securities are attractive to some institutional investors because they allow them to buy an asset with an income stream that more closely matches the floating-rate nature of some of their liabilities. Floating-rate securities expose the bondholder to lower interest rate risk than fixed-rate securities since their coupon resets to reflect the current market yield levels. In theory, a floating-rate security with frequent resets should trade at par if the market believes that the spread off the benchmark at the time of issuance has not changed. For example, suppose that a single-A-rated bank offers a floating-rate security whose coupon resets every 3 months to 40 basis points over the 3-month Treasury bill. If the perceived credit quality of this issuer deteriorates enough for the market to want 55 basis points over the 3-month Treasury bill for this bond at the reset date, the issue will sell below par. The opposite could occur if the credit quality improves and the market is willing to accept a lower spread. If the spread has remained constant, the issue should sell at par.

Certain floating-rate instruments are viewed by some investors as a passive substitute for short-term holdings, particularly that part of a short-term portfolio that is more or less consistently maintained at certain minimum levels. Thus floating-rate securities save on the costs of rolling over short-term securities as they reach maturity.

Why do corporations issue floating-rate securities? Closer matching of their income flows from variable-rate assets with floating-rate liabilities is of major importance, especially for lenders such as banks and finance companies. Issuers can fix or lock in a spread between the cost of borrowed funds and the rate at which they are loaned out. Another reason might be to avoid the uncertainties associated with what could be an unreceptive market at some future date. Floating-rate securities allow the issuer to tap a new source for intermediate-to-long-term funds at short-term rates, thereby necessitating fewer trips to the marketplace and avoiding related issuance costs.

There may be other features in a floating-rate issue. For example, many floating-rate issues include a put option. Some issues are exchangeable either automatically at a certain date (often 5 years after issuance) or at the option of the issuer into fixed-rate securities. A few issues are convertible into the common stock of the issuer.

MUNICIPAL BONDS

Municipal bonds are securities issued by state and local governments and their creations such as "authorities" and special districts. There are tax-exempt and taxable municipal bonds. "Tax-exempt" means that interest is exempt from federal income taxation. Interest may or may not be taxable at the state and local levels. The large majority of municipal bonds outstanding are tax-exempt. The Federal government, however, does have the right to tax the interest on municipal securities.

Types of Municipal Securities

In terms of security structures, there are basically two different types of municipal bonds: general obligation bonds and revenue bonds. Some securities have characteristics of both general obligation and revenue bonds.

General Obligation Bonds. General obligation bonds are debt instruments issued by states, counties, special districts, cities, towns, and school districts that are secured by the issuer's general taxing powers. Usually, a general obligation bond is secured by the issuer's unlimited taxing power.[10] For smaller government jurisdictions such as school districts and towns, the only available unlimited taxing power is on property. For larger general obligation bond issuers such

[10]Not all general obligation bonds are secured by unlimited taxing powers. Some have pledged taxes that are limited as to revenue sources and maximum property tax millage amounts. Such bonds are known as *limited-tax general obligation bonds.*

as states and big cities, the tax revenues are more diverse and may include corporate and individual income taxes, sales taxes, and property taxes. The security pledges for these larger issuers, especially states, are sometimes referred to as being *full faith and credit obligations.*

Revenue Bonds.   The second basic type of security structure is found in a revenue bond. Such bonds are issued for either project or enterprise financings in which the bond issuers pledge to the bondholders the revenues generated by the operating projects financed. Examples are airport revenue bonds, college and university revenue bonds, hospital revenue bonds, single-family mortgage revenue bonds, multifamily revenue bonds, industrial development and pollution control revenue bonds, public power revenue bonds, resource recovery revenue bonds, seaport revenue bonds, sports complex and convention center revenue bonds, student loan revenue bonds, toll road and gas tax revenue bonds, and water revenue bonds.

Hybrid and Special Bond Securities.   Some municipal bonds, though having certain characteristics of general obligation bonds and revenue bonds, have a unique structure. Five examples of such bonds are insured bonds, bonds backed by letters of credit, moral obligation bonds, refunded bonds, and "troubled city" bailout bonds.[11]

Insured bonds are backed by insurance policies written by commercial insurance companies as well as by the credit of the municipal issuer. The insurance provides prompt payment to the bondholders if a default should occur. The larger insurers of municipal bonds are American Municipal Bond Assurance Corporation, Bond Investors Guaranty Insurance Company, Financial Guaranty Insurance Corporation, and Municipal Bond Insurance Association.

Some municipal bonds, in addition to being secured by the issuer's cash flow revenues, are backed by commercial bank *letters of credit.* A *moral obligation bond* is a security structure for state-issued bonds that indicates that if revenues are needed for paying bondholders, the state legislature involved is legally authorized, *though not required,* to make an appropriation out of general state tax revenues.

Refunded bonds are bonds that were originally issued as general obligation or revenue bonds but are now secured by an "escrow fund"

---

[11]For a further discussion, see Sylvan G. Feldstein and Frank J. Fabozzi, *Dow Jones-Irwin Guide to Municipal Bonds* (Homewood, IL: Dow Jones-Irwin, 1987).

consisting entirely of direct U.S. government obligations that are sufficient for paying the contractual obligations to bondholders. These bonds are among the safest of all municipals if the escrow account is properly structured.

"Troubled city" bailout bonds are structured to appear as pure revenue bonds but in essence are not. Revenues come from general-purpose taxes and revenues that otherwise would have gone into the state's or the city's general fund. These bond structures were created to bail out underlying general obligation bond issuers from severe budget deficits. Examples are the New York State's Municipal Assistance Corporation of the City of New York Bonds (MAC) and the state of Illinois's Chicago School Finance Authority Bonds.

Municipal Notes.   Municipal securities issued for periods ranging not beyond 3 years are considered to be short-term in nature. Examples are tax anticipation notes (TANs), revenue anticipation notes (RANs), grant anticipation notes (GANs), bond anticipation notes (BANs), construction loan notes, and tax-exempt commercial paper.

Credit Risk

As with corporate bonds, investors in municipal bonds are exposed to default risk. While many institutional investors, underwriters, and traders rely on their own in-house municipal credit analysts for determining the creditworthiness of a municipal issue, other investors depend on the ratings assigned by the same commercial credit rating companies that rate corporate bonds.

Tax Risk

Investors who purchase tax-exempt municipal bonds are exposed to two types of risk that we shall refer to as *tax risk*. The first type of tax risk is the risk that the federal income tax rate will be reduced. The higher the marginal tax rate, the greater is the value of the tax-exemption feature. As the marginal tax rate declines, the price of a tax-exempt municipal bond will also decline. For example, when the Tax Reform Act of 1986 reduced marginal tax rates, tax-exempt municipal bonds began trading at lower prices.

The second type of tax risk is that the municipal bond that is issued as a tax-exempt issue will eventually be declared taxable by the Internal Revenue Service. This may occur because many municipal revenue bonds have elaborate security structures that could be subject to future adverse congressional actions and IRS interpretations. If the tax-exemption feature is lost, the municipal bond will decline in value until it provides a yield comparable to that for similar taxable bonds. In June of 1980, for example, the Battery Park City Authority sold $97.315 million in construction loan notes whose interest, in the opinion of legal counsel at the time of issuance, would be exempt from federal income taxation. In November of 1980, however, the IRS held that interest on these notes was not exempt. The issue was not resolved until September 1981, when the Authority and the IRS signed a formal agreement that the interest on the notes was tax-exempt.

Redemption Features

Municipal bonds are issued with one of two debt-retirement structures or a combination of both. Either a bond has a *serial* maturity structure or a *term* maturity structure. With a serial maturity structure, a portion of the debt obligation is retired each year. When there is a term maturity structure, the debt obligation is repaid on a final date. Usually term bonds have maturities ranging from 20 to 40 years and retirement schedules (known as sinking funds) that begin 5 to 10 years before the final term maturity.

Municipal bonds may be called prior to maturity, as part of a mandatory sinking fund or at the option of the issuer. Thus bondholders may be exposed to call risk.

Special Investment Features

In our earlier discussion of corporate bonds we explained zero-coupon bonds, floating-rate bonds, and putable bonds in the corporate market. There are bonds in the municipal bond market with these same features.

The municipal bond market has two types of zero-coupon bonds. One type is issued at a very deep discount and matures at par. The difference between the par value and the purchase price represents a predetermined realized compound yield. These zero-coupon bonds are the same as those issued in the taxable bond market for Treasuries and corporates. The second type of zero-coupon bond in the municipal bond market is called a *municipal multiplier* or *compound-interest bond.*

This type of bond is issued at par and does actually have interest payments. However, the interest payments are not distributed to the holder of the bond until maturity. Instead, the issuer agrees to reinvest the undistributed interest payments at the bond's yield to maturity when it was issued. For example, suppose that a 10%, 10-year coupon bond with a par value of $5,000 is sold at par to yield 10%. Every 6 months the maturity value of this bond is increased by 5% of the maturity value of the previous 6 months. So, at the end of 10 years, the maturity value of the bond will be equal to $13,266.[12] In the case of a 10-year zero-coupon bond priced to yield 10%, the bond would have a maturity value of $5,000 but sell for $1,884 when it is issued.[13]

The Primary and Secondary Markets

A substantial number of municipal obligations are brought to the market each week. A public offering may be marketed by either competitive bidding or direct negotiations with underwriters. In the former case, the issue is awarded to the bidder who submits the best bid. An official statement describing the issue and issuer is prepared for all new offerings.

Municipal bonds are traded in the over-the-counter market, which is supported by hundreds of municipal bond dealers across the country. Markets are maintained on local credits by regional brokerage firms and local banks, and by some of the larger Wall Street firms. General names are supported by the larger brokerage firms and banks, many of whom have investment banking relationships with issuers. There are brokers who serve as intermediaries in the sale of large blocks of municipal bonds among dealers and large institutional investors. In addition to these brokers and the daily offerings sent out over *The Bond Buyer's* "Munifacts" teletype system, many dealers advertise their municipal bond offerings for the retail market in what is known as *The Blue List*. This is a 100+-page booklet containing

---

[12]This is found by computing the future value of $5,000 20 periods from now, using a 5% interest rate; that is:

$$\$5,000 \times (1.05)^{20} = \$13,266$$

[13]This is found by computing the present value of $5,000 20 periods from now using a 5% interest rate; that is:

$$\$5,000 \times \frac{1}{(1.05)^{20}} = \$1,884$$

municipal securities offerings and prices that is published every week-day by the Standard & Poor's Corporation.

In the municipal bond markets an odd lot of bonds is $25,000 (five bonds) or less in par value for retail investors. For institutions, any-thing below $100,000 in par value is considered an odd lot. Dealer spreads depend on several factors. For the retail investor, the spread can range from as low as one-quarter of one point ($12.50 per $5,000 par value) on large blocks of actively traded bonds to 4 points ($200 per $5,000 of par value) or more for odd lot sales of inactive issues. For institutional investors, the dealer spread is much lower.

Bond Quotes.   The convention for both corporate and Treasury bonds is to quote prices as a percentage of par value, with 100 being equal to par. Municipal bonds, however, are generally traded and quoted in terms of yield (yield to call or yield to maturity). The price of the bond in this case is called a *basis price.* The exception is certain long-maturity revenue bonds. When a bond is traded and quoted in dollar prices (actually, as a percentage of par value), it is called a *dollar bond.*

EXHIBIT 7.1   Weekly Yield Ratios of Municipal Yields to Treasury Yields

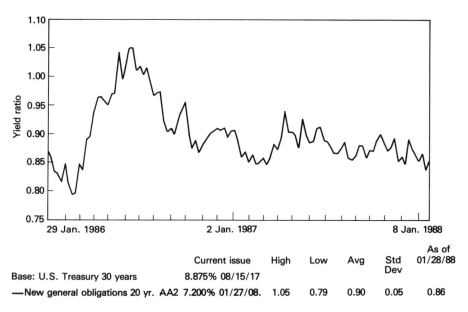

	Current issue	High	Low	Avg	Std Dev	As of 01/28/88
Base: U.S. Treasury 30 years	8.875% 08/15/17					
—New general obligations 20 yr. AA2	7.200% 01/27/08.	1.05	0.79	0.90	0.05	0.86

Source: Municipal Bond Research, Merrill Lynch Capital Markets.

Yield Relationships Between Tax-Exempt and Taxable Bonds

Because of the tax-exempt feature of municipal bonds, the yield on them is usually less than that on Treasuries. Exhibit 7.1 shows the weekly ratio of municipal yields to Treasury yields from January 1986 to January 1988. On January 29, 1988, the yield ratio was 0.86. The average for the period was 0.90. The yield ratio exceeded 1 in several months in 1986 because of proposed changes in the tax law that made the tax exemption of municipal bonds less attractive.

A common yield measure used to compare the yield on a tax-exempt municipal bond with that on a comparable taxable bond is the *equivalent taxable yield*. It is computed as follows:

$$\text{Equivalent taxable yield} = \frac{\text{Tax-exempt yield}}{(1-\text{Marginal tax rate})}$$

For example, suppose an investor in the 28% marginal tax bracket is thinking of acquiring a tax-exempt municipal bond that offers a yield of 8%. The equivalent taxable yield is 11.11%:

$$\text{Equivalent taxable yield} = \frac{.08}{(1-.28)} = .1111 \text{ or } 11.11\%$$

When computing the equivalent taxable yield, the traditionally computed yield to maturity is not the tax-exempt yield if the issue is selling at a discount because only the coupon interest is exempt from federal income taxes. Instead, the yield to maturity is calculated after an assumed tax on the capital gain is deducted and used in the numerator of the above formula.[14]

There is a major drawback in employing the equivalent taxable yield formula to compare the value of a taxable corporate or Treasury bond relative to a tax-exempt municipal bond. The yield to maturity, as we argued in Chapter 3, assumes that the entire coupon interest can be reinvested at the computed yield. Consequently, taxable bonds with the same yield to maturity cannot be compared because the total dollar returns may differ from the computed yield. The same problem arises when attempting to compare taxable and tax-exempt municipal bonds, especially since only a portion of the

---

[14]The yield to maturity after an assumed tax on the capital gain is calculated in the same manner as the traditional yield to maturity (explained in Chapter 3). But instead of using the maturity value in computing the internal rate of return, the net proceeds after an assumed tax on the capital gain is used.

coupon interest on taxable bonds can be reinvested, while for the tax-exempt municipal bond the entire coupon payment is available for reinvestment. The realized compound yield concept can be used to compare taxable and tax-exempt municipal bonds.

Yield Relationships Within the Municipal Bond Market

Yield spreads within the municipal bond market exist for the following reasons: (1) differences in security structure; (2) differences between credit ratings; (3) differences between in-state and general market; and (4) differences between maturities.

What we said earlier about the quality spreads between credit ratings for corporate bonds over the interest rate cycle is true for municipal bonds: quality spreads widen when interest rates are high but narrow when they are low. Another factor that causes changes in the quality spread is the temporary oversupply of issues within a market sector.

Bonds of municipal issuers located in certain states yield considerably less than issues of identical credit quality that come from other states that trade in the "general market." One reason for this is that states often exempt interest on in-state issues from state and local personal income taxes, while interest on out-of-state issues is generally not exempt. Consequently, in states with high income taxes such as New York and California, strong investor demand for in-state issues will reduce their yields relative to bonds of issuers located in states where state and local income taxes are not as important a consideration (for example, Illinois and Florida).

In the municipal bond market long-term bonds typically offer higher yields than short- and intermediate-term bonds. Another characteristic of the municipal bond market is that yield spreads between maturities are usually wider in the municipal bond market than in the taxable market. This means that the potential rewards for lengthening maturity are greater in the municipal bond market than in the taxable bond market.

INTERNATIONAL BONDS

The corporate and municipal bonds that we have discussed so far in this chapter are issued by U.S.-domiciled issuers and trade in the U.S. capital market. In this section we shall describe international bonds.

From the perspective of the U.S. investor, international bonds can be divided into two categories: dollar-denominated bonds (or U.S.-pay bonds) and nondollar-denominated bonds (or foreign-pay bonds).

Dollar-Denominated International Bonds

All the cash flows from dollar-denominated international bonds are in U.S. dollars. These bonds are further classified on the basis of the location of the primary trading market. When the primary trading market is outside the United States, dollar-denominated international bonds are referred to as *Eurodollar bonds;* when the primary trading market is in the United States, they are called *Yankee bonds.*

Eurodollar Bonds.   Eurodollar bonds are underwritten by an international syndicate and, because they are not registered with the Securities and Exchange Commission, are not sold at issuance to U.S. investors. While U.S. investors may buy Eurodollar bonds after they have been seasoned, the primary investors are non-U.S. investors. U.S. corporations, U.S. government-sponsored agencies, and municipalities issue Eurodollar bonds.

Eurodollar bonds can be further divided into Eurodollar fixed-rate bonds and Eurodollar floating-rate bonds. Unlike bonds issued in the United States, which pay interest semiannually, Eurodollar fixed-rate bonds pay interest annually. Therefore an adjustment is required in order to make a direct comparision between the yield to maturity on a U.S. fixed-rate bond and that on a Eurodollar fixed-rate bond. Given the yield to maturity on a Eurodollar fixed-rate bond issue, its bond-equivalent yield is computed as follows:

Bond-equivalent yield of a Eurodollar bond
$$= 2\,[(1+ ytm \text{ on Eurodollar bond})^{1/2} - 1]$$

For example, suppose that the yield to maturity on a Eurodollar bond issue is 10%. Then the bond-equivalent yield is:

$$\text{Bond-equivalent yield} = 2\,[(1.10)^{1/2} - 1]$$
$$= .09762$$

Notice that the bond-equivalent yield will always be less than the Eurodollar bond's yield to maturity.

To convert the bond-equivalent yield of a U.S. bond issue to an annual-pay basis so that it can be compared to the yield to maturity of a Eurodollar bond, the following formula can be used:

Yield to maturity on an annual-pay basis =

$$\left[\left(1 + \frac{ytm \text{ on a bond-equivalent basis}}{2}\right)^2 - 1 \right]$$

For example, suppose that the yield to maturity of a U.S. bond issue quoted on a bond-equivalent basis is 10%. The yield to maturity on an annual-pay basis would be:

$$[(1.05)^2 - 1] = .1025$$

The yield to maturity on an annual-pay basis is always greater than the yield to maturity on a bond-equivalent basis.

Eurodollar floating-rate bonds were first issued in 1970. At that time they constituted about 21% of all Eurodollar bond financing. By 1984, Eurodollar floating-rate bonds made up almost 50% of Eurodollar bond financing.[15] Typically, the coupon rate on a Eurodollar floating-rate bond is some stated margin over the London Interbank Offer Rate (LIBOR).

Innovation has characterized the Eurodollar floating-rate market. For example, in 1984 "mismatched" Eurodollar floating-rate notes were issued. With a mismatched floater, the frequency at which the coupon is reset is generally shorter than the frequency of the coupon payment. The benchmark rate that the coupon rate is tied to is generally equal to the coupon payment frequency. Thus the coupon payment may be every 6 months and the benchmark rate may be based on the rate on a 6-month instrument. The coupon rate, however, may be reset every month; the 6-month coupon payment is then the average of the previous six monthly coupon resets. When the yield curve is steep in the 1-month to 6-month portion of the yield curve, there is an opportunity for investors to enhance returns by buying mismatched floaters with funds borrowed at the 1-month rate and earning the higher coupon rate offered on the basis of the 6-month rates determined

---

[15]For a further discussion of the Eurodollar floating-rate market, see Sarah Allen and Beth L. Palumbo, "Eurodollar Floating Rate Notes," Chap. 5 in Frank J. Fabozzi, ed., *Floating Rate Instruments: Characteristics, Valuation and Portfolio Strategies* (Chicago, IL: Probus Publishing 1986).

monthly. This is in fact what occurred in the first quarter of 1985, which explains why the issuance of mismatched Eurodollar floating-rate notes exceeded that of other Eurodollar floating-rate notes in that period. Recognizing that the risk investors face with such a strategy is that the yield curve may become inverted in the short-term sector (that is, short-term money market rates may exceed long-term money market rates), issuers included protection for investors by having the coupon rate reset at the maximum of a short-term and long-term money market rate.[16]

Another innovation in the Eurodollar floating-rate market is an equity-linked floating-rate bond that, instead of offering a coupon payment for a specified number of years, offers a discount on the purchase of the issuer's stock. This allows investors to take advantage of a rising stock market.

Yankee Bonds.   Yankee bonds are issued by foreign-domiciled entities such as foreign governments, foreign corporations, and supranational agencies[17] (such as the World Bank, the Asian Development Bank, and the Inter American Bank). Yankee bonds are underwritten by a syndicate of U.S. investment banking firms and are registered with the SEC. While foreign buyers may participate in the Yankee bond market, the primary buyers are U.S. investors. Unlike Eurodollar fixed-rate bonds, which pay interest annually, fixed-rate Yankee bonds pay interest semiannually.

Nondollar-Denominated Bonds

All cash flows from nondollar-denominated bonds are denominated in a foreign currency or a basket of foreign currencies (such as the European Currency Unit (ECU)).[18] Trading of nondollar-denominated bonds is typically outside of the United States. In early

---

[16]Jeffrey Hanna and Gioia M. Parente, *Floating Rate Financing Quarterly* (Bond Research Department, Salomon Brothers Inc (April 22, 1985).

[17]For a discussion of supranational agencies and the securities they issue, see Lizabeth L. Palumbo, "Supranational Instruments for World Portfolios," Chap. 20 in Carl Beidleman, ed., *The Handbook of International Investing* (Chicago, IL: Probus Publishing, 1987).

[18]The ECU is the official composite currency unit of the European Monetary System. For a discussion of the ECU bond market, see Edward J. Rappa, Clive Bergel, and Richard Scofield, "The ECU: The Alternative European Currency," Chap. 19 in *The Handbook of International Investing;* and Tran Q. Hung, "The ECU Bond Market," Chap. 52 in *The Handbook of Fixed Income Securities*.

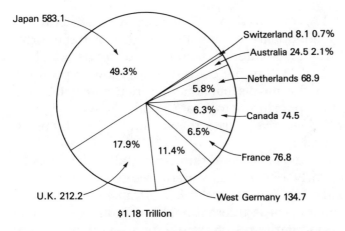

Japan 583.1

Switzerland 8.1 0.7%

Australia 24.5 2.1%

49.3%

Netherlands 68.9

5.8%

6.3%

Canada 74.5

6.5%

17.9%   11.4%

France 76.8

U.K. 212.2

West Germany 134.7

$1.18 Trillion

EXHIBIT 7.2   Size of World Government Bond Market (As of February 2, 1988)

Source: Salomon Brothers Inc.

1986, however, several issues of Australian dollar-denominated bonds were issued in the United States.

Exhibit 7.2 shows the size of the non-U.S. government bond markets converted into U.S. dollars as of February 2, 1988. The Japanese government is by far the largest issuer of nondollar bonds, followed by the United Kingdom and then West Germany. Because most corporations outside of the United States rely heavily on banks for fixed-income financing, corporate bond issues make up only a small segment of the bond markets in foreign countries. Salomon Brothers, for example, estimates that nondollar-denominated bonds issued by foreign governments constitute about 81% of the nondollar-denominated bond market.

A U.S. investor in a nondollar-denominated bond is exposed to exchange rate risk. That is, the dollar return that will be realized will depend on the exchange rate between the currency in which the cash flow will be paid and the U.S. dollar. An appreciation of the foreign currency relative to the U.S. dollar will increase the dollar return; a depreciation will decrease it.

The appeal of nondollar-denominated bonds to the U.S. investor is twofold. First, even after adjusting for foreign exchange rate fluctuations, nondollar-denominated bonds have offered higher returns than U.S. domestic bonds historically. For example, between January 1, 1975, and December 31, 1986, the dollar return on nondollar-denominated bonds was 11.4%, compared to 8.3% for U.S. domestic bonds.[19] The second appeal of nondollar-denominated bonds is that the correlation between returns on nondollar-denominated bonds and U.S. domestic bonds is low.[20] Within the context of Markowitz portfolio theory,[21] this low correlation means that nondollar-denominated bonds offer U.S. investors the opportunity to create a portfolio with a higher expected return for a given level of risk than could be done by using only U.S. domestic bonds.

The international bonds discussed thus far pay all cash flows in a foreign currency. In early 1983 bonds were introduced in the Swiss franc market that paid all coupon interest in Swiss francs but repaid the principal in U.S. dollars. These international bonds are called *dual currency bonds*. Their popularity resulted from the strength of the U.S. dollar at the time.

SUMMARY

In this chapter we described corporate, municipal, and international bonds. The investor who purchases any of these types of bonds is exposed to credit risk, call risk, and marketability risk. In addition, the investor in tax-exempt municipal bonds is subject to tax risk, and the investor in nondollar-denominated international bonds is exposed to exchange rate risk.

[19]Gary P. Brinson and Richard C. Carr, "International Equities and Bonds," in Frank J. Fabozzi, ed., *Portfolio and Investment Management* (Chicago, IL: Probus Publishing, 1989).

[20]Brinson and Carr, "International Equities and Bonds."

[21]Harry M. Markowitz, "Portfolio Selection," *Journal of Finance*, March 1971, pp. 77–91.

CORPORATE
AND MUNICIPAL BONDS:
Analysis and Strategies

In this chapter we discuss how to analyze bond swaps involving corporate and municipal bonds. We also provide an analytical framework for evaluating callable bonds and convertible bonds.

BOND SWAPS

Portfolio managers commonly swap an existing bond in a portfolio for another bond. Bond swaps can be categorized as follows: (1) pure yield pickup swaps; (2) substitution swaps; (3) rate anticipation swaps; (4) intermarket spread swaps; and (5) tax swaps.

Pure Yield Pickup Swap

Switching from one bond to another that has a higher yield is called a *pure yield pick-up swap*. The swap may be undertaken to achieve either higher current coupon income or higher yield to maturity, or both. No expectation about changes in interest rates, yield spreads, or credit quality is involved.

Rate Anticipation Swap

A portfolio manager who has expectations about the future direction of interest rates will use bond swaps to position the portfolio (on the basis of duration) to take advantage of the anticipated interest rate move. These are known as *rate anticipation swaps.* If rates are expected to fall, for example, bonds with higher duration will be swapped for existing bonds in the portfolio with low duration (to take advantage of the larger change in price). The opposite will be done if rates are expected to rise.

Substitution Swap

In a *substitution swap* a portfolio manager swaps one bond for another bond that is similar in terms of coupon, maturity, and credit quality, but offers a higher yield. This swap depends on a capital market imperfection. Such situations sometimes exist in the bond market owing to temporary market imbalances. The risk the portfolio manager faces in making a substitution swap is that the bond purchased may not be truly identical to the bond for which it is exchanged. For example, if credit quality is not the same, the bond purchased may be offering a higher yield because of higher risk rather than because of a market imbalance.

The analytical framework for evaluating a substitution swap is horizon analysis, which was discussed in Chapter 3. Suppose a pension portfolio that is exempt from income taxes includes a single-A-rated, 10%, 18-year corporate bond currently selling at par. We'll call this Bond A. Assume that the portfolio manager has the opportunity to swap into another bond, Bond B, that is also a single-A-rated corporate bond but is selling at 100.41 to yield 10.2%. Bond B is a 10.25% coupon bond with 18.5 years to maturity. The portfolio manager believes that Bond B is cheap because it is offering a higher yield (10.2%) than Bond A (10%), a comparable-quality corporate bond. The portfolio manager has an investment horizon of 6 months and expects that Bond B will fall into line with other single-A-rated bonds by the end of the investment horizon. Let's assume that the next coupon payment for both bonds is exactly 6 months from now, so that we need not consider reinvestment income.

Exhibit 8.1 shows the holding-period return for both bonds for three interest rate environments at the investment horizon (that is, 6 months from now): stable, falling 100 basis points, and rising 100 basis

EXHIBIT 8.1 Analysis of a Substitution Swap

Held in Portfolio (Candidate for Sale): Bond A
A corporate, 10%, 18-year, selling at 100.00 to yield 10%.

Candidate for Purchase: Bond B

A corporate, 10.25%, 18.5-year, selling at 100.41 to yield 10.2%.
Investment Horizon = 6 months.
Expectations:
The buy candidate currently is mispriced (underpriced).
The spread between the bond held in the portfolio and the buy candidate
will be zero at the horizon date.

Spread (in basis points)	Bond A (Sell)			Bond B (Buy)		
	Yield (%)	Price	RCY (%)	Yield (%)	Price	RCY (%)
	10.0	100.00	—	10.2	100.41	—
Rates Stable:						
Spread = 20	10.0	100.00	5.00	10.20	100.41	5.10
Spread = 0	10.0	100.00	5.00	10.00	102.07	6.76
Spread = 10	10.0	100.00	5.00	10.10	101.23	5.92
Spread = 30	10.0	100.00	5.00	10.30	99.59	4.29
Falling Rates:						
Spread = 20	9.0	108.73	13.73	9.20	109.15	13.81
Spread = 0	9.0	108.73	13.73	9.00	111.04	15.69
Spread = 10	9.0	108.73	13.73	9.10	110.09	14.74
Spread = 30	9.0	108.73	13.73	9.30	108.23	12.89
Rising Rates:						
Spread = 20	11.0	92.30	−2.70	11.20	92.71	−2.56
Spread = 0	11.0	92.30	−2.70	11.00	94.17	−1.11
Spread = 10	11.0	92.30	−2.70	11.10	93.44	−1.84
Spread = 30	11.0	92.30	−2.70	11.30	91.99	−3.28

points.[1] For each interest rate environment, four yield spreads are
shown. For the first, the yield spread is unchanged at 20 basis points
(10.2%–10%). The second yield spread is zero (i.e., Bond B's yield has

[1]Since there are no coupon payments to reinvest, the realized compound yield for both
bonds can be computed as follows:

$$\frac{\text{Price 6 months from now at assumed yield} - \text{Initial price} + \text{Semiannual coupon}}{\text{Initial price}}$$

The semiannual coupon for Bond A is $5 and for Bond B $5.125.

moved in the direction anticipated by the portfolio manager). The third yield spread assumes a narrowing of the yield spread to 10 basis points, which represents a partial adjustment rather than the full adjustment anticipated by the portfolio manager. Finally, the last yield spread assumes that the yield spread widens to 30 basis points rather than narrowing as expected.

In all interest rate environments, if the yield spread narrows, Bond B will outperform Bond A. However, if the yield spread widens, Bond A will outperform Bond B. If the spread is unchanged, Bond B will outperform Bond A.

Since we analyzed this swap from the perspective of a pension fund, the tax implications of selling Bond A were not considered since pension funds are exempt from income taxes. Managers of taxable entities would have to undertake a more comprehensive analysis that takes into account any tax implications, such as a realized gain or loss from the sale of Bond A.

Intermarket Spread Swaps

Intermarket spread swaps are undertaken when the portfolio manager believes that the current yield spread between two bonds in the market are out of line with their historical yield spread and that the yield spread will realign by the end of the investment horizon. Yield spreads between bonds exist because:

1. There is a difference in the credit quality of bonds (for example, between 15-year Treasury bonds and 15-year AAA utility bonds).
2. The type of issuer differs (for example, 20-year AAA utility bonds versus 20-year AAA industrial bonds, or 10-year AA general obligation bonds versus 10-year AA revenue bonds).

To illustrate an intermarket spread swap and how to analyze its investment merits, suppose a pension fund manager is holding Bond X, a single-A-rated corporate bond with a 7.5% coupon rate and 10 years to maturity that is selling at 93.35 to yield 8.5%. The pension fund manager observes that yields on 10-year double-A corporate bonds are 20 basis points lower. On the basis of historical patterns, he feels that a 20-basis-point yield spread between single-A and double-A corporates is too narrow and that a more appropriate spread is 30 basis points. Furthermore, he believes that the market will realign to a 30-basis-point spread in 6 months.

Suppose that the pension fund manager has the opportunity to swap Bond X for Bond Y, a double-A-rated corporate bond with a coupon rate of 7.5%, 10 years to maturity, and selling for 94.64 to yield 8.3%. The yield spread between Bond X and Bond Y is 20 basis points. Exhibit 8.2 shows the realized compound yield after 6 months for three interest rate environments: stable, falling 100 basis points, and rising 100 basis points. Four yield spreads at the end of 6 months are shown for each interest rate environment. Bond Y will outperform Bond X if the yield spread between single-

EXHIBIT 8.2   Analysis of an Intermarket Swap

Held in Portfolio (Candidate for Sale): Bond X
  A corporate, 7.5%, 10-year, selling at 93.35 to yield 8.5%.
Candidate for Purchase: Bond Y
  AA corporate, 7.5%, 10-year, selling at 94.64 to yield 8.3%.
Investment Horizon = 6 months.
Expectations:
  Spread between A and AA corporates will widen from 20 basis points to
  30 basis points.

Spread (in basis points)	Bond X (Sell)			Bond Y (Buy)		
	Yield (%)	Price	RCY (%)	Yield (%)	Price	RCY (%)
	8.5	93.35	—	8.3	94.64	—
Rates Stable:						
Spread = 10	8.5	93.57	4.25	8.4	93.57	2.83
Spread = 20	8.5	93.57	4.25	8.3	94.81	4.14
Spread = 30	8.5	93.57	4.25	8.2	95.44	4.81
Spread = 40	8.5	93.57	4.25	8.1	96.08	5.48
Falling Rates:						
Spread = 10	7.5	100.00	11.14	7.4	100.67	10.33
Spread = 20	7.5	100.00	11.14	7.3	101.35	11.05
Spread = 30	7.5	100.00	11.14	7.2	102.04	11.78
Spread = 40	7.5	100.00	11.14	7.1	102.73	12.51
Rising Rates:						
Spread = 10	9.5	87.66	−2.08	9.4	88.23	−2.81
Spread = 20	9.5	87.66	−2.08	9.3	88.81	−2.20
Spread = 30	9.5	87.66	−2.08	9.2	89.83	−1.12
Spread = 40	9.5	87.66	−2.08	9.1	89.97	−0.97

double-A-rated corporate bonds widens; it will underperform Bond X if the yield spread remains unchanged or narrows.

Of course, as we noted in the illustration of the substitution swap, tax consequences must be considered for any taxable entity contemplating an intermarket swap.

Tax Swaps

Bonds provide an ideal vehicle for managers of institutional taxable portfolios to postpone the payment of taxes from the present year to a future tax year by employing a tax swap. In a tax swap a bond issue that has declined in value is sold and a similar, but not identical, bond is purchased. Some or all of the loss realized from the sale of one bond issue can be used to reduce the taxable income realized from coupon payments or from capital appreciation on another security sold during the taxable year. For example, suppose that a portfolio includes bonds that have declined in value from $500,000 to $400,000 since they were purchased. If the portfolio manager sells these bonds for $400,000 and purchases a similar bond, a loss of $100,000 will be realized, which can be used to offset taxable income earned on the bonds in the portfolio. Yet the portfolio structure will be virtually unchanged since a similar bond has been substituted.

The reason bonds are attractive for tax swaps is that, unlike stocks, they allow investors to swap securities in a way that satisfies tax regulations for claiming a capital loss and at the same time leaves the composition of the portfolio virtually unchanged.

Tax laws discourage tax swaps on any security by refusing to recognize a tax loss if an investor purchases "substantially *identical* securities" within 30 days before or after securities are sold for a loss. The Internal Revenue Service calls this a "wash sale." Thus, if an investor sold *stock* to generate a loss, he would be prohibited from purchasing the same stock within 30 days before or after the sale and claiming a capital loss. And if the investor purchased some other stock to replace the stock sold, this swap would not be considered a "wash sale," but the composition of his portfolio would change. The replacement stock would not have the same investment characteristics as the stock sold because no stocks of different issuers are identical. But if, instead, an investor sold bonds to realize a loss, he could easily find a replacement bond with a similar coupon, duration or maturity, and credit rating, even though it might have a different issuer. Thus the actual composition of the portfolio would be virtually unchanged, but the Internal Revenue Service would not treat this tax swap involving two different issuers as a wash sale.

VALUATION OF CALLABLE BONDS

Most corporate bonds are callable prior to maturity. The traditional methodology for assessing the relative value of a callable bond, as explained in Chapter 3, is to compare the yield to call for different callable issues. However, as we explained in the same chapter, using such a framework will not permit a portfolio manager to assess the relative performance of callable bonds over a predetermined investment horizon. Specifically, the traditional methodology will not permit the portfolio manager to answer such questions as:

1. Is a current coupon bond callable in 5 years more attractive than a bond selling at a discount that is immediately callable?
2. Is a current-coupon bond callable in 2 years more attractive than a bond selling at a premium but not callable for 6 years?
3. For the same issuer, which one of several callable issues is the most attractive?

To develop an analytical framework for assessing relative value and evaluating the potential performance of callable bonds it is necessary to understand what the components of the bond owned are. A callable bond is a bond in which the bondholder has granted the issuer the option to repurchase the contractual cash flow of the bond from the time the bond is first callable until the maturity date. Consider, for example, a callable bond that has a 10% coupon, 25 years to maturity, and is callable in 5 years at 106. The holder of this bond then owns a 5-year noncallable bond and has sold an option granting the issuer the right to call away 20 years of cash flows 5 years from today. The exercise price is 106. An investor who owns a 15-year, 11% bond that is immediately callable at 100 (par) owns a 15-year noncallable bond and has sold an option granting the issuer the right to immediately call the entire 15-year contractual cash flow or any cash flow remaining at the time the issue is called for 100.

What portfolio managers need is a framework to address the following two questions. First, does the callable bond represent good value? And if it does, is the risk/return profile of the callable bond such that its potential performance makes it an attractive invest-ment for an investor's portfolio?[2]

Valuing the Noncallable Component of a Callable Bond

The position of an investor in a callable bond can be expressed as follows:

Long a callable bond = Long a noncallable bond + Short a call option

The value of a callable bond is equal to the price of the two com-ponents; that is:

Price of a callable bond = Price of a noncallable bond – Call option price

or

(8.1) $P_{cb} = P_{ncb} - P_{co}$

where
P_{cb} = price of a callable bond
P_{ncb} = price of a noncallable bond
P_{co} = price of a call option

Notice that the call option price is subtracted from the price of the noncallable bond. The reason is that when the bondholder sells a call option, he receives the option price. Effectively, what the owner of a callable bond is doing is entering into two separate transactions. First, he buys a noncallable bond from the issuer for which he pays some price. Then he sells the issuer a call option for which he receives an amount (the option price) from the issuer.

Given this relationship for the callable bond, an investor wants to know if the noncallable bond is correctly priced. In other words, is he being rewarded adequately for assuming the credit risk associated with owning the bond? Though the price of a noncallable bond is not

[2]The analytical framework discussed here is drawn from Gary D. Latainer and David P. Jacob, "Modern Techniques for Analyzing Value and Performance of Callable Bonds," in Frank J. Fabozzi and T. Dessa Garlicki, eds., *Advances in Bond Analysis and Portfolio Strategies* (Chicago, Il: Probus Publishing, 1987).

directly observable, it can be estimated by rewriting equation (8.1) as:

(8.2) $P_{ncb} = P_{cb} + P_{co}$

The price of a callable bond can be observed in the market. If the price of the call option can be estimated, then adding this estimated option price to the observed callable bond price will give us the price of a noncallable bond. In Chapter 12 we will provide an overview of option pricing. Using an option-pricing model, practitioners can estimate the price of the call option for a callable bond. The purpose here is not to discuss option-pricing models, but rather to demonstrate how the output of such models can be utilized in valuing the noncallable component of a callable bond.

Suppose, for example, a portfolio manager is considering a callable bond selling at par with a 10% coupon, 25 years to maturity, and callable in 5 years at 106. Suppose also that using an option-pricing model, the call option price is estimated to be $3.77. The price of the noncallable bond is then:

$$
\begin{aligned}
P_{ncb} &= \$100 + \$3.77 \\
&= \$103.77
\end{aligned}
$$

Given the price of the noncallable bond, it is simple to compute the yield on this bond if it is held to maturity. The yield is the interest rate that will make the cash flow for the bond if held to maturity equal to the price of the noncallable bond. The yield computed is referred to as the *call-adjusted yield*.

For our hypothetical callable bond the call-adjusted yield is computed by finding the interest rate that will make the present value of 50 coupon payments of $5 every 6 months plus $100 at the end of 50 6-month periods equal to $103.77. The calculated 6-month interest rate that satisfies this is 4.8%. Doubling this interest rate gives the call-adjusted yield of 9.6% on a bond-equivalent yield basis.

The call-adjusted yield is the implied yield on the noncallable bond. A noncallable bond is priced fairly if the call-adjusted yield for a callable bond is the proper yield for a noncallable bond with the same features and of the same issuer. A bond is rich or overvalued if the call-adjusted yield is less, and cheap or undervalued if the call-adjusted yield is more. Latainer and Jacob report that there have been times in the market when a callable bond has been so mispriced that the call-adjusted yield on the callable corporate bond has been below the yield on a comparable noncallable Treasury security.[3]

Call-Adjusted Duration

The call-adjusted yield is only one side of the valuation equation. The other is price volatility, which is commonly measured by modified duration (simply duration hereafter). In Chapter 4 we illustrated how to compute the duration of an option-free bond. To analyze the duration of a callable bond, we follow the same procedure.

Taking the first derivative of equation (8.1) with respect to yield (y), we have:

$$\frac{dP_{cb}}{dy} = \frac{dP_{ncb}}{dy} - \frac{dP_{co}}{dy}$$

Dividing both sides by the price of a callable bond gives us:

$$\frac{dP_{cb}}{dy}\frac{1}{P_{cb}} = \frac{dP_{ncb}}{dy}\frac{1}{P_{cb}} - \frac{dP_{co}}{dy}\frac{1}{P_{cb}}$$

Multiplying both the numerator and the denominator of the right-hand side of the equation by the price of a noncallable bond, we obtain:

$$\frac{dP_{cb}}{dy}\frac{1}{P_{cb}} = \frac{dP_{ncb}}{dy}\frac{1}{P_{ncb}}\frac{P_{ncb}}{P_{cb}} - \frac{dP_{co}}{dy}\frac{1}{P_{ncb}}\frac{P_{ncb}}{P_{cb}}$$

Let's look at each of the components:

$$\frac{dP_{cb}}{dy}\frac{1}{P_{cb}} = \text{Duration of callable bond} = D_{cb}$$

$$\frac{dP_{ncb}}{dy}\frac{1}{P_{ncb}} = \text{Duration of a noncallable bond} = D_{ncb}$$

Thus we have:

---

[3]Latainer and Jacob, "Modern Techniques for Analyzing Value and Performance of Callable Bonds," p. 272.

$$(8.3) \quad D_{cb} = D_{ncb} \frac{P_{ncb}}{P_{cb}} - \frac{dP_{co}}{dy} \frac{1}{P_{ncb}} \frac{P_{ncb}}{P_{cb}}$$

The change in the value of the call option for a change in yield is:

$$(8.4) \quad \frac{dP_{co}}{dy}$$

However, the change in the value of the call option depends on the change in the price of the noncallable bond for a given change in yield. That is:

$$P_{co} = f(P_{ncb}) \text{ and } P_{ncb} = g(y)$$

Using the function-of-a-function rule from calculus, equation (8.4) can be expressed as:

$$(8.5) \quad \frac{dP_{co}}{dy} = \frac{dP_{co}}{dP_{ncb}} \frac{dP_{ncb}}{dy}$$

The first term on the right-hand side of equation (8.5) is the change in the value of the call option for a change in the price of the noncallable bond. This is commonly referred to as the *delta* of an option. Thus:

$$(8.6) \quad \frac{dP_{co}}{dy} = (\text{delta}) \frac{dP_{ncb}}{dy}$$

Substituting equation (8.6) into equation (8.3) and rearranging terms, we obtain:

$$(8.7) \quad D_{cb} = D_{ncb} \frac{P_{ncb}}{P_{cb}} (1-\text{delta})$$

The duration for the callable bond given by equation (8.7) is commonly referred to as the *call-adjusted duration*. Equation (8.7) states that the call-adjusted duration depends on (1) the duration of a noncallable bond, (2) the ratio of price of a noncallable bond to a callable bond, and (3) the delta of the call option.[4] In Chapter 12 we will look at the delta of the call option. For now, we will just state two properties of delta:

1. For a callable bond selling at a deep discount from par because the coupon rate is substantially below the market yield, delta is zero and the price of a callable bond will be equal to the price of a noncallable bond (the ratio is equal to 1).
2. For a bond selling at a substantial premium because the coupon rate is above the required yield, delta is close to 1.

The first property states that for a bond selling at a substantial discount from par, the price of the call option does not respond to changes in the underlying noncallable bond. Substituting zero for delta and 1 for the ratio of the price of the noncallable bond to the price of the callable bond into equation (8.7), we find:

$$D_{cb} = D_{ncb} 1 (1 - 0) = D_{ncb}$$

Thus the duration of a callable bond is equal to the duration of a noncallable bond if the bond's coupon rate is considerably below the market yield and, as a result, is unlikely to be called. In contrast, if the bond's coupon rate is considerably higher than the market yield, the second property states that delta will be close to 1. Substituting 1 for delta in equation (8.7), we find:

$$D_{cb} = D_{ncb} \frac{P_{ncb}}{P_{cb}} (1 - 1) = 0$$

The call-adjusted duration of a callable bond that is expected to be called is therefore zero.

Anywhere between a deep-discount bond and a premium bond, the call-adjusted duration of a callable bond will be less than the duration of a noncallable bond.

Unlike an option-free bond which has the property that duration increases (decreases) when yield decreases (increases), this is not true for a callable bond. At some yield level, the duration will decrease as the yield decreases. This property of a callable bond is referred to as *negative convexity*.

---

[4]A call-adjusted convexity can also be derived. See Chap. 13 and Appendix A in Frank J. Fabozzi, *Fixed Income Mathematics* (Chicago, IL: Probus Publishing, 1988).

Performance Profiles of Callable Bonds

While call-adjusted yield can help identify relative value, a callable bond that is cheap still may not be appropriate for a portfolio manager whose performance evaluation is based on total return. Using horizon analysis, the performance of a callable bond can be compared to that of a noncallable bond under different market scenarios. However, the two bonds must have equivalent duration to be comparable. In the case of a callable bond, the appropriate duration measure is the call-adjusted duration.

To illustrate how to evaluate the performance of a callable bond relative to that of a noncallable bond of the same duration, consider a 12% coupon, 30-year bond callable after 5 years at 109.60.[5] Suppose also that: (1) the current interest rate is 12% (thus the bond is selling at par); (2) the call-adjusted duration is estimated to be 7.4 years; (3) the callable bond is fairly priced; and (4) the portfolio manager considering this bond is concerned with its performance over a 6-month investment horizon.

Exhibit 8.3 shows the performance profile of this callable bond relative to a noncallable bond of the same duration (7.4 years). This example assumes the callable bond is fairly priced. The horizontal axis measures the change from the current rate (12%) at the end of the 6-month horizon. The difference in the total return (realized compound yield) between the callable bond and the noncallable bond is shown on the vertical axis. This performance profile demonstrates that if interest rates do not move more than 100 basis points above or below the current rate of 12%, the callable bond will outperform the noncallable bond of equal duration. However, the callable bond will underperform the equivalent-duration noncallable bond if interest rates change by more than 100 basis points in either direction. Thus the attractiveness of this bond will depend on the portfolio manager's expectations about how much interest rates will have changed at the end of 6 months. If interest rates are expected to be stable, the callable bond will be more attractive relative to the noncallable bond.

Our example in Exhibit 8.3 assumed that the callable bond was fairly priced. Now let's look at the performance profile if the callable bond is priced 50 basis points too rich; that is, the call-adjusted

[5]This example is adapted from Latainer and Jacob, "Modern Techniques for Analyzing Value and Performance of Callable Bonds," p. 278.

EXHIBIT 8.3   6-Month Performance of a 30-Year, 12% Coupon Bond Callable After 5 Years at 109.6 Relative to an Equivalent-Duration Noncallable Bond

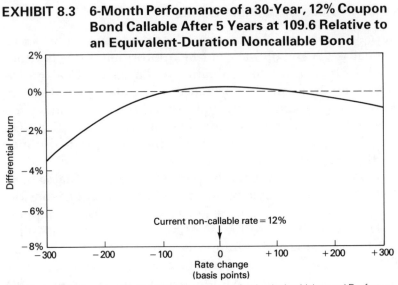

Source: Latainer and Jacob, "Modern Techniques for Analyzing Value and Perform-ance of Callable Bonds."

yield is 50 basis points less than that of a noncallable bond of the same issuer. The performance profile shown in Exhibit 8.4 assumes that this mispricing is corrected in 6 months. Notice that regardless of what happens to interest rates at the end of 6 months, this bond will underperform the equivalent-duration noncallable bond.

If, on the other hand, the callable bond is cheap by 50 basis points and corrects in 6 months, the callable bond will provide incremental returns even if interest rates rise or fall by 300 basis points, as shown in Exhibit 8.5. Remember that the performance profiles shown in Exhibits 8.4 and 8.5 assume that the mispricing will be corrected at the end of the 6-month period. If the bond continues to get cheaper or richer, the callable bond will underperform relative to the noncallable bond.[6]

---

[6]Latainer and Jacob tested this framework by looking at the 6-month performance of callable long telephone bond issues that were identified as being 25 basis points cheap or rich on the basis of the estimated call-adjusted yield. Their empirical results indicate that, on average, bonds identified as cheap provided incremental returns of 1.27% relative to bonds that were identified as rich. In addition, 70% of the callable bonds identified as cheap in their study would have provided a higher total return. See Latainer and Jacob, "Modern Techniques for Analyzing Value and Performance of Callable Bonds," pp. 285–289.

EXHIBIT 8.4   6-Month Performance of a 30-Year 12% Coupon Bond Callable After 5 Years at 109.6, Priced 50 Basis Points Rich, Relative to an Equivalent-Duration Noncallable Bond

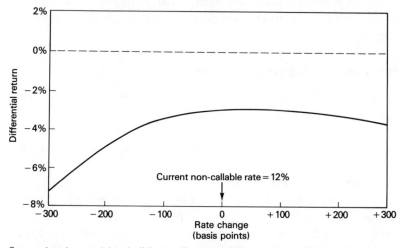

Source: Latainer and Jacob, "Modern Techniques for Analyzing Value and Performance of Callable Bonds."

EXHIBIT 8.5   6-Month Performance of a 30-Year, 12% Coupon Bond Callable After 5 Years at 109.6, Priced 50 Basis Points Cheap, Relative to an Equivalent Duration Noncallable Bond

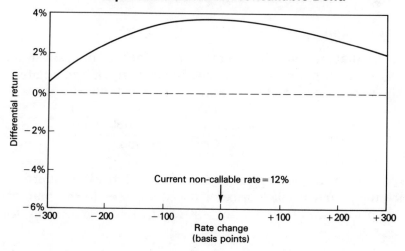

Source: Latainer and Jacob, "Modern Techniques for Analyzing Value and Performance of Callable Bonds."

VALUATION OF CONVERTIBLE BONDS

In the previous chapter we explained that a convertible bond grants the bondholder the option to convert the bond into common stock. The number of shares the bondholder will receive upon conversion is called the *conversion ratio*. In this section we explain how convertible bonds are valued.

Minimum Value of a Convertible Bond

The *conversion value* of a convertible bond is the value of the bond if it is converted immediately; that is:

Conversion value = Market price of common stock × Conversion ratio

The minimum price of a convertible bond is the greater of: (1) its value as a corporate bond without the conversion option, which is based on the convertible bond's cash flows if not converted (i.e., a plain vanilla bond); or (2) its conversion value. The former value is called the *straight value* of the bond. To estimate the straight value, the required yield on a nonconvertible bond with the same quality rating and similar investment characteristics must be determined. The straight value is the present value of the bond's cash flows at this estimated required yield. If the convertible bond did not sell for the greater of these two values, arbitrage profits could be realized.

Market Conversion Price

The price that an investor effectively pays for the common stock if he purchases the convertible bond and then converts it immediately is called the *market conversion price*[7] and is found as follows:

$$\text{Market conversion price} = \frac{\text{Market price of convertible bond}}{\text{Conversion ratio}}$$

The market conversion price is a useful analytical number because once the actual market price of the stock rises to the market conversion price, any further stock price increase is certain to

---

[7] The market conversion price is also called the *conversion parity price*.

increase the value of the convertible bond by at least the same amount as the increase in the price of the stock. Therefore the market conversion price can be viewed as a break-even point.

By purchasing the convertible bond rather than the stock, an investor typically pays a premium over the current market price of the stock. The conversion premium per share is equal to the difference between the market conversion price and the current market price of the common stock. The conversion premium is usually expressed as a percentage of the current market price as follows:

$$\text{Conversion premium ratio} = \frac{\text{Conversion premium per share}}{\text{Market price of common stock}}$$

Current Income of Convertible Bond versus Stock

As a partial offset to the price premium, the investor generally realizes higher current income from the coupon interest paid on the convertible bond than he would from dividends paid on the number of shares equal to the conversion ratio.

In evaluating a convertible bond, analysts typically compute the time it takes to recover the premium per share by computing the *premium payback period* (which is also known as *break-even time*). This is computed as follows:

$$\frac{\text{Market conversion premium per share}}{\text{Favorable income differential per share}}$$

where the favorable income differential per share is equal to:

$$\frac{\text{Coupon interest from bond} - (\text{Conversion ratio} \times \text{dividend per share})}{\text{Conversion ratio}}$$

Notice that the break-even time does *not* take into account the time value of money.

Downside Risk with a Convertible Bond

Investors usually use the straight value of the bond to measure the downside risk of a convertible bond. Recall that the price of the convertible bond cannot fall below this value. Thus, the straight value acts as a floor for the price of the convertible bond. The downside risk is measured as a percentage of the straight value. It is computed as follows:

$$\text{Premium over straight value} = \frac{\text{Market price of the convertible bond}}{\text{Straight value}} - 1$$

Despite the frequency of its use, this measure of downside risk is flawed because the straight value (the floor) changes as interest rates change. If interest rates decline, the straight value rises. Thus, the floor rises, and the downside risk is decreased.

As we will see in Chapter 12, convertible bonds have the same investment characteristics as options: substantial upside potential and limited losses. With convertible bonds the upside potential is reduced by the market conversion premium per share and the downside risk is limited by the convertible bond's straight value. Unlike options, the maximum loss is not known at the outset. It can be lower than the straight value of the convertible bond at the time of purchase if interest rates rise or the credit quality of the issuer deteriorates after purchase.

Illustration of Risk and Reward Characteristics of a Convertible Bond

To illustrate the risk and reward characteristics of a convertible bond, let's consider MidCon's convertible bond with a coupon of 10.25%, maturing March 31, 2009. The conversion ratio for this issue is 23.809; that is, if the bondholder exchanges the bond for MidCon's common stock, 23.809 shares will be received. The convertible bond was callable on March 31, 1987. The investment characteristics will be examined as of July 5, 1985. The market value of the bond on that date was $1,240.

On July 5, 1985, MidCon's common stock was $47.00. The conversion value was then:

$$
\begin{aligned}
\text{Conversion value} &= \text{Market price of common stock} \times \text{Conversion ratio} \\
&= \$47.00 \times 23.809 \\
&= \$1,119.02
\end{aligned}
$$

A straight bond (noncallable and nonconvertible) with 23 years and 9 months to maturity, a coupon rate of 10.25%, and the same credit quality as MidCon's convertible bond was estimated to offer a yield of approximately 12% on July 5, 1985. Pricing this MidCon bond issue at 12% gives a straight value of $863.[8] Thus the minimum price for this issue was $1,119.02, the greater of the conversion value and the straight value. The floor for this issue, assuming no change in interest rates, was $863.

The market conversion price is:

$$\text{Market conversion price} = \frac{\text{Market price of convertible bond}}{\text{Conversion ratio}}$$

$$= \frac{\$1,240}{23.809}$$

$$= \$52.08 \text{ per share of common stock}$$

The conversion premium per share is $5.08 ($52.08 – $47) and the conversion premium ratio is:

$$\text{Conversion premium ratio} = \frac{\text{Conversion premium per share}}{\text{Market price of common stock}}$$

$$= \frac{\$5.08}{\$47}$$

$$= 10.81\%$$

A conversion premium ratio of 10.81% means that an investor who had purchased this convertible bond and converted immediately rather than buying MidCon's common stock outright would have paid a premium of 10.81% over the market price of the common stock. This premium represents the cost of the call option.

The premium over straight value is:

Premium over straight value =

$$\frac{\text{Market price of the convertible bond}}{\text{Straight value}} - 1$$

---

[8]Technically, since this bond is callable, the determination of the straight value should be based on the callable bond analysis discussed in the previous section.

$$= \frac{\$1,240}{\$863} - 1$$

$$= .44 \text{ or } 44\%$$

Assuming that interest rates do not change, a premium over straight value of 44% means that the price of the issue can fall by 44% before it reaches its floor (straight value).

The market conversion premium for this bond is partially offset by the greater current income that would be realized from owning the convertible bond rather than the common stock. The current yield on the convertible bond is:

$$\text{Current yield} = \frac{\text{Annual coupon interest}}{\text{Price of the convertible bond}}$$

$$\frac{\$1,000 \times .1025}{\$1,240}$$

$$\frac{\$102.25}{\$1,240}$$

$$.0827 \text{ or } 8.27\%$$

The current yield on MidCon's common stock was 3.67%. In addition to the higher current yield obtained by investing in the convertible bond, it is important to realize that coupon interest is more secure than dividends, since coupon interest cannot be cut without the firm defaulting.

To see the typical trade-off between upside potential and downside risk, let's look at what would happen on March 31, 1987, if the price of the common stock changes. First, suppose that the common stock price rose to $64 per share. By owning the common stock outright, an investor would have realized a gain of:

$$\frac{\$64 - \$47}{\$47} = 36.2\%$$

The conversion value for the convertible bond would be $1,523.78 ($64 × 23.809) and thereby the investor would have realized a minimum gain of:

$$\frac{\$1,523.78 - \$1,240}{\$1,240} = 22.9\%$$

The increase would have been 22.9% plus any premium over the conversion value the market would be willing to place on the convertible bond. It's easy to understand why the price appreciation is less. The market conversion price was $52.08. Thus the increase in price of the common stock to $64 represented an increase of only 22.9%:

$$\frac{\$64 - \$52.08}{\$52.08} = 22.9\%$$

Hence the upside potential of a convertible bond is reduced by the premium per share paid by the investor. As we shall see in Chapter 12, this is an investment characteristic of a long call option position whose exercise price here is $52.08 combined with a long position in the underlying security.

Focusing on the downside risk, if the common stock price had declined to $32 on March 31, 1987, and the common stock was owned outright, the investor would have realized a loss of 32%. The minimum price of the convertible bond would be the greater of the conversion value and the straight value. The conversion value would be $761.88 ($32 × 23.809). The straight value would depend on the market yield for comparable-risk and -maturity bonds at the time. Following is a list of the straight values for the bond (the convertible bond has 22 years remaining to maturity—assuming it is not called) for various market yields and the corresponding losses:

Market Yield (%)	Straight Value ($)	Loss (%)
8	$1,231.10	1
9%	1,118.90	10%
10	1,022.10	18
11	938.30	24
12	865.40	30

For all these market yields, the loss is less than the 32% loss that occurs if the common stock is owned and its price falls to $32. Consequently, we can see the downside protection offered by the convertible bond. However, the downside protection is not known in advance, as it would be for call options in which the loss is limited to the option price.

The floor for a convertible bond depends on market yields. In fact, in our illustration, if the yield was less than 7.8%, the straight value would be greater than $1,240, resulting in a small gain rather than a loss.

Takeover Risk and Convertible Bonds

Corporate takeovers add another risk to investing in convertible bonds. If an issuer is acquired by another company or by its own management (as in a leveraged buyout), the stock price may not appreciate sufficiently for the holders of the convertible bond to recoup any premium over the conversion value they paid. If the stock of the acquired company no longer trades, as in the case of a leveraged buyout, the investor may be left with a bond that pays a lower coupon rate than comparable-risk bonds.

Take, for example, the situation facing the holders of the convertible bonds of Wherehouse Entertainment, Inc.[9] The convertible bonds have a par value of $1,000 and can be converted into just over 36 shares, so the conversion price is roughly $27.60 per share. By February 1987, the stock price was $13 per share. Investors who purchased the convertible bond before the leveraged buyout paid a premium over the stock market price of Wherehouse. After the leveraged buyout, the convertible bondholders lost that premium because there was no market price for the stock. As a result, they faced two unappealing choices. They could convert the bond into common stock and lose the entire premium over conversion value that they had paid. Or they could continue to hold the convertible bond, which would then be effectively a straight bond. The coupon rate on the convertible bond is 6.25%, which is far below the estimated coupon rate for a straight bond of comparable risk.

VALUATION OF MORE COMPLEX STRUCTURES: THE CASE OF LYONs

An interesting example of complex structure bonds that have been created for corporate issuers is the Liquid Yield Option Notes (LYONs). These corporate bonds were created by Merrill Lynch White Weld Capital Markets Group in 1985 and were first issued by Waste Management, Inc., and Staley Continental, Inc., in the spring of 1985.

---

[9]This example is taken from David Zigas, "The One-Two Punch Pummeling Convertibles," *Business Week*, February 8, 1988, p. 82.

A LYON is a zero-coupon corporate bond that is (1) callable by the issuer, (2) convertible into the common stock of the issuer, and (3) putable to the issuer at specified dates and prices that escalate over time. Thus the price of a LYON can be decomposed as follows:[10]

Price of a zero-coupon bond of the same maturity with no default risk

minus

Price of the credit risk

minus

Price of the option sold to the issuer for the right to call the bond

plus

Price of the call option purchased from the issuer for the right to buy (convert to) common stock

plus

Price of the option purchased from the issuer for the right to put the bond at specified dates

OPPORTUNITIES IN HIGH-YIELD BONDS

As explained in the previous chapter, high-yield or junk bonds are issues with quality ratings below triple B. Several studies have demonstrated that *diversified* portfolios of high-yield bonds have historically generated returns more than sufficient to compensate for the additional credit risk associated with any individual issue.[11] This performance is chiefly due to two factors.

First, studies have found that defaults by corporate issuers have been lower than expected. This can be seen in Exhibit 8.6, which shows the percentage of all publicly issued corporate straight debt that has defaulted over various periods. Are these percentages considerably higher for high-yield bonds? A study by Drexel Burnham Lambert focusing on the default experience of high-yield bonds[12] found that between January 1977 and February 1985 the average amount of high-yield debt outstanding lost in bankruptcies each year was 0.45%. When

---

[10]For an analytical framework for evaluating a LYON, see John J. McConnell and Eduardo Schwartz, "LYON Taming," *Journal of Finance*, July 1986, pp. 561–576. McConnell and Schwartz apply their framework to the pricing of the LYON issued by Waste Management, Inc.

[11]For a summary of these studies, see Howard S. Marks, "High Yield Bond Portfolios," Chap. 35 in Frank J. Fabozzi and Irving M. Pollack, eds., *The Handbook of Fixed Income Securities* (Homewood, IL: Dow Jones-Irwin, 1987).

[12]*The Case for High Yield Bonds* (Beverly Hills, CA: Drexel Burnham Lambert, 1985).

EXHIBIT 8.6   Default Rate as a Percentage of All Straight Corporate Debt

Period	Default Rate
1900–1909	0.90%
1910–1919	2.00
1920–1929	1.00
1930–1939	3.20
1940–1949	0.40
1950–1959	0.04
1960–1965	0.03
1966–1970	0.20
1971–1975	0.11
1976–1980	0.06
1980–1984	0.12

Source: *The Case for High Yield Bonds* (Beverly Hills, CA: Drexel Burnham Lambert, 1985), p. 10.

those issues that defaulted but did not go bankrupt were included, the percentage rose to slightly over 0.5%. Thus, while the default rate for high-yield bond issues was considerably greater than that for all straight corporate debt in the same period (shown in Exhibit 8.6), it has been modest in percentage terms. In addition, any estimate of the impact of default on return must consider that a money manager can sell the bond after a default or a bankruptcy. A study by Altman and Nammacher, for example, found that if bonds are sold immediately after bankruptcy, an average of 41% of the par value is recouped.[13]

The second factor affecting the performance of diversified portfolios of high-yield bonds is the substantial yields offered by these bonds. The DBL 100 Bond Index (a high-yield bond index) and the Salomon Brothers All High Yield Bond Index show that the yield spread over Treasury bonds between 1980 and 1985 ranged from 319 to 526 basis points.

In summary, the low default rate experience of high-yield bonds coupled with their high promised yield spread to Treasuries has generated the consistently above-average returns that have been noted in empirical studies for diversified portfolios of high-yield bonds. In addition, a study by Blume and Keim has found that during the period from January 1980 to June 1984 the volatility of returns (as measured by

[13]Edward I. Altman and Scott A. Nammacher, "The Default Rate Experience on High Yield Corporate Debt," *Financial Analysts Journal*, July–August 1985, pp. 25–41.

[14]Marshall E. Blume and Donald B. Keim, "Risk and Return Characteristics of Lower Grade Bonds," Rodney L. White Center for Financial Research, University of Pennsylvania, 1985, Tables 1 and 3.

the standard deviation of monthly returns) was less for lower-rated bonds than for higher-rated bonds.[14]

SUMMARY

Money managers undertake bond swaps in order to enhance the performance of a portfolio over some investment horizon. There are five types of bond swaps: (1) pure yield pickup swaps; (2) substitution swaps; (3) rate anticipation swaps; (4) intermarket spread swaps; and (5) tax swaps. This chapter showed how the horizon analysis framework is used to analyze a potential bond swap.

An investor in a callable bond is long a noncallable bond and short a call option on the bond. The chapter illustrated how, by analyzing these two components, the value of a callable bond can be determined. Macaulay duration is not appropriate for callable bonds. Instead, a call-adjusted duration, which depends on the delta of the embedded call option, should be determined. Callable bonds may also exhibit negative convexity.

Techniques for valuing a convertible bond were also discussed. A convertible bond is nothing more than a long position in a bond (in fact, a callable bond) and a long position in call options on the common stock. Breaking down complex bond structures into component parts and evaluating each part is the proper method of analysis. We illustrated this with a LYON bond structure.

Studies of the high-yield (junk) bond market have found that diversified portfolios of these issues have consistently provided above-average returns. This can be attributed to the low default rate experience of high-yield bonds and their large yield spread relative to Treasury bonds and higher quality corporate bonds.

9

MORTGAGES

The purpose of this chapter is to describe the major types of mortgages that serve as the underlying collateral in mortgage-backed securities. These are: level-payment, fixed-rate mortgages; graduated-payment mortgages; and adjustable-rate mortgages. The cash flow characteristics of these mortgages are also presented here. In the next chapter we shall discuss the mortgage-backed securities themselves: mortgage pass-through securities; collateralized mortgage obligations; and stripped mortgage-backed securities.

WHAT IS A MORTGAGE?

A mortgage is a pledge of real estate to secure the payment of the loan originated for the purchase of that real property. The mortgage gives the lender (*mortgagee*) the right to foreclose on the loan and seize the property in order to ensure that the loan is paid off if the borrower (*mortgagor*) fails to make the contracted payments.

When the lender makes the loan on the basis of the borrower's credit and the collateral for the mortgage, the mortgage is said to be a *conventional mortgage*. The lender also may take out mortgage insurance to guarantee the obligations of the borrower.[1] The two forms of mortgage insurance that are guaranteed by the U.S. government for borrowers who qualify are Federal Housing Administration (FHA) and Veteran's Administration (VA) insurance. There are also private mortgage insurers. The cost of mortgage insurance is paid to the guarantor by the mortgage originator but passed along to the borrower in the form of higher mortgage payments.

The types of real estate properties that can be mortgaged are divided into two broad categories: residential and nonresidential. The former category includes houses, condominiums, cooperatives, and apartments. Residential real estate can be subdivided into single-family (one-to-four family) structures and multifamily structures (apartment buildings in which more than four families reside). The second type of real estate property is nonresidential property, which includes commercial and farm properties.

MORTGAGE ORIGINATORS

The major mortgage originators are savings and loan associations, savings banks, commercial banks, mortgage bankers, and insurance companies. In 1986 the first four accounted for about 98% of single-family mortgage originations. The largest originator was savings and loan associations (40%), followed by mortgage bankers (30%), commercial banks (21%), and savings banks (8%). Insurance companies originate a substantial amount of commercial real estate mortgages. Exhibit 9.1 shows the dollar amount of mortgage originations in 1986 by lender and type of property.

Mortgage originators may generate income from mortgages in one or more of the following ways. First, they typically charge an origination fee. This fee is expressed in terms of *points*, each of which represents 1% of the borrowed funds. For example, an origination fee of 2 points on a $100,000 mortgage is $2,000. Second, the mortgage originator obtains a servicing fee. Servicing of the mortgage involves collecting monthly payments from mortgagors and forwarding the proceeds to the owners of the loan; sending payment notices to mortgagors; reminding mortgagors when payments are overdue; maintaining records of mortgage balances; furnishing tax information

---

[1]There is also mortgage insurance that may be obtained by the borrower in the form of life insurance.

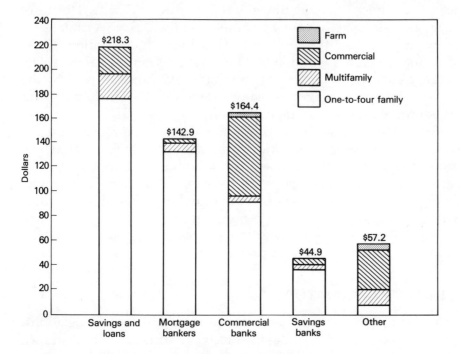

Source: Department of Housing and Urban Development.
Reprinted from: Peter G. Brown, Thomas A. Zimmerman, and K. Jeanne Person, Introduction to Mortgages and Mortgage-Backed Securities. New York: Salomon Brothers Inc, September 1987.

EXHIBIT 9.1   Mortgage Originations by Lender and Property Type, 1986 (Dollars in Billions)

to mortgagors; administering an escrow account for real estate taxes and insurance purposes; and, if necessary, initiating foreclosure proceedings. The servicing fee is a fixed percentage of the outstanding mortgage balance, typically 1/4% (25 basis points) to 1/2% (50 basis points) per annum. The mortgage originator may sell the servicing of the mortgage to another party, who then receives the servicing fee. Finally, the mortgage originator may hold the mortgage in its investment portfolio.

Regulatory and tax considerations encourage thrifts (savings and loan associations and savings banks) to invest in mortgages or mortgage-backed securities.[2] In fact, thrifts have become increasingly de-

---

[2]The tax benefits have been reduced by the 1986 tax act. See Kenneth Rosen and Janet Spratlin, "The Impact of Tax Reform on the Mortgage Market," Chapter 45 in Frank J. Fabozzi, ed., The Handbook of Mortgage-Backed Securities, 2nd ed. (Chicago, IL: Probus Publishing, 1988).

pendent on the fees generated from originating and servicing mortgages. Mortgage bankers do not invest in mortgages. Instead, they derive their income from the origination fees. Commercial banks derive their income from all three sources—origination, servicing, and investment. However, unlike thrifts, they realize no regulatory benefits from investing in mortgages or mortgage-backed securities.

Mortgage originators can either (1) hold the mortgage in their portfolio, (2) sell the mortgage to an investor who wishes to hold the mortgage in its portfolio or who will package the mortgage into a mortgage pass-through security, or (3) package the mortgage into a mortgage pass-through security themselves. When a mortgage originator intends to sell the mortgage, it will obtain a commitment from the potential investor (buyer). Two federally sponsored credit agencies and private conduits buy mortgages and then repackage them. These two agencies, the Federal Home Loan Mortgage Corporation and the Federal National Mortgage Association, purchase only *conforming* mortgages. A *conforming mortgage* is one that meets the underwriting standards established by these agencies for inclusion in a pool of mortgages underlying a pass-through security that the agencies guarantee. The private conduits, such as Bear Stearns Mortgage Capital, Citimae, Residential Funding Corporation, Sears Mortgage Securities Corporation, and Shearson Lehman Mortgage Corporation, purchase both conforming and nonconforming mortgages (mortgages that do not conform to the standards required by the two agencies).

The mortgage rate that the mortgage originator sets on the loan depends on the mortgage rate required by the investor who plans to purchase the mortgage. Exhibits 9.2 and 9.3 are pages from the Knight-Ridder MoneyCenter that provide information about the terms for mortgages to be delivered to the Federal Home Loan Mortgage Corporation and Bear Stearns Mortgage Capital. Notice that there are different mortgage rates for delivery at different times (30 days, 60 days, or 90 days). The mortgage originator also has a choice of mandatory delivery or optional delivery. The latter means that the originator has the right, but not the obligation, to deliver the mortgage; that is, the mortgage originator has a put option.[3] As with all options, the originator pays for this option. The price or fee is shown on the two exhibits. Other information on these two exhibits will become clearer as we discuss the various types of mortgages in the remainder of this chapter.

[3]Put options are decribed in Chapter 12.

EXHIBIT 9.2   Example of FHLMC Single Family Commitments

331 Fixed Format Page KNIGHT-RIDDER MoneyCenter					5-Apr-88 4:21P

FHLMC Single Family Commitments　　　　**4/05**

	SFFR		GRADUATED PAYMENT MORTGAGES			
			30 YEAR		15 YEAR	
DELIVERY	30 YEAR	15 YEAR	5% CAP	7.5% CAP	5% CAP	7.5% CAP
------						
10 DAY	10.04	9.72	10.34	10.41	10.02	10.10
30 DAY	10.12	9.81	10.42	10.50	10.11	10.19
60 DAY	10.20	9.91	10.50	10.57	10.21	10.29
90 DAY	10.28	10.00	10.58	10.66	10.30	10.38
120 DAY	10.36	10.09	10.66	10.74	10.39	10.47
120 DAY OPTIONAL						
PLAN A - RATE	10.36	10.09	NA	NA	NA	NA
FEE	1.475	1.475	NA	NA	NA	NA
PLAN B - RATE	10.86	NA	NA	NA	NA	NA
FEE	0.550	NA	NA	NA	NA	NA
240 DAY OPTIONAL						
RATE	10.84	NA	NA	NA	NA	NA
FEE	1.750	NA	NA	NA	NA	NA

Knight-Ridder MoneyCenter

EXHIBIT 9.3 Example of Private Conduit Commitments

Bear Stearns Mortgage Capital Corporation - Mandatory Commitments

4/4

	30-Year Fixed	15-Year Fixed	7-Year Roll	Bear
Max Rate	10.600	10.250		
Min Rate	9.600	9.250		

Term	Max Price	Net Yield	Max Price	Net Yield	Max Price	Max Price
Days 10	100.000	10.600	100.000	10.250		
30	99.750	10.638	99.750	10.306		
60	99.375	10.696	99.375	10.391		
90	99.000	10.754	99.000	10.477		

Yield Equivalency Factors: 7-Year: Bear:

All rates posted are net of servicing Optional Delivery Commitment
prices for these programs on Page 379.

175

EXHIBIT 9.3   Example of Private Conduit Commitments (Continued)

Bear Stearns Mortgage Capital Corporation - Optional Commitments   4/4

7-Year Roll

30-Year Fixed Rate

Term:MaxRate	MinRate	MaxPrice	Yield	Fee	MaxRate	MinRate	MaxPrice	Fee
60 13.500	11.500	99.000	13.673	0.375				
90 13.500	11.500	99.000	13.673	0.750				
120 13.500	11.500	99.000	13.673	1.250				
180 13.500	11.500	98.500	13.761	2.000				
270 13.500	11.500	98.000	13.849	2.750				

15-Year Fixed Rate

Bear

Term: MaxRate	MinRate	MaxPrice	Yield	Fee	MaxRate	MinRate	MaxPrice	Fee
60 13.250	11.250	99.000	13.492	0.375				
90 13.250	11.250	99.000	13.492	0.750				
120 13.250	11.250	99.000	13.492	1.250				
180 13.250	11.250	98.500	13.614	2.000				
270 13.250	11.250	98.000	13.737	2.750				

Convert-to-Mandatory Fee   30-Day:0.375   60-Day:0.750   90-Day:1.125

176

LEVEL-PAYMENT, FIXED-RATE MORTGAGES

The mortgage loan specifies the interest rate of the loan, the frequency of payment, and the number of years to maturity. A level-payment, fixed-rate mortgage has the following characteristics: (1) the term of the loan is fixed; (2) the interest rate is fixed; and (3) the amount of the monthly mortgage payment is fixed for the entire term of the loan (i.e., the mortgage is "level-pay"). The level-payment, fixed-rate mortgage is the most common type of underlying mortgage for pass-through securities. The term of the mortgage is typically 30 years; however, in recent years an increasing number of 15-year mortgages have been securitized.

Cash Flow of a Level-Payment, Fixed-Rate Mortgage

Each monthly mortgage payment for a level-payment, fixed-rate mortgage is due on the first of each month and has two constituents:

1. Interest of one-twelfth of the fixed annual interest rate times the amount of the outstanding mortgage balance at the beginning of the previous month (interest "in arrears").
2. A repayment of a portion of the outstanding mortgage balance (principal).

The difference between the monthly mortgage payment and the portion of the payment that represents interest equals the amount that is being applied to reduce the outstanding mortgage balance. The monthly mortgage payment is designed so that after the last scheduled monthly payment of the loan is made, the amount of the outstanding mortgage balance will be zero (i.e. the mortgage is fully repaid).

To see what the mortgage payments look like for a level-payment, fixed-rate mortgage, consider a 30-year (360 months), $100,000 mortgage with a 10% mortgage interest rate. The monthly mortgage payment would be $877.57. (How the monthly mortgage payment is determined will be explained later.)

Exhibit 9.4 shows how for the first 36 months each monthly mortgage payment is divided between interest and repayment of principal. At the beginning of month 1, the mortgage balance is $100,000, the amount of the original loan. The mortgage payment for month 1 includes interest on the $100,000 borrowed for the month.

EXHIBIT 9.4 Amortization Schedule for a Level-Payment, Fixed-Rate Mortgage (First 36 Months)

Mortgage Loan = $100,000
Interest Rate = .10
Term of Loan = 30 Years (360 months)

(1)	(2) Beginning Mortgage- Balance	(3) Monthly Mortgage Payment	(4) Interest for Month	(5) Principal Repayment	(6) Ending Mortgage Balance
Month					
1	$100,000.00	$877.57	$833.33	$44.24	$99,955.76
2	99,955.76	877.57	832.96	44.61	99,911.16
3	99,911.16	877.57	832.59	44.98	99,866.18
4	99,866.18	877.57	832.22	45.35	99,820.83
5	99,820.83	877.57	831.84	45.73	99,775.10
6	99,775.10	877.57	831.46	46.11	99,728.99
7	99,728.99	877.57	831.07	46.50	99,682.49
8	99,682.49	877.57	830.69	46.88	99,635.61
9	99,635.61	877.57	830.30	47.27	99,588.34
10	99,588.34	877.57	829.90	47.67	99,540.67
11	99,540.67	877.57	829.51	48.06	99,492.61
12	99,492.61	877.57	829.11	48.46	99,444.14
13	99,444.14	877.57	828.70	48.87	99,395.27
14	99,395.27	877.57	828.29	49.28	99,346.00
15	99,346.00	877.57	827.88	49.69	99,296.31
16	99,296.31	877.57	827.47	50.10	99,246.21
17	99,246.21	877.57	827.05	50.52	99,195.69
18	99,195.69	877.57	826.63	50.94	99,144.75
19	99,144.75	877.57	826.21	51.36	99,093.39
20	99,093.39	877.57	825.78	51.79	99,041.60
21	99,041.60	877.57	825.35	52.22	98,989.37
22	98,989.37	877.57	824.91	52.66	98,936.71
23	98,936.71	877.57	824.47	53.10	98,883.62
24	98,883.62	877.57	824.03	53.54	98,830.08
25	98,830.08	877.57	823.58	53.99	98,776.09
26	98,776.09	877.57	823.13	54.44	98,721.65
27	98,721.65	877.57	822.68	54.89	98,666.77
28	98,666.77	877.57	822.22	55.35	98,611.42
29	98,611.42	877.57	821.76	55.81	98,555.61
30	98,555.61	877.57	821.30	56.27	98,499.34
31	98,499.34	877.57	820.83	56.74	98,442.59
32	98,442.59	877.57	820.35	57.22	98,385.38
33	98,385.38	877.57	819.88	57.69	98,327.69
34	98,327.69	877.57	819.40	58.17	98,269.52
35	98,269.52	877.57	818.91	58.66	98,210.86
36	98,210.86	877.57	818.42	59.15	98,151.71

Since the interest rate is 10%, the monthly interest rate is 0.0083333 (.10 divided by 12). Interest for month 1 is therefore $833.33 ($100,000 times 0.0083333). The difference between the monthly mortgage payment of $877.57 and the interest of $833.33 ($44.24) is the portion of the monthly mortgage payment that represents repayment of principal.

The mortgage balance at the end of month 1 (beginning of month 2) is then $99,955.76 ($100,000 minus $44.24). The interest for the second monthly mortgage payment is $832.96, the monthly interest rate (0.008333) times the mortgage balance at the beginning of month 2 ($99,955.76). The difference between the $877.57 monthly mortgage payment and the $832.96 interest is $44.61, representing the amount of the mortgage balance paid off with that monthly mortgage payment. The last monthly mortgage payment will be sufficient to pay off the remaining mortgage balance. When a loan repayment schedule is structured in this way, so that the payments made by the borrower will completely pay off the interest and principal, the loan is said to be *self-amortizing*. Exhibit 9.4 is therefore referred to as an *amortization schedule*.

As Exhibit 9.4 clearly shows, *the portion of the monthly mortgage payment applied to interest declines each month and the portion that goes to reducing the mortgage balance increases.* The reason for this is that as the mortgage balance is reduced with each monthly mortgage payment, the interest on that balance declines. Since the monthly mortgage payment is fixed, an ever-larger part of the monthly payment is applied to reduce the principal as time goes by.

Determining the Monthly Mortgage Payment

In Chapter 2 we reviewed the calculation of the present value of an ordinary annuity. To compute the monthly mortgage payment for a level-payment, fixed-rate mortgage requires the application of the present value of an ordinary annuity formula (equation (2.5)) which is given below as equation (9.1):

$$(9.1)\ P_A\ =\ A\left[\frac{1-\dfrac{1}{(1+r)^n}}{r}\right]$$

where A = amount of the annuity (in $)
        n = number of periods
        P_A = present value of an annuity (in $)
        r = periodic interest rate.

We can redefine the four variables in equation (9.1) in terms of a level-payment, fixed-rate mortgage as follows:

A = monthly mortgage payment (in $)
n = number of months
P_A = the original mortgage balance (in $)
r = simple monthly interest rate (annual interest rate/12)

To determine the amount of the monthly mortgage payment, equation (9.1) must be solved for A. Solving, we get:

$$(9.2) \quad A = \frac{P_A}{\left[\dfrac{1 - \dfrac{1}{(1 + r)^n}}{r} \right]}$$

Alternatively, equation (9.2) can be expressed as follows:

$$(9.3) \quad \text{Monthly mortgage payment} = \frac{\text{Amount of funds borrowed}}{\substack{\text{Present value of an annuity} \\ \text{of \$1 per month}}}$$

To see how to apply equation (9.3) to obtain the monthly mortgage payment, we will use our $100,000, 30-year, 10% mortgage. For this mortgage:

n = 360
P_A = $100,000
r = .0083333 (= .10/12)

Then the present value of an annuity of $1 per month is:

$$\left[\frac{1 - \dfrac{1}{(1.0083333)^{360}}}{0.0083333} \right] = 113.95119$$

The monthly mortgage payment is then:

$$\frac{\$100,000}{113.95119} = \$877.57$$

GRADUATED-PAYMENT MORTGAGES

With a graduated-payment mortgage (GPM), both the interest rate and the term of the mortgage are fixed, as they are with a level-payment, fixed-rate mortgage. However, the monthly payment for a GPM is smaller in the initial years than for a level-payment, fixed-rate mortgage with the same mortgage rate, but larger in the remaining years of the mortgage term.

The monthly payments in the earlier years of a GPM are generally not sufficient to pay the entire interest due on the outstanding mortgage balance. The difference between the monthly mortgage payment and the accumulated interest (based on the outstanding mortgage balance) is added to the outstanding mortgage balance, so that in the earlier years of a GPM there is *negative amortization*. The higher-level mortgage payments in the later years of the GPM are designed to fully amortize the outstanding mortgage balance, which is, by then, greater than the original amount borrowed.

The Federal Housing Administration (FHA) introduced GPMs in late 1976. They were created to give people with rising incomes the opportunity to purchase a home at a monthly mortgage payment that they could afford. The theory was that as their incomes rose over time, they would be able to afford the progressively higher mortgage payments. GPMs became eligible for pooling in certain types of pass-through securities in 1979. GPMs have faded in popularity in recent years with the growing popularity of adjustable rate mortgages (discussed in the next section). As a result, GPMs are slowly becoming illiquid.

GPM Plans

The terms of a GPM plan include: (1) the mortgage rate; (2) the term of the mortgage; (3) the number of years over which the monthly mortgage payment will increase (and when the level payments will begin); and (4) the annual percent increase in the mortgage payments. For example, the most popular 30-year GPM plan calls for monthly payments that increase by 7.5% per year for 5 years, then stay constant for the remaining 25 years of the mortgage. The monthly mortgage payments under this GPM program for a $100,000, 30-year, 10% mortgage would be: (1) $667.04 per month in the first year; (2) $717.06 per month in the second year; (3) $770.84 in the third year; (4) $828.66 in the fourth year; (5) $890.80 in the fifth year; and (6) beginning with the sixth year, $957.62 for the remainder of the term of the mortgage. For a level-payment, fixed-rate, 30-year mortgage, the monthly mortgage payment would be $877.57. Exhibit 9.5 compares the amount of the outstanding mortgage balance at the end of each year for a level-payment, fixed-rate mortgage and this particular GPM. Notice that there is negative amortization of the GPM for the first 4 years. Not until year 10 does the outstanding mortgage balance fall below the original mortgage balance.

Five 30-year GPM plans currently available can be summarized as follows:

	Plan				
	I	II	III	IV	V
Annual increase in monthly payment	2.5%	5.0%	7.5%	2.0%	3%
Years of increase	5	5	5	10	10

The level payment for a $100,000, 30-year, 10% fixed-rate mortgage is $877.57. For the five GPM plans, the initial and final monthly mortgage payment for a $100,000, 30-year, 10% mortgage are:

	I	II	III	IV	V
Initial payment	$800.58	$730.58	$667.04	$780.04	$734.58
Final payment	$905.76	$932.44	$957.62	$950.86	$987.20

The first three GPM plans qualify for inclusion in certain types of mortgage pass-through securities discussed in the next chapter. The majority of the GPMs underlying certain types of pass-through securities are Plan III graduated-payment mortgages because, as can be seen from the preceeding table, Plan III GPMs have the lowest initial monthly mortgage payment and thus are the most popular. Although GPMs from all three plans may be found within a pool of mortgages that are collateral for a pass-through security, analysts typically assume all GPMs are of the Plan III type.

EXHIBIT 9.5   Comparison of Outstanding Mortgage Balance for a Level-Payment, Fixed-Rate Mortgage and a Popular GPM

Term of mortgage = 30 years
Original balance   = $100,000
Mortgage rate   = 10%
GPM: Monthly mortgage payment increases by 7.5% per year for 5 years

Year	— Outstanding Mortgage Balance at End of Year —	
	Level-Payment, Fixed-Rate	GPM
1	$99,444	$102,090
2	98,830	103,769
3	98,152	104,949
4	97,402	105,526
5	96,574	105,383
6	95,660	104,385
7	94,649	103,282
8	93,533	102,064
9	92,300	100,719
10	90,938	99,233
11	89,433	97,591
12	87,771	95,777
13	85,934	93,773
14	83,906	91,559
15	81,665	89,113
16	79,189	86,412
17	76,454	83,427
18	73,432	80,130
19	70,094	76,488
20	66,407	72,464
21	62,333	68,019
22	57,833	63,108
23	52,862	57,684
24	47,370	51,691
25	41,303	45,071
26	34,601	37,757
27	27,197	29,678
28	19,018	20,752
29	9,982	10,892
30	0	0

ADJUSTABLE-RATE MORTGAGES

An adjustable-rate mortgage (ARM) is a mortgage in which the interest rate on the loan is adjusted periodically. The interest rate may adjust every 6 months, every year, every 2 years, or every 3 years. The interest rate at the reset date is equal to a benchmark index plus a spread. The benchmark index used is either the interest rate on U.S. Treasury securities or a calculated measure such as a cost-of-funds index for a thrift.[4] The benchmark for an ARM generally coincides with the term of adjustment. For example, for a 1-year ARM, the benchmark would be a 1-year Treasury rate or a cost-of-funds index for 1 year. Exhibit 9.6 shows the characteristics of outstanding ARMs as of 1985 with respect to the benchmark index and the length of the adjustment period.

ARMs have become popular with lenders because they shift interest rate risk from the lender to the borrower. Thrifts prefer to hold ARMs in their portfolio rather than fixed-rate mortgages such as level-payment and graduated-payment mortgages because ARMs provide a better matching with their liabilities. Since liabilities are closely tied to the calculated cost-of-funds indexes, thrifts prefer ARMs benchmarked to these indexes. ARMs are used as collateral in the pass-through securities that we shall describe in the next chapter.

EXHIBIT 9.6   Attributes of ARMs

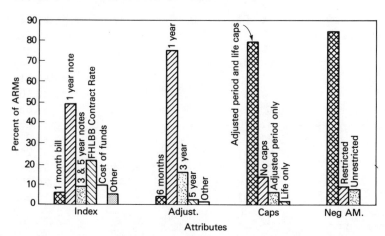

Source: Kenneth H. Sullivan and Andrew D. Langerman, "Adjustable Rate Mortgages," in *Floating Rate Instruments,* Frank J. Fabozzi, ed. (Chicago, IL: Probus Publishing, 1986).

[4]The two most popular calculated indexes are the 11th Federal Home Loan Bank District cost-of-funds and the Federal Home Loan Bank Board contract rate.

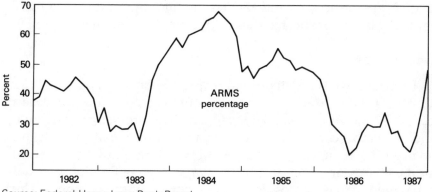

Source: Federal Home Loan Bank Board.

Reprinted from: Brown, Zimmerman, and Person, *Introduction to Mortgages and Mortgage-Backed Securities* (Salomon Brothers Inc).

EXHIBIT 9.7   ARMs Market Share: Percentage of Conventional Mortgage Originations, January 1982–July 1987

Exhibit 9.7 shows the percentage of conventional mortgage originations that were ARMs for the period January 1982 to July 1987. The percentage went as high as about 70%, and as low as 20%; it varied with the level of interest rates. When interest rates were relatively high, in 1983 and 1984, homeowners preferred ARMs to fixed-rate mortgages. When interest rates declined, in 1985 and 1986, homeowners preferred locking in the relatively low rates via fixed-rate mortgages, and consequently, ARMs originations as a percentage of conventional mortgage originations decreased dramatically.

To encourage borrowers to use ARMs rather than fixed-rate mortgages, mortgage originators generally offer an initial mortgage rate that is lower than the prevailing market mortgage rate. This below-market initial mortgage rate, set according to competitive market conditions, is commonly referred to as a *teaser rate*. At the reset date, the benchmark index plus the spread determines the new mortgage rate. For example, suppose that 1-year ARMs are typically offering a 200-basis-point spread over the 1-year Treasury rate. If the current 1-year Treasury rate is 6.5%, then the initial mortgage rate should be 8.5%. But the mortgage originator might set an initial mortgage rate of 7.5%, 100 basis points below the existing market mortgage rate for 1-year ARMs.

The basic ARM resets periodically and has no other terms that affect the monthly mortgage payment. Typically, however, ARMs do have other terms that affect the monthly mortgage payment, and hence the cash flow of the mortgage from the investor's perspective. These include (1) periodic caps and (2) lifetime rate caps and floors. Attributes of ARMs with respect to these two terms are shown in Exhibit 9.6.

Periodic Caps

There are two types of periodic caps: rate caps and payment caps. Rate caps limit the amount that the interest rate may increase or decrease at the reset date. The rate cap is expressed in percentage points. The most common rate cap on annual-reset loans is 2%. There is no negative amortization in an ARM with a rate cap. Payment caps limit the change in the monthly mortgage payment at the reset date. The payment cap is expressed as a percentage of the payment. Thus, while there is no restriction on how much the mortgage rate may change, there is a restriction on how much the amount of the monthly mortgage payment may change. A payment cap may produce negative amortization because the cap on the monthly mortgage payment may result in a payment that is not sufficient to cover the higher mortgage interest.

The impact of the two types of periodic caps on the cash flows and mortgage balance is illustrated in Exhibit 9.8. The first ARM in the exhibit is based on a 2% rate cap structure, while the second ARM is based on a 7.5% payment cap structure. The underlying mortgage for both ARMs is a 30-year, $100,000 mortgage with a spread of 200 basis points over the index rate. The initial index rate is 8.5%, which means that the initial mortgage rate should be 10.5%. In Exhibit 9.8 it is assumed that the initial mortgage rate for both mortgages is a teaser rate of 8.5%. The second column in the exhibit shows the assumed index rate for each year. In the first year the monthly mortgage payment and the end-of-year mortgage balance are identical for both mortgages.

In the second year the index rate is assumed to increase to 9.5%. In the absence of any rate cap, the mortgage rate would be 11.5%. Because of the 2% rate cap, however, the mortgage rate for the first ARM in the second year is restricted to 10.5%, an increase of only 200 basis points over the initial mortgage rate. With the 7.5% payment cap, the mortgage rate increases to 11.5%. To amortize the mortgage balance at the end of the first year at an 11.5% mortgage rate, the monthly mortgage payment would have to increase from $768.91 (the first-year monthly mortgage payment at an 8.5% mortgage rate) to $986.80. However, the 7.5% payment cap restricts the monthly mortgage pay-

EXHIBIT 9.8 Rate Cap Structure versus Payment Cap Structure*

			Rate Cap Structure			Payment Cap Structure		
Year	Index Rate	Index Plus Margin	Mortgage Rate	Beginning Balance	P&I Payment	Mortgage Rate	Beginning Balance	P&I Payment
1	8.50%	10.50%	8.50%	$100,000	$ 768.91	8.50%	$100,000	$ 768.91
2	9.50	11.50	10.50	99,244	912.39	11.50	99,244	826.58
3	10.50	12.50	12.50	98,690	1,060.63	12.50	100,819	888.57
4	12.50	14.50	13.50	98,275	1,135.87	13.50	102,874	955.21
5	11.50	13.50	13.50	97,888	1,135.87	13.50	105,455	1,026.86
6	9.00	11.00	11.50	97,446	990.51	11.00	107,492	1,053.54
7	7.00	9.00	9.50	96,729	853.90	9.00	106,631	974.53
8	4.00	6.00	7.50	95,624	728.07	6.00	105,315	704.40
9	5.00	7.00	7.00	94,004	698.85	7.00	103,121	757.23
10	6.00	8.00	8.00	92,139	755.93	8.00	101,192	814.02

*$100,000 original principal balance 30-year original term.

Source: Bella S. Borg and Andrew S. Carron, "The Valuation of Adjustable Rate Mortgages," Chap. 29 in Frank J. Fabozzi, ed.. The Handbook of Mortgage-Backed Securities, 2nd ed. (Chicago, IL: Probus Publishing 1988).

ment to $826.58 (1.075 times $768.91). Monthly interest alone for the first month of the second year on the mortgage balance at the beginning of the second year is $951.09 ($99,244 × 0.115/12). The difference of $124.51 between the interest for that month of $951.09 and the new monthly mortgage payment of $826.58 is added to the mortgage balance. That is, the 7.5% payment cap has resulted in negative amortization for this ARM. In the second month of the second year, the interest is greater than $951.09 because the mortgage balance has increased. Thus more than $124.51 would be added to the mortgage balance. At the end of the second year, the mortgage balance is $100,819.

Lifetime Caps and Floors

Most ARMs have an upper limit on the interest rate that can be charged over the life of the loan. This lifetime loan cap is expressed in terms of the initial rate, the most common lifetime cap being 5%. For example, if the initial mortgage rate is 7% and the lifetime cap is 5%, the maximum interest rate that the lender can charge at any time over the life of the loan is 12%. Many ARMs also have a lower limit on the interest rate that can be charged over the life of the loan.

IMPORTANCE OF THE PREPAYMENT OPTION

In our earlier illustration of the cash flow from a level-payment mortgage, we assumed that the homeowner would not pay off any portion of the mortgage balance before the scheduled due date. But homeowners do pay off all or part of their mortgages prior to the maturity date. Payments made in excess of the scheduled principal repayments are called *prepayments.*

Effectively, the lender (mortgagee) has granted the homeowner the right to prepay the mortgage balance at any time. Since the cash flow of a mortgage will depend on whether the homeowner exercises the option to prepay all or part of the mortgage before maturity and, when those prepayments occur, it is important to understand why people prepay.

Homeowners prepay their mortgages for one of several reasons. First, they prepay the entire mortgage when they sell their home (except in specific cases where mortgages may be assumed). Homes are sold for many reasons, among them a change of employment that requires moving, the purchase of a more expensive home ("trading up"), and a divorce settlement that requires the sale of the marital residence. Second, if interest rates drop substantially after the mortgage was obtained, it may be beneficial for the homeowner to refinance the loan (even after paying all refinancing costs) at the lower interest rate. Third, for homeowners who cannot meet their mortgage obligations, their property is repossessed and sold. In the case of a conventional mortgage, the proceeds from the sale are used to pay off the mortgage. For an insured mortgage, the insurer will pay off the mortgage balance. Finally, if property is destroyed by fire or another insured catastrophe occurs, the insurance proceeds are used to pay off the mortgage.

The risk that homeowners will prepay the mortgage at an inopportune time for the investor (lender) is called *prepayment risk* or *call risk*. The latter term is used because the lender has effectively granted the homeowner a call option, much like the option bondholders grant corporations to call bonds prior to maturity. An investor in a mortgage wants to be compensated for accepting prepayment or call risk. The question is: What is fair compensation for accepting this risk?

Because of this call option, a valuation approach based on options theory has been advocated to value mortgages and mortgage-backed securities. While the approach is useful, it does have limitations because, in terms of option theory, homeowners may "irrationally" exercise the prepayment option or may not exercise it when it is rational to do so. More specifically, from an options perspective, the rational exercise of the prepayment option by the homeowner should occur when there is an economic benefit to refinancing the mortgage— that is, when the current market interest rate for mortgages is less than the mortgage rate on the loan outstanding by an amount sufficient to cover refinancing costs. In this case, the option is said to be "in the money." Yet there are homeowners who, for whatever reason, do not exercise this option, viz. the existence of 16% mortgages at a time when the current mortgage rate was 8%. Similarly, when mortgage rates were 16%, there were homeowners who paid off their 8% mortgages. From an options perspective, such mortgages were "out of the money" and should not have been exercised. But for the reasons cited previously, prepaying their mortgages may have been rational from these homeowners' point of view.

SUMMARY

To understand mortgage-backed securities, it is necessary to comprehend the cash flow characteristics of the underlying collateral. In this chapter we reviewed the three major types of mortgages (level-payment, fixed-rate mortgages; graduated-payment mortgages; and adjustable-rate mortgages). We also discussed mortgage originators, their sources of income and their activities, and introduced the concept of prepayments.

10

MORTGAGE-BACKED SECURITIES

A mortgage-backed security is an instrument whose cash flow (and thus its value) depends on the cash flow from the underlying pool of mortgages. Mortgage-backed securities include mortgage pass-through securities, collateralized mortgage obligations, and stripped mortgage-backed securities. As we explained in the previous chapter, the cash flow of a mortgage cannot be known with certainty because of prepayments. This characteristic is shared by mortgage-backed securities. However, as we shall see, with collateralized mortgage obligations and stripped mortgage-backed securities the underlying cash flow can be altered so as to generate price/yield relationships that differ from the cash flow of the underlying mortgages.

MORTGAGE PASS-THROUGH SECURITIES

One problem with investing in mortgages is that they lack liquidity. Another is that holding one mortgage exposes the investor to substantial prepayment risk (although this risk can be reduced by holding a portfolio of mortgages). A more efficient way of investing in mortgages is to invest in a pass-through security. This security is created when one or more holders of mortgages form a collection (pool) of mortgages and sell shares or participations in the pool. A pool may consist of several thousand mortgages or only one mortgage. The cash flow of pass-through securities depends on the cash flow of the underlying mortgages. As we explained in the previous chapter, the cash flow consists of monthly mortgage payments representing interest, the scheduled repayment of principal, and any prepayments.

The amount and the timing of the cash flow from the pool of mortgages and the cash flow passed through to investors owning a pass-through security, however, are not identical. The monthly cash flow for a pass-through security is less than the monthly cash flow of the underlying mortgages by an amount equal to servicing and other fees. The other fees are those charged by the issuer or guarantor of the pass-through security for guaranteeing the issue (discussed later in this chapter).[1] Typically, the coupon rate on a pass-through security is 0.5% less than the coupon rate on the underlying pool.

The timing of the cash flow is also different. The monthly mortgage payment is due from each mortgagor on the first day of each month. There is a delay in passing through the corresponding monthly cash flow to the security holders. The number of days that the payment is delayed varies by the type of pass-through security.

Types of Pass-Through Securities

There are three major types of pass-through securities guaranteed by the following organizations: Government National Mortgage Association, Federal Home Loan Mortgage Corporation, and Federal National Mortgage Association. As we explained in Chapter 5, the last two are federally sponsored credit agencies. The Government National Mortgage Association is a wholly owned U.S. government corporation within the Department of Housing and Urban Development (HUD). The securities associated with these three entities are known as *agency pass-through securities*. About 98% of all pass-through securities are agency pass-through securities; the balance are privately issued pass-through securities called *conventional mortgage pass-through securities*.

Exhibit 10.1 shows the total stock of single-family mortgages for the period 1975 through the first quarter of 1987 and the amount that has been securitized (that is, has been placed in a pool of mortgages collateralizing a pass-through security). By 1987, more than one-third

---

[1]Actually, the servicer pays the guarantee fee to the issuer or guarantor.

EXHIBIT 10.1 Securitized Single-Family Mortgages Outstanding, 1975–First Quarter 1987 (Dollars in Billions)

	Total Stock of 1–4 Family Mortgages	Securitized Residential Mortgages*	Pct. of Mtg. Outstanding Securitized	Publicly Offered Pass-Throughs			
				GNMA	FNMA	FHLMC	Conventional
1975	$ 477	$ 17.8	3.7%	$ 16.2	—	$ 1.6	—
1976	540	28.4	5.3	25.6	—	2.8	—
1977	633	49.7	7.9	42.9	—	6.8	—
1978	743	65.7	8.8	53.0	—	12.0	$ 0.7
1979	861	92.1	10.7	75.8	—	15.3	1.0
1980	955	112.2	11.7	93.9	—	17.0	1.3
1981	1,032	127.9	12.4	105.8	$ 0.7	19.9	1.5
1982	1,075	178.0	16.6	118.9	14.5	42.9	1.7
1983	1,192	246.2	20.7	159.8	25.1	58.0	3.3
1984	1,321	290.7	22.1	180.0	36.2	70.9	3.6
1985	1,470	372.0	25.3	212.1	55.0	100.5	4.4
1986	1,667	534.7	32.1	260.9	97.2	168.6	8.0E+
1987†	1,713	582.0	34.0	277.4	107.7	186.4	10.5E+

*Summation of publicly offered GNMA, FNMA, FHLMC, and conventional mortgage pass-throughs.
+Through the first quarter of 1987.
†Estimate.

Source: Board of Governors of the Federal Reserve, U.S. Department of Housing and Urban Development, GNMA, FNMA, FHLMC, and Lepercq de Neuflize & Co., Inc.

Reprinted from: Kenneth T. Rosen, *Securitization and the Mortgage Market* (New York: Salomon Brothers Inc, August 1987).

had been securitized. The last four columns of the exhibit show in what type of mortgage pass-through these mortgages were securitized.

Agency Pass-Through Securities

Exhibit 10.2 summarizes the different types of agency pass-through securities. For each security, the exhibit indicates the types of mortgages, the term of the mortgages, the minimum pool size, the geographic characteristics of the mortgages in the pool, the portion of mortgage coupon allowed as a servicing fee, the range of coupons available, and the actual penalty (in days) due to the payment delay. For all agency pass-throughs, there are also pools collateralized with adjustable-rate mortgages (ARMs).

The minimum purchase price of all agency pass-through securities when they are originally issued is $25,000, with increments of $5,000 for the securities issued by the Government National Mortgage Association and the Federal National Mortgage Association, and increments of $25,000 for the securities issued by the Federal Home Loan Mortgage Corporation. Unlike coupon Treasury, corporate, and municipal bonds, which pay interest semiannually, all agency pass-through securities make monthly cash flow payments.

Of the three agencies, the Government National Mortgage Association (GNMA), popularly known as "Ginnie Mae," guarantees the largest amount of pass-through securities of the three agencies.[2] Only FHA-insured mortgages and VA-guaranteed mortgages are included in GNMA pools. The two major types of Ginnie Mae securities are GNMA Is and GNMA IIs. Ginnie Mae securities can be further divided into GNMA ARMs, GNMA Midgets, GNMA GPMs, GNMA Mobile Homes, GNMA Buydowns, and GNMA FHA Projects. Ginnie Mae securities are summarized in Exhibit 10.2. Unlike the other two agency pass-through securities, Ginnie Mae pass-throughs are guaranteed by the full faith and credit of the United States government with respect to timely payment of both interest and principal. "Timely payment" means that the interest and principal will be paid when due.

The second-largest type of agency pass-through securities are those issued by the Federal Home Loan Mortgage Corporation, popu-

---

[2]Ginnie Mae is often referred to as an issuer of pass-through securities. Technically, however, Ginnie Mae does not issue the securities; instead, an originator of mortgages files the necessary documents with Ginnie Mae and, if approved, issues pass-throughs guaranteed by Ginnie Mae.

larly known as "Freddie Mac." The securities issued by Freddie Mac are called *participation certificates.* Most of the pools of mortgages consist of conventional mortgages, although participation certificates with underlying pools consisting of FHA-insured or VA-guaranteed mortgages have been issued. There are participation certificates that guarantee the timely payment of both interest and principal. Most Freddie Mac participation certificates, however, guarantee only the timely payment of interest. The scheduled principal is passed through as it is collected, with Freddie Mac only guaranteeing that the scheduled principal will be paid no later than 1 year after it is due. Recall from Chapter 5 that a guarantee by Freddie Mac is *not* the guarantee of the U.S. government. Yet most market participants view Freddie Mac participation certificates as similar, although not identical, in creditworthiness to Ginnie Mae pass-throughs which are fully guaranteed by the U.S. government. Nonetheless, Freddie Mac pass-throughs offer a higher yield than Ginnie Mae securities with the same coupon and remaining term. In certain interest rate environments, the higher yield for Freddie Mac participation certificates is due to the prepayment characteristics of the underlying pool of mortgages. Conventional mortgages tend to prepay more variably than the FHA/VA mortgages that collateralize Ginnie Mae pass-throughs.

The other issuer of agency pass-through securities is the Federal National Mortgage Association (FNMA), popularly known as "Fannie Mae." Its pass-through securities, called *mortgage-backed securities,* are similar in many respects to Freddie Mac participation certificates. However, Fannie Mae guarantees the timely payment of both interest and principal on all its securities. Like Freddie Mac participation certificates, Fannie Mae mortgage-backed securities are not the obligation of the U.S. government.

Conventional Pass-Through Securities

Conventional pass-through securities, also called *private pass-through securities* or *private-label pass-through securities,* are issued by thrifts, commercial banks, and private conduits. In the last chapter we discussed private conduits that purchase nonconforming mortgages in order to package them to sell pass-through securities against them. The conventional pass-through security was first introduced by Bank of America in 1977. Exhibit 10.3 shows the major issuers of conventional pass-through securities.

EXHIBIT 10.2 Features of Mortgage Pass-Through Securities

	GNMA I	GNMA II	FHLMC Regular PC	FHLMC SWAP	FNMA MBS
Number of Lenders in Pool	Single	Single and Multiple	Multiple	Single and Multiple	Multiple
Mortgages	FHA, VA, FMHA	FHA, VA, FMHA	Conventional and seasoned FHA and VA	Conventional and seasoned FHA and VA	Conventional and seasoned FHA and VA
Pool Types*	Single-family level-payment (SF), graduated-payment (GP), and growing equity mortgages (GA, GD), mobile home (MH), construction (CL), project (PL), and buydown loans (BD).	Same as GNMA I except includes adjustable-rate mortgages or ARMs (AR) and excludes PL, CL, and BD pools. (Buydown mortgages can be included in SF pools.)	FHA/VA (15), conventional 30-year (16, 17); conventional 15-year (20), Multi-family Plan B (22, 49), ARM (35, 41).	FHA/VA (14), conventional 30-year (18, 25, 27, and 28 guarantee the timely payment of interest, 26 the timely principal and interest), Multifamily (23, 24), conventional 15-year (21), Multifamily variable interest rate or VIRs (31).[+]	Conventional long-term level-pay (CL), intermediate (CI), conventional long-term fully assumable (CA), conventional short-term (CS), FHA/VA long-term project loans (MA), and growing equity (GEM).
Pool Terms	Separate programs for SF and GP series with 15- and 30-year terms; MH 12- (A), 15- (B), 18- (C), 20-year (D) terms; GA and GD terms vary.	AR pools have 30-year terms	FHA/VA and ARM securities have 30-year terms. Multi-family pool terms vary with series: 22 series have 15-year terms, 49 series have 10-year terms.	Unless defined otherwise, these series have 30-year terms.	Long-term is 30 years, intermediate 15 years, and short-term 7 years. GEM series have 15-year terms, MA 40 years.
Mortgage Seasoning	Only new mortgages (less than 24 months).	Only new mortgages (less than 24 months).	No limit on seasoning.	No limit on seasoning.	No limit on seasoning.

196

	GNMA I	GNMA II	FHLMC Regular PC	FHLMC SWAP	FNMA MBS
Mortgage Coupon Range	0.5% over security rate (approx. 3.5% above for mobile home).	0.5%–1.5% over security rate (approx. 3.5% above for mobile homes).	No restrictions.[†]	0.5%–2.5% above the pass-through rate.[†]	0.5%–2.5% above the pass-through rate.
Guarantee	Full and timely payment of principal and interest (backed by full faith and credit of U.S. Govt.).	Full and timely payment of principal and interest (backed by full faith and credit of U.S. Govt.).	Timely payment of interest and eventual payment of principal. Mortgages insured by eligible insurers.	Timely payment of interest; certain series guarantee timely payment of principal and interest.	Full and timely payment of principal and interest.
Payment Delay	45 stated / 15 actual	50 stated / 20 actual	75 stated / 45 actual	75 stated / 45 actual	55 stated / 25 actual
Assumability	Yes	Yes	No	No	No
Minimum Pool Size	$1 million	$1 million[§]	$50 million	$1 million[†]	$1 million
Maximum Mortgage Amount	$67,500[||]	$67,500[||]	$153,100[¶]	$153,100[¶]	$153,000[¶]

*Series types or prefixes are given in parentheses.

+A series of "Mini" FHLMC Swap securities was established in 1986 with pool minimum of $250,000 and backed by 30-year (43 timely interest, 46 timely principal and interest); 15-year (44 timely interest and 47 timely principal and interest); and FHA/VA (45 timely interest and 48 timely principal and interest). These securities are not considered good for delivery in generic trades.

[†]After June 1, 1987, mortgage rates on Regular or Cash PC pools may be 0.0–2.0% above the security rate but the range between maximum and minimum mortgage rates in the pool may not exceed 1.0%; the range between maximum and minimum mortgage rates for Guarantor pools may not exceed 1.0%.

[§]$1 million minimum pool size for SF pools; $500,000 for GP, GT, GA, GD, AR, or AZ pools; $350,000 for MH pools.

[||]Maximum FHA loan in High-Cost Regions is $90,000 (e.g., New York, Los Angeles); maximum VA loan $135,000 (current October 1, 1986).

[¶]FHLMC and FNMA loan limits range from $153,100 for single-family unit to $294,150 for 4-family units. In Alaska, Guam, and Hawaii the loan maximums range from $229,650 to $441,225 (effective January 1, 1987).

Source: Kenneth Sullivan and Linda Lowell, "Mortgage Pass-Through Securities" Chap. 5 in *The Handbook of Mortgage-Backed Securities.*

While conventional mortgage pass-through securities are not guaranteed by the U.S. government (as Ginnie Maes are) or by the agencies themselves (as Fannie Mae and Freddie Mac securities are), they are often supported by credit enhancements. These take the form of either (1) letters of credit or guarantees from commercial banks that provide for payment up to some specified percentage, (2) pool insurance from a mortgage insurance company, or (3) subordinated interests. Mortgage pool insurance is the most common form of credit enhancement, accounting for loss coverage on about 49% of all conventional mortgage pass-through securities.[3] Conventional pass-through securities provide a cash-advance provision, whereby the issuer states that in the event of deliquent mortgage payments, it intends to use its own funds to pay holders of the pass-through security.

Agency pass-through securities are not rated by commercial rating agencies such as Moody's and Standard & Poor's because they think it inappropriate to do so. In contrast, conventional mortgage pass-through securities are rated. As of late 1986, the credit enhancements have allowed more than 70% of all conventional mortgage pass-through securities to be rated double A or better at the time of issuance.[4] Also, unlike agency pass-through securities, conventional mortgage pass-through securities must be registered with the Securities and Exchange Commission.

Despite the credit enhancement, investors face default risk when investing in these conventional pass-through securities. They must therefore be compensated for accepting both prepayment risk and default risk.

Measuring Yields on Pass-Through Securities

Even in the absence of prepayments, the investor in a mortgage pass-through security would face reinvestment risk—that is, the risk of reinvesting the monthly mortgage cash flow at a rate less than the yield offered on the security at the time of purchase. However, prepayments do occur, so an investor in pass-through securities does not know what the cash flow will be and thus cannot determine a precise return on the security when contemplating purchase. Still, market conventions for

---

[3]Howard Altarescu, Erik Anderson, Mike Asay, and Hal Hinkle, "The Conventional Mortgage Pass-Through Market," Chap. 8 in Frank J. Fabozzi, ed., *The Handbook of Mortgage-Backed Securities*, 2nd ed. (Chicago, IL: Probus Publishing, 1988).

[4]Ibid.

EXHIBIT 10.3   Market Share of Major Conventional Pass-Through Issuers 1977 to September 1987 (By Dollar Amount Issued [in Billions])

Issuer	Amount Issued ($ Millions)	Percent of $ Issued
Citicorp[1]	$ 6,982	35.0%
Salomon Brothers[2]	3,538	17.7
Sears Mortgage Securities	1,903	9.5
Norwest Mortgage Securities	1,477	7.4
Bank of America	1,002	5.0
Travelers	950	4.8
Imperial	779	3.9
Home Savings of America	711	3.6
Security Pacific	603	3.0
Banco Mortgage Securities	448	2.2
All Others (16 issuers)	1,561	7.8
Total:	$19,954	

[1]Citicorp—Citibank, N.A.; Citicorp Homeowners; Citicorp Mortgage Securities, Inc.
[2]Salomon Brothers—Residential Funding Mortgage Securities I, Inc.; Salomon Brothers Mortgage Securities IV, Inc.
Source: Howard Alterescu, Eric Anderson, Mike Asay, and Hal Hinkle, "The Conventional Pass-Through Market," Chap. 8 in Frank J. Fabozzi (ed.), *The Handbook of Mortgage-Backed Securities* (Chicago, IL: Probus Publishing, 1988, Second Edition).

quoting and measuring (and therefore comparing) yields have developed. These measures assume that the investor will hold the security until the last mortgage in the pool is fully repaid.

As the mortgage-backed security market developed, it became conventional to quote yields on the basis of a "12-year prepaid life assumption." This convention assumed that all the mortgages in a pool would prepay exactly after 12 years. That is, the assumption was that the cash flow from the underlying pool would be the regularly scheduled monthly mortgage payments for the first 12 years, and then, at the end of year 12, all the mortgages in the pool would pay off. The quoted yield based on a 12-year prepaid life assumption was used for both new mortgage pools and seasoned pools.[5] Therefore, if a mortgage pass-through security with an original stated maturity of 30 years was issued 10 years ago, the quoted yield would assume that the pool still had a remaining term of 30 years, that there would be no prepayments for the mortgages in the pool for 12 years and then all the mortgages

---

[5]*Seasoning* refers to the time since origination or the age of a mortgage pool.

would prepay. Although this yield measure standardized the way in which yields on pass-through securities were quoted, it was not useful for making investment decisions because there is little justification for its underlying assumptions.

Money managers must make some assumption about prepayment rates for an individual pool in order to estimate the cash flow that can be expected from the pass-through security for which that pool is the underlying. Using the estimated cash flow, a yield can be computed.[6] A yield computed in this manner is called a *cash flow yield*. Cash flow yields are typically based on one of the following benchmarks for projecting cash flows: FHA experience, constant prepayment rate, or Public Securities Association (PSA) standard prepayment model.[7]

FHA Experience.   At one time, the most commonly used benchmark for estimating prepayment rates was the prepayment experience for 30-year mortgages derived from a Federal Housing Administration (FHA) probability table on mortgage survivals. Using FHA experience, cashflows are forecasted for a pool, assuming that the prepayment rate is the same as the FHA experience ("100% FHA") or some multiple of FHA experience (faster than FHA experience or slower than FHA experience). For example, taking the square root of the FHA experience is referred to as "50% FHA"; squaring the FHA experience as the prepayment rate is referred to as "200% FHA."

Despite their popularity, prepayment rate forecasts based on FHA experience are not necessarily indicative of the prepayment rate for a particular pool because FHA experience represents an estimate of prepayments on all FHA-insured mortgages over various interest rate periods. Since prepayment rates are tied to interest rate cycles, what does one average prepayment rate over various cycles mean? To many market participants, not much. Consequently, since a cash flow forecast derived from estimated prepayments using FHA experience may be misleading, the resulting cash flow yield may not be meaningful for making investment decisions.

---

[6]See Chapter 3 for an explanation of how to compute the yield for any investment.

[7]The formulas for computing the cash flow yields based on FHA experience and constant prepayment rate can be found in Lakhbir S. Hayre and Cyrus Mohebbi, "Mortgage Pass-Through Securities," in Frank J. Fabozzi (ed.), *Advances and Innovations in the Bond and Mortgage Markets* (Chicago, IL: Probus Publishing, 1988) or Frank J. Fabozzi, *Fixed Income Mathematics* (Chicago, IL: Probus Publishing, 1988), Chap. 15.

Constant Prepayment Rate (CPR).[8]   Another approach to estimating prepayments and cash flow yield is to assume that some fraction of the remaining principal in the pool will be prepaid each month. The prepayment rate assumed for a pool is based on the characteristics of the pool and the economic environment. The advantage of this approach is its simplicity. What's more, it permits quick analysis when changes in economic conditions affect prepayment rates. This method also accounts for the particular characteristics unique to a specific pool.

PSA Standard Prepayment Model.   Although initially developed for the evaluation of collateralized mortgage obligations (discussed later in this chapter), the Public Securities Association (PSA) standard prepayment model can be applied to project cash flows for any mortgage-related security. The Public Securities Association is an organization that represents dealers in U.S. government securities and mortgage-backed securities. The PSA standard prepayment model, generally referred to as *PSA*, is expressed as a monthly series of annual prepayment rates. The basic PSA model assumes that prepayments will occur less frequently for newly originated mortgages, and then will speed up as the mortgages become seasoned. More specifically, the PSA model assumes the following prepayment rates for 30-year mortgages: (1) an annualized rate of 0.2% for the first month, increased by 0.2% per annum per month for the next 2.5 years until the rate reaches 6% per year; and (2) 6% per year for the remaining years of the mortgage. This base benchmark is referred to as "100% PSA"; slower or faster speeds are referred to as some percentage of PSA. For example, 50% PSA means one-half the CPR of the PSA prepayment rate; 150% PSA means one and one-half the CPR of the PSA prepayment rate.

The PSA prepayment model is a benchmark, not a model for forecasting prepayments. While it has helped standardize quotations on mortgage-backed securities and is easy for market participants to understand, it has several shortcomings that limit its usefulness as a

---

[8]There is no standardized terminology for this approach to computing cash flow yield. Salomon Brothers, Inc refers to it as *constant prepayment rate* (CPR). Drexel Burnham Lambert uses the term *conditional prepayment rate* (CPR), while Bear Stearns & Co. uses the term *constant percentage prepayment* (CPP). In all cases, the prepayment rate assumed is an annual rate.

tool for analysis.[9] Most importantly, it implicitly assumes that all mortgage-backed securities have the same pattern of prepayment. No recognition is given to the characteristics of the underlying pool. For example, discount, premium, and current-coupon pools will have different prepayment patterns, as will GNMAs and conventional pass-through securities and 15-year and 30-year securities.

Bond-Equivalent Yield

When comparing the yield estimated for a pass-through security to that of a Treasury or corporate bond, the yield of the pass-through security cannot be computed by merely multiplying the monthly yield by 12. The reason is that a Treasury bond and a corporate bond pay interest semiannually, while a pass-through has a monthly cash flow. This gives the investor of a pass-through security the opportunity to generate greater annual interest by reinvesting monthly cash flows. Therefore the yield on a pass-through security must be calculated so as to make it comparable to the yield to maturity for a bond. This is done by computing the *bond-equivalent yield* for a pass-through security, assuming that the monthly cash flows from the pass-through are reinvested at the cash flow yield until the end of each semiannual period. The formula used is:

$$\text{Bond-equivalent yield} = 2\,[(1 + r_M)^6 - 1\,]$$

where r_M = monthly interest rate that will equate the present value of the projected monthly cash flows to the price of the pass-through security

$[(1 + r_M)^6 - 1\,]$ = the bond-equivalent semiannual yield on the monthly pay pass-through security.

For example, if r_M is 1%, then the bond-equivalent yield is:

$$\text{Bond-equivalent yield} = 2\,[(1.01)^6 - 1]$$
$$= 2\,[1.06152 - 1]$$
$$= .1230 \text{ or } 12.30\%$$

---

[9]For a more detailed discussion, see David J. Askin and William J. Curtin, "Unsafe at any Speed? Derivative Mortgage-Backed Securities and the PSA Prepayment Model," Drexel Burnham Lambert *Monthly Prepayment Report*, April 1987.

Realized Compound Yield

In Chapter 3 we illustrated the two shortcomings of the yield to maturity as a measure of a bond's potential return: (1) the coupon payments must be reinvested at a rate equal to the yield to maturity; and (2) the bond must be held to maturity. These same shortcomings apply to the cash flow yield measures for pass-through securities: (1) the projected cash flows are assumed to be reinvested at the cash flow yield; and (2) the pass-through is assumed to be held until the entire pool of mortgages pays off. The importance of reinvestment risk—the risk that the cash flow will be reinvested at a rate less than the cash flow yield—is particularly important for pass-through securities because they make payments monthly.

An alternative procedure is to use the realized compound yield framework to assess the performance of a pass-through over some predetermined investment horizon. As we explained in Chapter 3, in order to compute the realized compound yield over some investment horizon, a reinvestment rate and yield for the bond at the end of the investment horizon must be assumed. For a pass-through security, the same information is needed. In addition, a prepayment rate must be assumed. The money manager can assess performance (as measured by the realized compound yield) under different scenarios for these three assumptions.

Obtaining Prepayment Estimates

The major dealers in pass-through securities and some independent investment services have econometric models that estimate prepayment rates. These models take into account the economic and specific geographic factors that influence prepayment rates.[10] Recently, the major dealers have made access to their projected prepayment rates (not the econometric model) easier by supplying them to services used by investors. Exhibit 10.4 shows the projected prepayment rate in terms of PSA by 13 major dealers as reported on the Knight-Ridder MoneyMarket Center.

---

[10]For a detailed discussion of prepayment forecasting, see: David Askin, William J. Curtin, and Linda Lowell, "Forecasting Prepayment Rates for Mortgage-Backed Securities," Chap. 23 in *The Handbook of Mortgage-Backed Securities;* and Chuck Ramsey and J. Michael Henderson, "Specified Pools," Chap. 6 in *The Handbook of Mortgage-Backed Securities.*

EXHIBIT 10.4 PSA Prepayment Assumptions as Reported by Major Dealers

Mortgage Prepayment Rate Tables – Public Securities Association

The following tables contain projected prepayment rates as formulated and reported by each dealer listed. These projections represent individual dealer's views of future prepayment rates, as of the date specified. Projections may change without notice and provide no assurance as to actual prepayment experience. Each dealer must be consulted about the timeliness of its projections and the underlying assumptions. Historical prepayment information reflects the arithmetic mean of historical prepayment rates for the preceding three months, as reported by listed dealers. The median information reflects the median of projected prepayment rates and the low/high information reflects the lowest and highest projected prepayment rates, as reported by listed dealers. All rates are reported as percentages of PSA. PSA, the Public Securities Association prepayment model, is an industry developed reference standard that neither reflects historical nor predicts future rates. Although PSA has received the information contained in the tables from sources PSA believes to be reliable, PSA has not verified such information and assumes no responsibility for its accuracy. The information contained in the tables may be revised or corrected at any time and does not constitute a basis for the valuation of pricing of any security.   (Continued on page 291.)

204

EXHIBIT 10.4 PSA Prepayment Assumptions as Reported by Major Dealers (Continued)

291 Fixed Format Page KNIGHT-RIDDER MoneyCenter	5-Apr-88 4:57P

Mortgage Prepayment Rate Tables
Public Securities Association

Quoting or publishing information from the tables is prohibited without the express written consent of PSA.

Abbreviations:

BS	= Bear Stearns	KP	= Kidder Peabody
CITI	= Citicorp	ML	= Merrill Lynch
DBL	= Drexel Burnham Lambert	MS	= Morgan Stanley
DW	= Dean Witter	PW	= Paine Webber
FBC	= First Boston Corp.	PB	= Prudential Bache
GS	= Goldman Sachs & Co.	SAL	= Salomon Brothers
		SL	= Shearson Lehman

N = New = Final Maturity >330 months (GNMA); WAM >330 months (FHLMC/FNMA).
Otherwise pools are classified as seasoned (S).
GNMA I 30Y-SF = GNMA I 30 Year Single-Family.
FHLMC 30Y-GU = FHLMC 30 year Guarantor.
FNMA 30Y = FNMA 30 Year

(See tables on pages 292-299.)

Knight-Ridder MoneyCenter

205

292 Fixed Format Page	KNIGHT-RIDDER MoneyCenter	5-Apr-88 4:57P

PSA: Mortgage Prepayment Rate Tables

GNMA I:3M-PSA: 4/05/88

30Y-SF:	3/88:MED	LOW-HIGH:	DBL :	FBC :	GS :	KP :	ML :	MS
7.5 S:	78 : 95	85-125 :	85-90 :	120-125 :	93 :	105 :	85 :	95
8.0 N:	37 : 85	75-110 :	85-90 :	105-110 :	82 :	75 :	85 :	85
8.0 S:	82 :100	90-135 :	90-90 :	130-135 :	97 :	105 :	90 :	100
8.5 N:	48 : 90	75-115 :	95-100 :	110-115 :	89 :	75 :	85 :	90
8.5 S:	88 :105	85-135 :	95-105 :	130-135 :	104 :	105 :	95 :	105
9.0 N:	55 :100	75-125 :	105-110 :	120-125 :	97 :	75 :	95 :	95
9.0 S:	90 :112	100-135 :	110-110 :	130-135 :	112 :	105 :	100 :	110
9.5 N:	80 :118	75-135 :	115-120 :	125-130 :	109 :	75 :	110 :	110
9.5 S:	92 :120	105-140 :	115-120 :	135-140 :	124 :	105 :	115 :	120
10.0 N:	105 :133	85-150 :	125-140 :	130-135 :	129 :	85 :	140 :	130
10.0 S:	104 :140	100-150 :	130-145 :	135-140 :	144 :	100 :	140 :	135
10.5 N:	171 :167	115-210 :	160-195 :	150-175 :	161 :	115 :	180 :	167
Update:	:	4/04/88 :	3/31/88 :	4/04/88 :	3/31/88:	4/01/88:	3/15/88:	4/04/88

*See notes on pages 290-291.

*Tables continued on page 293.

Knight-Ridder MoneyCenter

| 293   Fixed Format Page   KNIGHT-RIDDER   MoneyCenter | | | | | | 5-Apr-88   4:57P | |

4/05/88

PSA: Mortgage Prepayment Rate Tables — Cont.

GNMA I:3M-PSA :

30Y-SF:	3/88 :	PW :	PB :	SAL :	SL :	BS :	CITI :	DW
7.5 S:	78 :	110 :	94 :	115 :	90 :	90-100:	95 :	95
8.0 N:	37 :	90 :	80 :	95 :	80 :	80-90 :	90 :	75
8.0 S:	82 :	116 :	97 :	120 :	90 :	100-110:	105 :	95
8.5 N:	48 :	105 :	85 :	110 :	80 :	90-100:	100 :	85
8.5 S:	88 :	130 :	101 :	125 :	85 :	110-120:	110 :	100
9.0 N:	55 :	115 :	95 :	125 :	95 :	100-110:	110 :	100
9.0 S:	90 :	130 :	110 :	130 :	100 :	120-130:	120 :	115
9.5 N:	80 :	130 :	117 :	135 :	120 :	115-125:	120 :	105
9.5 S:	92 :	140 :	119 :	135 :	120 :	130-140:	130 :	120
10.0 N:	105 :	145 :	138 :	145 :	150 :	135-145:	130 :	130
10.0 S:	104 :	150 :	136 :	145 :	150 :	140-150:	140 :	140
10.5 N:	171 :	205 :	182 :	160 :	200 :	175-210:	150 :	150
Updated:	:3/07/88:	3/22/88	:3/31/88:	4/01/88:	3/08/88:	4/01/88:	3/15/88	

*See notes on pages 290-291.
*Tables continued on page 294.

EXHIBIT 10.4 PSA Prepayment Assumptions as Reported by Major Dealers (Continued)

295 Fixed Format Page KNIGHT-RIDDER MoneyCenter   5-Apr-88 4:58P

PSA: Mortgage Prepayment Rate Tables – Cont.

GNMA I:3M-PSA :   4/05/88

30Y-SF:	3/88 :	PW :	PB :	SAL :	SL :	BS :	CITI :	DW
11.0 S:	144 :	255 :	232 :	185 :	245 :	230-255:	190 :	220
11.5 S:	211 :	280 :	282 :	235 :	295 :	270-315:	255 :	280
12.0 S:	233 :	325 :	355 :	300 :	335 :	340-390:	330 :	395
12.5 S:	301 :	335 :	381 :	335 :	355 :	410-440:	385 :	420
13.0 S:	324 :	345 :	397 :	370 :	405 :	450-475:	415 :	435
Updated:	:3/07/88:	3/22/88 :	3/31/88:	4/01/88:	3/08/88:	4/01/88:	3/15/88	

*See notes on pages 290–291.

Knight-Ridder MoneyCenter

208

| 294 | Fixed Format Page | KNIGHT-RIDDER | MoneyCenter | | | | 5-Apr-88 | 4:57P |

PSA: Mortgage Prepayment Rate Tables – Cont.

GNMA I:3M-PSA :

30Y-SF:	3/88:MED	LOW-HIGH:	DBL :	FBC :	GS :	KP :	ML :	MS
								4/05/88
11.0 S:	144 :230	175-275	:225-275:	210-250 :	222 :	175 :	260 :	225
11.5 S:	211 :293	230-375	:285-350:	305-375 :	318 :	230 :	375 :	300
12.0 S:	233 :355	300-500	:405-475:	440-500 :	410 :	300 :	450 :	350
12.5 S:	301 :400	335-620	:450-480:	560-620 :	463 :	355 :	475 :	400
13.0 S:	324 :435	345-655	:455-470:	645-655 :	493 :	405 :	500 :	450
Update:	:	4/04/88	:3/31/88:	4/04/88	:3/31/88:	4/01/88:	3/15/88:	4/04/88

*See notes on pages 290-291.
*Tables continued on page 295.

Price Performance of Premium Pass-Through Securities

The price performance of a pass-through security will depend on investors' expectations of the prepayment rate which, in turn, will depend on investors' expectations about future interest rates (mortgage rates).

When any bond or pass-through security is purchased at a discount, the investor's return will be improved if the security is repaid at par (or greater) as quickly as possible. For example, if an investor buys a pass-through security for $90 today and all homeowners prepay the next day at $100, the investor will have earned an extremely attractive return. In addition, since current interest rates are higher than the coupon rate on the pass-through security, an investor can reinvest the $100 at a higher rate. Thus faster prepayment rates will make a discount pass-through security more attractive, thereby increasing its price.

In contrast, when a pass-through is purchased at a premium, the investor faces the risk that homeowners will prepay their mortgages quickly. In the extreme case, suppose that an investor buys a pass-through security for $110 and the next day homeowners prepay their mortgages at par ($100). This is obviously an unattractive outcome for the investor. In addition, the investor will have to reinvest the proceeds received ($100) at a lower interest rate. Thus, for a pass-through security selling at a premium, when prepayments are expected to increase, the price of a pass-through may not rise; in fact, it may decline.

When will homeowners be more likely to prepay their mortages? Obviously, when interest rates decline. Whenever interest rates decline, the price of an option-free bond rises. However, because of the embedded call option in a pass-through security, its price will not react in the same way. The premium pass-through's price may rise slightly, fall, or remain unchanged.

We have seen this price performance characteristic for securities selling at a premium before. Recall that in Chapter 8 we discussed the price performance characteristic of callable corporate bonds trading at a premium. This characteristic, which is referred to as *price compression*, is due to the negative convexity of the price/yield relationship for bonds with embedded call options as interest rates decline.[11] Pass-through securities, like callable corporate bonds, have an embedded call (prepayment) option.

[11]See p. 156.

Yield Spread to Treasuries

By now it should be clear that it is impossible to determine an exact yield for a pass-through security; the yield depends on the actual prepayment experience of the mortgages in the pool. Nevertheless, it is often stated that pass-through securities offer a higher yield than Treasury securities. Typically, the comparison is made between Ginnie Mae pass-through securities and Treasuries, since both are free of default risk. The difference between the two yields should therefore primarily represent compensation for prepayment risk. The question is whether the amount of the premium the investor receives in terms of higher yield for bearing prepayment risk is adequate. This is where option-pricing models applied to pass-through securities have been used.[12] By using an option pricing model, it is possible to determine if the pass-through security is offering the proper compensation for accepting prepayment risk.

We talk about comparing the yield of a mortgage pass-through security to that of a comparable Treasury, but what does "comparable" mean? The stated maturity of a mortgage pass-through security is inappropriate because of prepayments. Instead, market participants have used two measures: duration and average life. As explained in Chapter 4, duration is a measure of the interest rate sensitivity of a bond. The standard Macaulay duration is inappropriate for bonds with an embedded option such as mortgage pass-through securities. Call-adjusted duration, discussed in Chapter 8, is a more appropriate measure of duration. A second measure commonly used is the "average life," which is the average time to receipt of principal payments (scheduled and projected prepayments), weighted by the amount of principal expected.[13]

---

[12]See David J. Askin, Woodward C. Hoffman, and Steven Meyer, "Evaluation of the Option Component of Mortgages," Chap. 28 in *The Handbook of Mortgage-Backed Securities*; Gifford Fong, Ki-Young Chung, and Eric M. P. Tang, "The Valuation of Mortgage-Backed Securities: A Contingent Claims Approach," Chap. 30 in *The Handbook of Mortgage-Backed Securities*; and David P. Jacob, Graham Lord, and James A. Tilley, "Price, Duration and Convexity of Mortgage-Backed Securities," in Frank J. Fabozzi, ed., *Mortgage-Backed Securities: New Strategies, Applications and Research* (Chicago, IL: Probus Publishing 1987).

[13]Mathematically, the average life is expressed as follows:

$$\text{Average life} = \sum_{t=1}^{T} \frac{t \text{ (Principal received at time } t)}{\text{Total principal received}}$$

where T is the number of months.

COLLATERALIZED MORTGAGE OBLIGATIONS

There is considerable uncertainty about the maturity of any mortgage pass-through security. Consequently, market participants interested in purchasing a short-term security—say 1- to 3-years—find these securities unattractive. Some long-term investors also find these securities unattractive because their maturities can be substantially reduced by fast prepayments. A collateralized mortgage obligation (CMO) reduces the uncertainty concerning the maturity of a mortgage-backed security and thereby provides a risk/return pattern not available with typical mortgage pass-through securities. The growth of the CMO market since the first CMO issue was introduced in June of 1983 by Freddie Mac has been phenomenal, as can be seen from Exhibit 10.5.[14]

A CMO is a security backed by a pool of mortgages and/or by a portfolio of pass-through securities. Because CMOs derive their cash flows from the underlying mortgage collateral, they are referred to as "derivative" securities. CMOs are structured so that there are several classes of bondholders with varying *stated* maturities. The principal payments from the underlying collateral are used to sequentially retire the bonds.[15]

For example, in a typical CMO structure there are four classes of bonds, generally referred to as class-A, class-B, class-C and class-Z.[16] The first three classes, with class-A representing the shortest bond, receive periodic interest payments from the underlying collateral; class-Z (also called the Z-bond) is an accrual bond that receives no periodic interest until the other three classes are retired. When principal payments—both scheduled payments and prepayments—are received by the trustee for the CMO, they are applied to retire the class-A bonds. After all the class-A bonds have been retired, all principal payments received are applied to retire the class-B bonds. Once all the class-B bonds have been retired, class-C bonds are paid off from all

---

[14]For an in-depth discussion of the history and empirics of CMOs, see Richard Roll, "Collateralized Mortgage Obligations: Characteristics, History, Analysis," in *Mortgage-Backed Securities.*

[15]In structuring a CMO, the issuer has to take account of certain federal income tax provisions. The Real Estate Mortgage Investment Conduit (REMIC) provision of the 1986 tax act gives issuers greater flexibility in structuring CMOs. For a further discussion, see Kenneth T. Rosen and Janet Spratlin, "The Impact of Tax Reform on the Mortgage Market," Chap. 45 in *The Handbook of Mortgage-Backed Securities.*

[16]In a particular CMO issue the letters for each class may be different from those used here, but the principle concerning the sequential retirement of the bonds for each class is the same. The classes are commonly referred to as *tranches.*

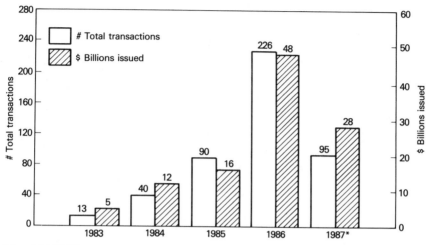

*As of 04/30/87
Source: Lakhbir S. Hayre, David Foulds, and Lisa Pendergast, "Introduction to Collateralized Mortgage Obligations," Chap. 14 in Frank J. Fabozzi, ed., *The Handbook of Mortgage-Backed Securities*, (Chicago, IL: Probus Publishing, 1988).

EXHIBIT 10.5   Growth of the CMO Market

principal payments. Finally, after the first three classes of bonds have been retired, the cash flow payments from the remaining underlying collateral are used to satisfy the obligations on the Z-bonds (original principal plus accrued interest).

An example of a CMO with four classes is the M.D.C. Mortgage Funding Corporation, Series J CMO, a $100 million issue priced on July 7, 1986.[17] The underlying collateral is GNMA pass-throughs with a weighted-average coupon of 9.5% and 297 months remaining to maturity. The original maturity for the GNMA pass-throughs was 360 months. Basic information for each class is summarized in the upper panel of Exhibit 10.6.

[17]This information is taken from Lakhbir S. Hayre, David Foulds, and Lisa Pendergast, "Introduction to Collateralized Mortgage Obligations," Chap. 14 in *The Handbook of Mortgage-Backed Securities.*

EXHIBIT 10.6   Summary Information for M.D.C. Mortgage Funding, Series J

Class	Par (in millions)	Stated Maturity	Coupon	Price
A	$35.5	5/99	8.05%	99.87500
B	15.5	2/02	8.75	99.84575
C	40.5	2/07	9.35	99.71875
Z	9.0	8/16	9.50	93.15625

Class	Expected Maturity	Average Life (years)	Duration	Projected Yield	Benchmark Treasury	Spread over Treasury
A	5/91	2.30	2.10	8.87%	2-year	120 BP*
B	8/93	5.80	4.61	8.72	5-year	160 BP
C	11/99	10.10	6.58	9.38	10-year	210 BP
Z	8/11	18.50	17.05	10.00	20-year	235 BP

*Basis points.

The cash flows for each class can only be projected by assuming some prepayment rate for the underlying mortgage collateral. The prepayment benchmark used by mortgage-backed securities dealers to quote CMO yields is the PSA standard prepayment model discussed in the previous section. The issuer of this CMO based the price on a prepayment rate of 110% PSA. The cash flows for the four classes based on this assumed prepayment rate are shown in Exhibit 10.7. For the Z-bond, the interest is accrued and added to the principal. Exhibit 10.8 shows how the principal balance increases and is then paid off. The expected maturity, average life, duration, projected yield, and spread over Treasuries based on 110% PSA are summarized in the lower panel of Exhibit 10.6.

The spread over Treasuries for each class of this CMO issue represents compensation for prepayment risk and credit risk. The prepayment risk is lower than for a mortgage pass-through security. As we will see shortly, spreads over Treasuries may be wider or narrower than those of the MDC Series J CMO.

Credit Risk and Yield Spreads

The credit quality for most CMOs is high enough to be rated triple A by the major commercial rating agencies. The credit risk is deter-

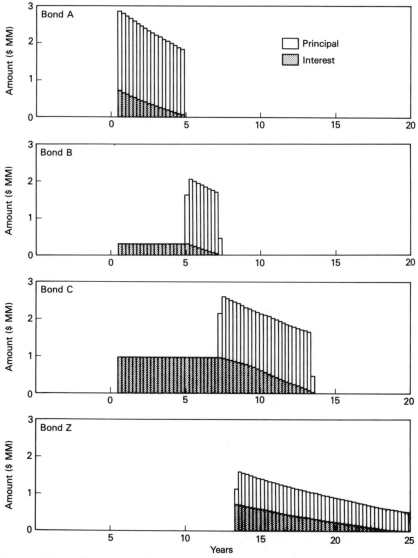

Source: Hayre, Foulds, and Pendergast, "Introduction to Collateralized Mortgage Obligations."

EXHIBIT 10.7   Cash Flow Distribution to MDC J Bonds at 110% PSA

mined by the way in which the CMO is structured and the quality of the underlying mortgage collateral; generally, the creditworthiness of the issuer is not considered.

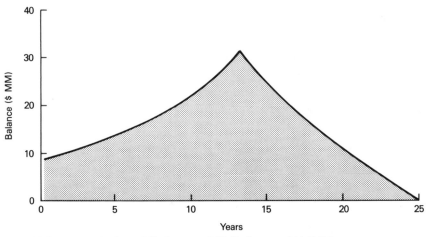

EXHIBIT 10.8   Z-Bond Balance: MDC J at 110% PSA

Source: Hayre, Foulds, and Pendergast, "Introduction to Collateralized Mortgage Obligations."

With respect to the collateral, most CMOs are backed by agency pass-through securities or FHA/VA-guaranteed mortgages. For these CMOs, credit risk is minimal. The majority of those CMOs not backed by agency pass-throughs or FHA/VA-guaranteed mortgages are issued by Freddie Mac, and therefore carry its guarantee and are perceived to have low credit risk. CMOs that do not fall into one of these two categories typically carry pool insurance that guarantees the timely payment of interest and principal. Exhibit 10.9 shows the spread

EXHIBIT 10.9   CMO Spreads in 1987

Benchmark Treasury (Years)	Collateral Type		
	GNMA (Basis points)	FHLMC/FNMA (Basis points)	Mortgages (Whole Loans) (Basis points)
1 Yr.	80	90	115
2	105	115	140
3	110	120	145
5	120	130	155
7	135	145	170
10	145	155	180
20	135	145	170

*Basis points.

Source: Hayre, Foulds, and Pendergast, "Introduction to Collateralized Mortgage Obligations."

over comparable Treasuries in 1987 for CMOs classified by the type of underlying mortgage collateral.

The other key element in determining the credit quality of the CMO is the manner in which the cash flows are structured. In order to receive a triple-A quality rating, the cash flows must be sufficient to meet all of the obligations under any prepayment scenario. Also, the reinvestment rate assumed to be earned on the cash flow until it is distributed to bondholders must be low.

Because of the safeguards built into a CMO structure, a triple-A rating for a CMO is generally viewed as a higher-quality rating than a triple-A rating for most corporate securities. Exhibit 10.10 shows the yield spread of triple-A corporate bonds over Treasuries and the yield spread of CMOs over triple-A corporate bonds in 1987. Notice that even though CMOs have a lower credit risk, they generally offer a higher yield relative to comparable corporate bonds. The yield spread is due to the prepayment risk. Once again, the question is whether the size of the yield spread is sufficient to compensate for the prepayment risk. If the yield spread is more than sufficient, then the investor has the opportunity to earn an enhanced return.

Other CMO Structures

So far, we have discussed the "plain vanilla" CMO structure. Other CMO structures have been introduced since June 1983. These include CMOs with a floating-rate class, and CMOs referred to as Y bonds with a class that, under all but extreme prepayment rates, provide a more stable cash flow.

Floating-rate CMOs. In September 1986 Shearson Lehman Brothers introduced a CMO (SLB CMO Trust D, $150 million) in

EXHIBIT 10.10   Yield Spreads in 1987

Maturity (Years)	Spread of Corporate AAAs over Treasuries (Basis points)	Spread of CMO Bonds over Corporate AAAs (Basis points)
5	40	80–115
7	60	75–100
10	80	65–100
20	90	45–80

Source: Hayre, Foulds, and Pendergast, "Introduction to Collateralized Mortgage Obligations."

which the first class received interest that was reset quarterly at a spread of 37.5 basis points over the 3-month London Interbank Offer Rate (LIBOR). This CMO structure, referred to as a *floating-rate CMO*, appealed to financial institutions and foreign investors who sought investments in which yield on funds invested would vary with the rate on their liabilities. As an indication of the popularity of this structure, almost one-half of the 150 CMOs issued in the 6-month period following the introduction of the floating-rate CMO included a floating-rate class.[18] The design of the floating-rate CMO has since changed to make it comparable in investment characteristics to other short-term instruments that attract funds from financial institutions.

One feature of the floating-rate CMO intended to ensure that the collateral would be sufficient to meet all obligations of the CMO issue was a cap placed on the maximum lifetime interest rate that could be paid on the floating-rate class. This feature made floating-rate CMOs less attractive for financial institutions and foreign investors using them for asset/liability management. To overcome this drawback, two types of structures were introduced: inverse floaters and deep-discount, low-coupon fixed-rate bonds.

The *inverse floater*, introduced in October 1986 with the CMO Trust 13 ($490 million), has two floating-rate classes. One class receives interest based on a fixed spread over LIBOR. The other class, the inverse floating-rate class, has an interest rate that moves in the opposite direction to the change in LIBOR. Thus, if LIBOR increases (decreases), the coupon rate on the floating-rate class increases (decreases), while the coupon rate on the inverse floating-rate class decreases (increases). While there is still a cap on the coupon rate for the floating-rate class, it is greater than the cap that would exist in the absence of the inverse floating-rate class.

The formula for the coupon rate on the inverse floating-rate class is set in such a way that the weighted-average coupon of the two floating-rate classes can be supported by the underlying collateral. For example, for the CMO Trust 13, the formula for the coupon rate for the floating rate class is:

LIBOR + .50

---

[18]Ravi Dattatreya and Lakhbir S. Hayre, "Floating-Rate Collateralized Mortgage Obligations," Chap. 15 in *The Handbook of Mortgage-Backed Securities*.

For the inverse floating-rate class, the coupon rate is:

$$14.60 - 2.163 \ (\text{LIBOR} - 6)$$

A floor of a 1.75% coupon rate was set on the inverse floating-rate class, and a cap of a 12.5% coupon rate was set on the floating-rate class. Since the size of the floating-rate class and inverse floating-rate class was $340 million and $140 million, respectively, the weighted average coupon rate was:

$$\frac{340}{480} \ (\text{coupon rate on floater}) + \frac{140}{480} \ (\text{coupon rate on inverse floater})$$

If LIBOR is 10%, for example, the weighted-average coupon is 9.11%. If the coupon rate cap is reached when LIBOR reaches 12.5%, the coupon rate on the inverse floating-rate class is the floor, 1.75%. The weighted-average coupon rate is 9.17%, the maximum weighted-average coupon rate for this CMO structure. Since there was $500 million of 9% coupon Freddie Mac participation certificates collateralizing this $490 million CMO issue, the collateral was sufficient to satisfy a maximum weighted-average coupon rate of 9.17%.

When a *low-coupon, deep-discount bond class* is included in a CMO issue, these bonds are retired simultaneously with the floating-rate class. This CMO structure was first introduced with the CMO Trust 14 ($1.3 billion) in November 1986.

Y Bonds.   In March 1987 the M.D.C. Mortgage Funding Corporation CMO Series 0, included a class of bonds referred to as "stabilized mortgage reduction term bonds," or "SMRT" bonds, and in its CMO Series P a class referred to as "planned amortization class bonds" or "PAC" bonds. The Oxford Acceptance Corporation III, Series C CMOs, included a class of bonds referred to as "planned redemption obligation bonds" or "PRO" bonds. The common characteristic of these three types of bonds is that, within a wide range of prepayment rates, the cash flow pattern is known with greater certainty than for other classes in a typical CMO issue.

The greater predictability of the cash flow for these classes of bonds, referred to generically as *Y bonds,* occurs because there is a sinking-fund schedule that must be satisfied to retire the obligations of this class. The Y-class bondholders therefore have priority over all other classes in the CMO issue in receiving principal payments from the underlying collateral.

The greater certainty of the cash flow for the Y bonds comes at the expense of the non-Y-bond classes. This is illustrated in Exhibit 10.11, which compares the average lives for all classes in a CMO structure with a Y bond (M.D.C. Series P) and a non-Y bond (BCP Series A), based on different PSA prepayment rates. As can be seen, the variation in the average lives of the non-Y classes in the CMO issue with the Y bonds is greater than for the corresponding classes in the CMO issue without the Y bonds.

CMO Residuals

The excess of the cash flow generated by the underlying collateral over the amount needed to pay interest, retire the bonds, and pay administrative expenses is called the *CMO residual*. Investors can purchase an equity position in the residual cash flow as it accumulates over time. The excess cash flow is not known with certainty. It depends on several factors: (1) current and future interest rates; (2) the coupon rate on the underlying mortgage collateral; (3) the type of collateral; (4) the prepayment rate on the underlying collateral; and (5) the structure of the CMO issue.[19]

The most significant source of excess cash flows is the spread between the coupon on the underlying mortgage collateral and the weighted-average coupon for the CMO issue. In a positive yield curve environment, the shorter-term and intermediate-term bond classes

EXHIBIT 10.11   Average Lives at Various PSA Assumptions

| MDC Series P (With "Y") | | | | | BCP Series A (Non-"Y") | | | | |
Class	0%	100%	300%	500%	Class	0%	100%	300%	500%
P-1	17.3	6.8	1.8	1.1	A-1	11.5	5.0	2.3	1.6
P-2	21.6	14.6	5.5	2.7	A-2	18.8	11.2	5.3	3.5
P-3 (Y)	9.0	5.6	5.6	5.8	A-3	20.8	14.1	7.6	5.1
P-4 (Z)	25.9	22.0	14.0	4.3	A-4 (Z)	25.7	21.8	13.7	9.2

Source: Michael Winchell, " Y Bonds," in *Mortgage Products Special Report,* Bear Stearns & Co., March 12, 1987.

[19]For a discussion of CMO residuals, see Gale M. Belonsky, "CMO Residuals," Chap. 17 in *The Handbook of Mortgage-Backed Securities.*

will expect lower yields than longer-term bond classes. Since the underlying collateral is a longer-term security, the issuer of the CMO is effectively doing the same thing that we discussed in the stripping of Treasury coupon securities in Chapter 5. That is, it is buying long-term cash flows at the yield offered at the long-term end of the yield curve and selling these cash flows at the yield offered at the short-term of the yield curve.

The second major source of residual cash flow is the difference between the actual reinvestment income earned on the cash flow invested before the payout to the bondholders and the assumed reinvestment rate. Recall from our earlier discussion of the rating of CMO issues that a conservative (low) reinvestment assumption must be made. When the actual reinvestment rate is greater than the assumed rate, residual cash flow will result.

Exhibit 10.12 shows the projected annual residual cash flow for the First Boston Corporation Mortgage Securities CMO Trust V. The underlying collateral is Freddie Mac participation certificates with a weighted-average coupon rate of 9.4%. The residual cash flow is based on two assumptions: (1) the underlying participation certificates will prepay at 185% PSA; and (2) the reinvestment rate is 6%. Using these assumptions, the projected residual cash flow available for distribution each year is shown in the last column of Exhibit 10.12. The value of the CMO residual is then the present value of the distributable cash flow. The required yield that an investor would use to discount the cash flow should reflect the high uncertainty in realizing the projected cash flow.

STRIPPED MORTGAGE-BACKED SECURITIES

Stripped mortgage-backed securities, introduced by Fannie Mae in 1986, are another example of derivative mortgage securities. A mortgage pass-through security divides the cash flow from the underlying pool of mortgages among the security holders on a pro rata basis. A stripped mortgage-backed security is created by altering that distribution of principal and interest from a pro rata distribution to an unequal distribution. By doing so, at least one of the securities created will have a price/yield relationship that is different from the price/yield relationship of the underlying mortgage pool. Certain stripped mortgage-backed securities provide means by which investors can hedge

EXHIBIT 10.12 Example of Residual Cash Flow*

FBC Mortgage Securities Trust V
(FHLMC 9.4% WAC Collateral, Priced at 185% PSA)

For the Year Ending January 20	Principal and Interest on FHLMC Certificates	Reinvestment Income at 6.00%	Principal and Interest on Bonds	Bond and Trust Expenses	Draws from Reserve Funds†	Bond Administrator Fee‡	Distributable Cash Flow
1988	$75,964	$431	$72,049	$87	$0	$39	$4,220
1989	94,515	539	90,520	100	0	50	4,383
1990	83,718	477	80,257	94	0	50	3,794
1991	74,083	422	71,099	89	0	50	3,267
1992	65,523	374	62,970	84	0	50	2,793
1993	57,919	330	55,753	80	0	50	2,366
1994	51,165	292	49,350	77	0	50	1,980
1995	45,166	258	43,670	73	0	50	1,630
1996	39,838	227	38,636	70	0	50	1,309
1997	35,107	200	34,175	68	0	50	1,015
1998	30,906	176	30,219	65	0	50	748
1999	27,177	155	26,719	63	0	50	500
2000	23,867	136	23,590	62	0	50	302
2001	20,929	119	20,700	60	0	50	238
2002	18,322	105	18,126	59	0	50	191
2003	16,009	91	15,843	57	0	50	150
2004	13,958	80	13,819	56	0	50	113
2005	12,139	69	12,023	55	0	50	80
2006	10,527	60	10,431	54	0	50	51
2007	9,097	52	9,020	54	0	50	25

For the Year Ending January 20	Principal and Interest on FHLMC Certificates	Reinvestment Income at 6.00%	Principal and Interest on Bonds	Bond and Trust Expenses	Draws from Reserve Funds	Bond Administrator Fee‡	Distributable Cash Flow
2008	7,831	45	7,771	53	0	49	4
2009	6,710	38	6,664	52	0	32	0
2010	5,718	33	5,684	52	0	15	0
2011	4,840	28	4,817	51	2	1	0
2012	4,063	23	4,050	51	15	0	0
2013	3,377	19	3,373	51	27	0	0
2014	2,333	14	2,337	50	40	0	0
2015	1,574	9	1,582	50	48	0	0
2016	420	3	422	38	603	340	227
Total	$842,799	$4,804	$815,668	$1,858	$736	$1,427	$29,387

*Dollars in thousands rounded to the nearest thousand.
†Draws from the Reserve Funds are sufficient to cover shortfalls as well as to release funds from the Bond Reserve Fund upon the retirement of the bonds.
‡Fees due to the Bond Administrator that are not payable from funds released from the lien of the Indenture are deferred until sufficient cash flow from the Reserve Funds becomes available.

Source: Andrew S Carron and Eric I. Hemel, "High Yield Mortgages," in Frank J. Fabozzi, ed., Institutional Investors Focus in Investment Management (Cambridge, MA: Ballinger Publishing, 1989).

prepayment risk or capitalize on expected changes in prepayment rates based on interest rate changes.

Partially Stripped Mortgage-Backed Securities

The first generation of stripped mortgage-backed securities were "partially stripped" mortgage-backed securities. We can see what this means by looking at the stripped mortgage-backed securities issued by Fannie Mae in mid-1986.[20]

The Class B stripped mortgage-backed securities were backed by FNMA 9% mortgage pools. Mortgage rates were about 10% at the time the stripped mortgage-backed security was created, so the mortgage pool would have sold at a discount from par. The mortgage payments from the underlying mortgage pool are distributed to Class B-1 and Class B-2 bondholders in the following way. Both classes receive an equal amount of the principal. However, the interest payments are divided so that Class B-1 receives one-third, while Class B-2 receives two-thirds. Since the coupon for the underlying mortgage pool is 9%, Class B-1 receives 3% interest and one-half the principal, making it a 6% coupon security. The Class B-1 security was sold at a discount (remember that the mortgage rate at the time was 10%), backed by a mortgage pool with a coupon of 9%. Class B-2 receives two-thirds of the 9% coupon from the underlying pool, or 6%, and one-half the principal, producing a 12% coupon security that was sold at a premium but backed by a 9% mortgage pool.

To understand why this was done, we must look at how the investment characteristics of these two classes differ from pass-through securities backed with the same coupon rate. First consider Class B-1. Because this security is selling at a discount, the investor would like to see fast prepayments. Since the underlying mortgage pool is a 9% coupon, if market mortgage rates fall by, say, 300 basis points, prepayments should increase. In contrast, consider a 6% pass-through security in which the underlying pool has a 6.5% coupon rate in a 10% interest rate environment. While this pass-through would sell at a discount and benefit by faster prepayments, if market mortgage rates declined by 300 basis points to 6%, there would be no reason for prepayments to speed up, since the mortgages in the underlying pool have a 9% coupon. Consequently, Class B-1 should outperform

[20]For a further discussion, see Richard Roll, "Stripped Mortgage-Backed Securities," Chap. 18 in *The Handbook of Mortgage-Backed Securities.*

the 6.5% coupon pass-through security. Also, as long as market interest rates do not fall below 6%, the Class B-1 security should outperform Treasury securities with the same coupon and average life.

Now let's look at Class B-2, selling at a premium. The risk of investing in a high-coupon mortgage-backed security is the price compression (negative convexity) that results when interest rates fall. So, investing in a 12% coupon pass-through security in a 10% market rate environment means that the high current interest will not be received for long because prepayments will speed up, particularly if market mortgage rates drop further. The investor then receives par for a security that he paid a premium for. Compare this situation with the Class B-2 security paying high coupon interest. Since the coupon on the underlying mortgage pool is 9%, prepayments should not accelerate if market mortgage rates stay at 10% or decrease by, say, 100 to 200 basis points from their current level. Thus Class B-2 should outperform a 12% coupon mortgage pass-through security.

Interest Only/Principal Only Securities

Two issues of stripped mortgage-backed securities (Class A and Class E) issued by Fannie Mae created a low-coupon security and an extremely high-coupon security. For example, using FNMA 11% coupon pools, Fannie Mae created Class A-1 with a 5% coupon and Class A-2 with a 605% coupon rate. This was done by giving 4.95% of the interest from the underlying mortgage pool with a coupon of 11% to Class A-1 and 6.05% to Class A-2. However, Class A-1 was given 99% of the principal payments, while Class A-2 was given only 1%. Class A-1 selling at a discount would benefit from fast prepayments. Class A-2, which is receiving very high coupon interest, would benefit from slow prepayments. If market mortgage rates declined, an increase in prepayment rates would be expected. This, in turn, would decrease the value of the Class A-2 security.

Notice this investment characteristic of the Class A-2 security: as interest rates decline, its price should decline. In contrast, if market mortgage rates increase, prepayments should slow down, thereby benefiting the owner of a Class A-2 security. Therefore, as interest rates rise, the price of the Class A-2 security should rise.

In early 1987 stripped mortgage-backed securities began to be issued in which all of the interest is allocated to one class (called the *interest-only* or *IO class*) and all of the principal to the other class (called the *principal-only* or *PO class*). The IO and PO classes share the same investment characteristics as the Class A-1 and Class A-2 securities that we just discussed. Both the IO and PO classes have substantial price volatility. In the extreme case where prepayments turn out to be much faster than had been anticipated in pricing the IO class, an investor may not recover the amount invested in the IO class.[21]

Strategies with Stripped Mortgage-Backed Securities

Several strategies involving stripped mortgage-backed securities have been suggested. First, since the IO class should move in the same direction as the change in interest rates, IOs are recommended for hedging the prepayment risk in a portfolio of mortgage-backed securities. Thus, while the IO class is a high-risk security in terms of its price volatility, if properly used in a portfolio, it can reduce the overall interest rate risk of the portfolio.[22] The second strategy is to use IOs and POs to synthetically create customized pass-through securities with performance characteristics that conform to a money manager's expectations about interest rates and prepayments.[23] While there are other, more complex strategies, these are the two that are used most often.[24]

SUMMARY

In this chapter we discussed three types of mortgage-backed securities: mortgage pass-through securities, collateralized mortgage obligations, and stripped mortgage-backed securities. Mortgage pass-through securities provide a more efficient and lower risk vehicle for investing in a pool of mortgages than investing in individual mortgages. However,

---

[21]For a more detailed discussed of the price characteristics of IOs and POs and their valuation, see Andrew S. Carron, "Mortgage Strips," Chap. 19 in *The Handbook of Mortgage-Backed Securities;* Steven J. Carlson and Timothy D. Sears, "Stripped Mortgage Pass-Throughs: New Tools for Investors," Chap. 21 in *The Handbook of Mortgage-Backed Securities;* and R. Blaine Roberts, "The Relative Valuation of IO/PO Stripped Mortgage-Backed Securities," Chap. 20 in *The Handbook of Mortgage-Backed Securities.*

[22]For illustrations of how to use IOs for hedging, see Carlson and Sears, "Stripped Mortgage Pass-Throughs: New Tools for Investors."

[23]For illustrations of how this can be done, see Marilyn J. Dicks and Janet Piez, "Using Stripped Mortgage-Backed Securities to Create Customized Mortgage Pass-Throughs," Chap. 22 in *The Handbook of Mortgage-Backed Securities.*

[24]For a discussion of more complex strategies, see Michael Winchell, *Trading Strategies for Stripped Mortgage-Backed Securities,* Mortgage Products Special Report (New York: Bear Stearns, February 11, 1987).

the cash flow characteristics are the same as for the underlying mortgage pool. Collateralized mortgage obligations and stripped mortgaged-backed securities redirect the cash flows from the underlying mortgage pool, allowing price/yield relationships for at least one of the securities created to differ from those for the underlying mortgage pool.

11

INTEREST RATE FUTURES:
Contracts, Pricing,
and Applications

Futures contracts and options offer money managers opportunities for controlling risk. In this chapter we focus on futures contracts. We describe the salient features of currently traded contracts, how they are priced, and their use in portfolio management.

FUTURES CONTRACTS

A futures contract is a firm legal agreement between a buyer (seller) and an established exchange or its clearing house in which the buyer (seller) agrees to take (make) delivery of *something* at a specified price at the end of a designated period of time. When an investor takes a position in the market by buying a futures contract, the investor is said to be in a *long position* or *long the futures*. If, instead, the investor's opening position is the sale of a futures contract, the investor is said to be in a *short position* or *short the futures*.

Before 1972 the *something* that parties agreed to take or make delivery of was either traditional agricultural commodities (such as meat and livestock), imported foodstuffs (such as coffee, cocoa, and sugar), or industrial commodities. Collectively, such futures contracts are known as *commodity futures*.

Futures contracts based on a financial instrument or a financial index are known as *financial futures*. Financial futures can be classified as (1) interest rate futures, (2) stock index futures, and (3) currency futures. The first financial futures contracts were currency futures contracts, which were introduced in 1972 by the International Monetary Market (IMM) of the Chicago Mercantile Exchange (the "Merc" or CME). In October 1975 the Chicago Board of Trade (CBT) pioneered trading in a futures contract based on a fixed-income instrument—Government National Mortgage Association certificates. Three months later the IMM began trading futures contracts based on 13-week Treasury bills. Other exchanges soon followed with their own interest rate futures contracts. In 1982 three futures contracts based on broadly based common stock indexes made their debut.

Most financial futures contracts have contract expiration months of March, June, September, and December. This means that at a predetermined time in the contract expiration month the contract stops trading and a price is determined by the exchange for settlement of the contract. The contract with the closest settlement date is called the *nearby futures contract*. The *next futures contract* is the one that settles just after the nearby contract. The contract furthest away from settlement is called the *most distant futures contract*.

CURRENTLY TRADED INTEREST RATE FUTURES CONTRACTS

The focus of this chapter is on interest rate futures contracts. The most actively traded interest rate futures contracts at the time of this writing were:

Underlying:	*Exchange:*
Treasury bills	IMM
Eurodollar CDs	IMM and London International Futures Exchange
Treasury bonds	Chicago Board of Trade
Treasury notes	Chicago Board of Trade
Municipal bond index	Chicago Board of Trade

Treasury Bill Futures Contract

This futures contract is based on 13-week (3-month) Treasury bills with a face value of $1 million. The Treasury bills delivered can be newly issued 13-week bills or seasoned bills with 13 weeks remaining to maturity.

Recall from Chapter 5 that in the cash market Treasury bills are quoted in terms of the annualized yield on a bank-discount basis, where:[1]

$$Y_D = \frac{D}{F} \times \frac{360}{t}$$

Y_D = annualized yield on a bank-discount basis
D = dollar discount, which is equal to the difference between the face value and the price
F = face value
t = number of days remaining to maturity.

The dollar discount (D) is found by:[2]

$$D = Y_D \times F \times \frac{t}{360}$$

In contrast, the Treasury bill futures contract is not quoted directly in terms of yield. Instead, it is quoted on an index basis that is related to the yield on a bank-discount basis as follows:

$$\text{Index price} = 100 - (Y_D \times 100)$$

Notice that by quoting the futures contract in this way, there is an inverse relationship between the price of the futures contract and the yield. Market participants are more comfortable with this way of pricing futures contracts.

Given the price of the futures contact, the yield on a bank-discount basis for the futures contract is determined as follows:

$$Y_D = \frac{100 - \text{Index price}}{100}$$

For example, if the index price is 93.00, then the yield on a bank-discount basis for this Treasury bill futures contract is:

[1]See equation (5.1) on page 85.
[2]See equation (5.2) on page 86.

$$Y_D = \frac{100 - 93.00}{100} = .07 \text{ or } 7\%$$

The invoice price that the buyer of $1 million face value of 13-week Treasury bills must pay at settlement is found by first computing the dollar discount as follows:

$$D = Y_D \times \$1,000,000 \times \frac{t}{360}$$

where t is either 90 or 91 days

Typically, the number of days to maturity of a 13-week Treasury bill is 91 days. The invoice price is then:

Invoice price = $1,000,000 − D

For example, for the Treasury bill futures contract with an index price of 93.00 (and a yield on a bank discount basis of 7%), the dollar discount, assuming that the 13-week Treasury bill to be delivered has 91 days to maturity, is:

$$D = .07 \times \$1,000,000 \times \frac{91}{360}$$

$$= \$17,964.44$$

The invoice price is:

Invoice price = $1,000,000 − $17,964.44 = $982,305.46

The minimum price index fluctuation or "tick" for this futures contract is .01. A change of .01 for the minimum index price translates into a change in the yield on a bank-discount basis of 1 basis point (.0001). The change in the value of 1 basis point will change the dollar discount, and therefore the invoice price, by:

$$.0001 \times \$1,000,000 \times \frac{t}{360}$$

For a 13-week Treasury with 91 days to maturity, the change in the dollar discount is:

$$.0001 \times \$1,000,000 \times \frac{91}{360} = \$25.28$$

For a 13-week Treasury with 90 days to maturity, the change in the dollar discount would be $25.

Thus a "tick" on a Treasury bill futures contract is $25.28 for a 91-day Treasury bill but only $25 for a 90-day Treasury bill. Despite the fact that a 13-week Treasury bill typically has 91 days to maturity, market participants commonly refer to the value of a basis point for this futures contract as $25.

Eurodollar CD Futures Contract

Eurodollar certificates of deposit (CDs) are U.S. dollars on deposit outside the United States. The rate paid on Eurodollar CDs is the London Interbank Offer Rate (LIBOR). The 3-month Eurodollar CD is the underlying instrument for the Eurodollar CD futures contract. As with the Treasury bill futures contract, this contract is for $1 million of face value and is traded on a price index basis with a minimum price fluctuation (tick) of .01 (or .0001 in terms of LIBOR).

The unique feature of the Eurdollar CD futures contract is that it is impossible to deliver a Eurodollar CD. Since at settlement the seller of the futures contract cannot deliver a 3-month Eurodollar CD, the settlement procedure requires that the parties settle in cash for the value of a Eurodollar CD based on LIBOR at the settlement date. Because of this feature, Eurodollar CD futures contracts are referred to as *cash settlement contracts.*

Treasury Bond Futures Contract

The underlying instrument for a Treasury bond futures contract is $100,000 par value of a hypothetical 20-year, 8% coupon bond. While prices and yields of the Treasury bond futures contract are quoted in terms of this hypothetical Treasury bond, the seller of the futures contract has the option of several acceptable Treasury bonds to deliver. The Chicago Board of Trade allows the seller to deliver any Treasury bond that has at least 15 years to maturity from the date of delivery if not callable; if the issue is callable, it must not be callable for at least 15 years from the first day of the delivery month.

The minimum price fluctuation for the Treasury bond futures contract is a 32nd. The dollar value of a 32nd for a $100,000 par value (the par value for the underlying Treasury bond) is $31.25. Thus the minimum price fluctuation is $31.25 for this contract.

Delivery Procedure.   To make delivery equitable to both parties and to tie cash to delivery prices, the CBT introduced *conversion factors* for determining the invoice price of each acceptable deliverable Treasury issue against the Treasury bond futures contract. The conversion factor is determined by the CBT before a contract with a specific maturity begins trading. The conversion rate is based on the price that a deliverable bond would sell for at the beginning of the delivery month if it were to yield 8%. The conversion factor is constant throughout the maturity date of the futures contract.

The invoice price paid by the buyer for the Treasury bonds delivered by the seller is then determined using the following formula:

Invoice price = Contract size × Futures contract settlement price
× Conversion factor

For example, suppose the Treasury bond futures contract settles at 96 (.96 in decimal form) and that the short position elects to deliver a Treasury bond issue with a conversion factor of 1.15. Since the contract size is $100,000, the invoice price is:

$100,000 × .96 × 1.15 = $110,400

This invoice price is for the principal only. The buyer of the futures contract must also pay the seller accrued interest on the bond delivered.

Since it is the short position who selects the issue to deliver, he will choose the issue that is cheapest to deliver. The cost to deliver is the difference between the cost of purchasing the Treasury issue and the invoice price for the principal; that is:

Cost to deliver = Cost of purchasing issue – Invoice price

This is equivalent to selecting the issue that would generate the greatest profit as measured by the invoice price for the principal minus the cost of purchasing the issue. Notice that computation of the cost of delivery does not consider the accrued interest that the seller (short position) must pay to acquire the issue. The reason is that the cost would be offset by the long position when the issue is purchased from the short.

In addition to the option of which acceptable Treasury issue to deliver—sometimes referred to as the *swap option*—the short position has two more options granted under the delivery guidelines of the CBT. The short position is permitted to decide when in the delivery month a delivery will take place. This is called the *timing option*. The other option is the right of the short position to give notice of intent to deliver up to 8:00 P.M. Chicago time after the closing of the exchange (2:00 P.M. Chicago time) on the date when the futures settlement price has been fixed. This option is referred to as the *wild card option*. Because of the swap, timing, and wildcard options (referred to in sum as the *delivery option*), the long position can never be sure of which Treasury bond will be delivered or when it will be delivered.

Treasury Note Futures Contract

Modeled after the Treasury bond futures contract, the underlying instrument for the Treasury note futures contract is $100,000 par value of a hypothetical 10-year, 8% Treasury note. There are several acceptable Treasury issues that may be delivered by the short position. An issue is acceptable if the maturity is not less than 6.5 years and not greater than 10 years from the first day of the delivery month. The delivery options granted to the short position and the minimum price fluctuation are the same as for the Treasury bond futures contract.

Bond Buyer's Municipal Index Futures Contract

Traded on the CBT, the underlying instrument for this contract is a basket of 40 municipal bonds. The Bond Buyer serves as the index manager for the contract and prices each bond in the index according to prices received daily from municipal dealers. Each price is multiplied by a conversion factor that equates the bond to an 8% issue. The converted prices are then summed and divided by 40, for an average converted price on the index. The index is revised bimonthly when newer issues are added and older issues or issues that no longer meet the criteria for inclusion in the index are dropped.[3] A smoothing coefficient is calculated on the index revision date so that the index will not change merely because of a change in its composition. The average converted dollar price for the index is multiplied by this coefficient to

---

[3]The inclusion criteria, as well as the revision process and pricing of the index, are spelled out in a publication entitled *The Chicago Board of Trade's Municipal Bond Futures Contract*, 1987.

get the index value for a particular date. Since delivery on all 40 bonds in the index is not possible, the contract is a cash settlement contract, the settlement price being based on the value of the index on the delivery date. The size of the contract is $100,000 par value.

Mechanics of Futures Trading

Margin Requirements.   When a position is first taken in a futures contract, the investor must deposit a minimum dollar amount per contract as specified by the exchange. This amount is called the *initial margin* and is put up as a "good faith" deposit for the contract.[4] The initial margin may be in the form of an interest-bearing security such as a Treasury bill. As the price of the futures contract fluctuates, the value of the investor's equity in the futures position changes. At the close of each trading day, an investor's position is "marked to market," so that any gain or loss from the position is reflected in the investor's equity account. The price used to mark the position to market is the settlement price for that day.

Maintenance margin is the minimum level specified by the exchange by which an investor's equity position may fall as a result of an unfavorable price movement before the investor is required to deposit additional margin. The additional margin deposited is called *variation margin.* If required, the amount of variation margin the investor must deposit is an amount necessary to bring the equity in his account back to its initial margin level. Unlike initial margin, variation margin must be in cash, not interest-bearing instruments. If there is excess margin in the account due to fluctuations in the price of the futures contract, that amount may be withdrawn by the investor.

Although there are also initial and maintenance margin requirements for buying cash securities on margin, the concept of margin differs for futures. When securities are acquired on margin, the difference between the price of the security and the initial margin is borrowed from the broker. The security purchased serves as collateral for the loan and interest on that loan is paid by the investor. For futures contracts, the initial margin, in effect, serves as "good faith" money, indicating that the investor will satisfy the obligation of the contract. No money is borrowed by the investor.

---

[4]Individual brokerage firms are free to set margin requirements above the minimum established by the exchange.

Liquidating a Position.   The investor has two choices in liquidating a position. To liquidate a position before the delivery date, the investor must take an offsetting position in the same contract. For a long position, this means selling an identical number of contracts; for a short position, it means buying an identical number of contracts.

The alternative is to wait until the delivery date. At that time the investor liquidates a long position by accepting delivery of the underlying instrument at the agreed-upon price, and liquidates a short position by delivering the instrument at the agreed-upon price. For those interest rate futures contracts that do not have an underlying instrument that is deliverable (i.e., Eurodollar CD and municipal index), settlement is in cash at the settlement price on the delivery date.

The Role of the Clearing Corporation.   Every time an investor takes a position in the futures market, there is another party taking the opposite position and agreeing to satisfy the terms set forth in the contract. Because of the *clearing corporation* associated with each exchange, the investor need not worry about the financial strength and integrity of the party taking the opposite side of the contract. When an order is initially executed, the relationship between the two parties is severed. The clearing corporation interposes itself as the buyer for every sale and the seller for every purchase. Thus the investor is free to liquidate his position without involving the other party in the original contract, and without worry that the other party may default.

FUTURES VERSUS FORWARD CONTRACTS

A forward contract, just like a futures contract, is an agreement for the future delivery of *something* at a specified price at the end of a designated period of time. Futures contracts are standardized agreements as to the delivery date (or month) and quality of the deliverable, and are traded on organized exchanges. A forward contract is usually nonstandardized, and secondary markets are often nonexistent or extremely thin.

Although both futures and forward contracts set forth terms of delivery, futures contracts are not intended to be settled by delivery. In fact, generally less than 2% of outstanding contracts are delivered. In contrast, forward contracts are intended for delivery.

Futures contracts are marked to market at the end of each trading day. Forward contracts are not. Consequently, there are interim cash flows with futures contracts because additional margin may be required when there are adverse price movements, or cash may be withdrawn when there are favorable price movements. There are no interim cash flows with forward contracts because no variation margin is required.

Finally, the parties in a forward contract are exposed to credit risk because either may default on his obligation. In contrast, for futures contracts credit risk is minimal because the clearing corporation associated with the exchange guarantees the other side of the transaction.

PRICING OF FUTURES CONTRACTS

To understand how futures contracts should be priced, consider the following example. Suppose that a 20-year, $100 par value bond with a coupon rate of 12% is selling at par and the next coupon payment for this bond will occur 3 months from now. Also suppose that this bond is the deliverable for a futures contract that settles in 3 months. If the current 3-month interest rate at which funds can be loaned or borrowed is 8% per year, what should the price of this futures contract be?

Suppose the price of the futures contract is $107. Consider the following strategy:

> Sell the futures contract at $107
> Purchase the bond for $100
> Borrow $100 for 3 months at 8% per year

The borrowed funds are used to purchase the bond, resulting in no initial cash outlay for this strategy. Three months from now, the bond purchased must be delivered to settle the futures contract and the loan must be repaid. This strategy will produce the following outcome:

1. From settlement of the futures contract:

Proceeds from delivery of bond to settle the futures contract	= 107
Accrued interest paid by buyer at settlement (3% for 3 months)	= 3
Total proceeds	= 110

2. From the loan:

Repayment of principal of loan	= 100
Interest on loan (2% for 3 months)	= 2
Total outlay	= 102
Profit	= 8

Notice that this strategy will guarantee a profit of $8. Moreover, this profit is generated with *no investment* outlay because the proceeds obtained to purchase the bond were borrowed. The profit will be realized *regardless of what the futures price at the settlement date is.* Obviously, in a well-functioning market, arbitrageurs would buy the futures and sell the bond, forcing the futures price down and bidding up the bond price so as to eliminate this profit.

In contrast, suppose that the futures price is $92 instead of $107. Let's consider the following strategy:

Buy the futures contract at $92
Sell (short) the bond for $100
Invest (lend) $100 for 3 months at 8% per year

Once again, there is no initial cash outlay for the strategy. Three months from now the bond must be purchased to settle the long position in the futures contract. The bond accepted for delivery will then be used to cover the short position in the bond (i.e., to cover the short sale in the cash market). The outcome in 3 months would be as follows:

1. From settlement of the futures contract:

Price paid for purchase of bond to settle futures contract	= 92
Accrued interest paid to seller (3% for 3 months)	= 3
Total outlay	95

2. From the loan:

Proceeds received from maturing of investment	= 100
Interest earned from the 3-month investment (2% for 3 months)	= 2
Total proceeds	= 102
Profit	= 7

The $7 profit from this strategy is a pure arbitrage profit. It requires no initial cash outlay and will be realized regardless of what the futures price is at the settlement date.

Is there a futures price that will eliminate the arbitrage profit? Yes there is. There will be no arbitrage profit if the futures price is $99. Let's look at what would happen if the two previous strategies were followed and the futures price was $99. First, consider the following strategy:

Sell the futures contract at $99
Purchase the bond for $100
Borrow $100 for 3 months at 8% per year

In 3 months the outcome would be as follows:

1. From settlement of the futures contract:

Proceeds from delivery of bond to settle the futures contract	=	99
Accrued interest paid by buyer at settlement (3% for 3 months)	=	3
Total proceeds	=	102

2. From the loan:

Repayment of principal of loan	=	100
Interest on loan (2% for 3 months)	=	2
Total outlay	=	102
Profit	=	0

There is no arbitrage profit with this strategy.

Next consider the following strategy:

Buy the futures contract at $99
Sell (short) the bond for $100
Invest (lend) $100 for 3 months at 8% per year

The outcome in 3 months would be as follows:

1. From settlement of the futures contract:

Price paid for purchase of bond to settle futures contract	=	99
Accrued interest paid to seller (3% for 3 months)	=	3
Total outlay	=	102

2. From the loan:

Proceeds received from maturing of investment	=	100
Interest earned from the 3-month investment (2% for 3 months	=	2
Total proceeds	=	102
Profit	=	0

Thus neither strategy results in a profit. Hence the futures price of $99 is the equilibrium price because any higher or lower futures price will permit arbitrage profits.

Theoretical Futures Price Based on Arbitrage Model

Considering the arbitrage arguments we just presented, the equilibrium futures price can be determined on the basis of the following information:

1. The price of the bond in the cash market.
2. The yield (as measured by the coupon) on the bond earned until the settlement date. In our example, the yield on the bond is the accrued coupon interest. Since the bond pays an annual coupon rate of 12%, the yield on the bond for 3 months is 3%.
3. The interest rate for borrowing and lending until the settlement date. The borrowing and lending rate is referred to as the *financing cost*. In our example, the financing cost is 2% for the 3 months.

We will let:

r = financing cost (%)
y = yield (%)
P = cash market price ($)
F = futures price ($)

and then consider the following strategy:

Sell the futures contract at F
Purchase the bond for P
Borrow P until the settlement date at r

The outcome at the settlement date is:
1. From settlement of the futures contract:

Proceeds from delivery of bond to settle the futures contract	$= F$
Accrued interest paid by buyer at settlement	$= y\,P$
Total proceeds	$= F + y\,P$

2. From the loan:

Repayment of principal of loan	$= P$
Interest on loan	$= rP$
Total outlay	$= P + rP$

The profit will equal:

> Profit = Total proceeds – Total outlay
> Profit $= F + yP - (P + rP)$

In equilibrium the theoretical futures price occurs where the profit from this strategy is zero. Thus to have equilibrium, the following must hold:

$$0 = F + yP - (P + rP)$$

Solving for the theoretical futures price, we have:

(11.1) $F = P + P(r - y)$

Alternatively, consider the following strategy:

> Buy the futures contract at F
> Sell (short) the bond for P
> Invest (lend) P at r until the settlement date

The outcome at the settlement date would be:

1. From settlement of the futures contract:

Price paid for purchase of bond to settle futures contract	$= F$
Accrued interest paid to seller	$= yP$
Total outlay	$= F + yP$

2. From the loan:

Proceeds received from maturing of investment	$= P$
Interest earned	$= rP$
Total proceeds	$= P + rP$

The profit will equal:

> Profit = Total proceeds – Total outlay
> Profit $= P + rP - (F + yP)$

Setting the profit equal to zero so that there will be no arbitrage profit and solving for the futures price, we would obtain the same equation for the futures price as equation (11.1).

Let's apply equation (11.1) to our previous example in which:

$$r = .02$$
$$y = .03$$
$$P = \$100$$

Then the theoretical futures price is:

$$F = \$100 + \$100 \,(.02 - .03)$$
$$= \$100 - \$1 = \$99$$

This agrees with the equilibrium futures price we demonstrated earlier.

In equation (11.1) the theoretical futures price may sell at a premium to the cash market price (higher than the cash market price) or at a discount from the cash market price (lower than the cash market price), depending on $P\,(r - y)$. The term $r - y$ is called the *net financing cost* because it adjusts the financing cost for the yield earned. The net financing cost is more commonly called the *cost of carry,* or simply *carry.* *Positive carry* means that the yield earned is greater than the financing cost; *negative carry* means that the financing cost exceeds the yield earned. The relationships can be expressed as follows:

Carry	Futures Price
Positive ($y > r$)	Will sell at a discount to the cash price ($F < P$)
Negative ($y < r$)	Will sell at a premium to the cash price ($F > P$)
Zero ($r = y$)	Will be equal to the cash price ($F = P$)

In the case of interest rate futures, carry (the relationship between the short-term financing cost and the yield on the bond) depends on the shape of the yield curve. When the yield curve is upward sloping, the short-term financing cost will be less than the yield on the bond, resulting in positive carry for interest rate futures in which the underlying bond is long-term. The futures price will then sell at a discount to the cash price for the bond. The opposite will hold true when the yield curve is inverted.

A Closer Look at the Theoretical Futures Price

To derive the theoretical futures price using the arbitrage argument, we made several assumptions. We will now discuss the implications of these assumptions for the divergence between the actual futures price and the theoretical futures price.

Interim Cash Flows.   No interim cash flows due to variation margin or coupon interest payments were assumed in the model. However, we know that interim cash flows can occur for both of these reasons. Because we assumed no variation margin, the theoretical futures price is technically the theoretical price for a forward contract because a forward contract is not marked to market at the end of each trading day.[5] If interest rates rise, then the short position will receive margin as the futures price decreases; the margin can then be reinvested at a higher interest rate. In contrast, if interest rates fall, there will be variation margin that must financed by the short position; however, because interest rates have declined, the financing can be done at a lower cost.[6]

Incorporating interim coupon payments into the pricing model is not difficult. However, the value of the coupon payments at the settlement date will depend on the interest rate at which they can be reinvested—that is, on the reinvestment rate. The shorter the maturity of the futures contract and the lower the coupon rate, the less important the reinvestment income is in determining the futures price.

The Short-Term Interest Rate (Financing Cost).   In deriving the theoretical futures price it is assumed that the borrowing and lending rates are equal. Typically, however, the borrowing rate is greater than the lending rate.

We will let:

---

[5]For a technical discussion of the difference between futures and forward prices, see John C. Cox, John E. Ingersoll, and Stephen A. Ross, "The Relationship Between Forward and Futures Prices," *Journal of Financial Economics* (1981), pp. 321–346; Scott F. Richard and M. Sundaresan, "A Continuous Time Equilibrium Model of Forward Prices and Futures Prices in a Multigood Economy," *Journal of Financial Economics* (1981), pp. 347–372; and Robert A. Jarrow and George S. Oldfield, "Forward and Futures Contracts," *Journal of Financial Economics* (1981), pp. 373–382. For a procedure to adjust the forward price to account for variation margin, see Nick Hanson and Robert Kopprasch, "Pricing of Stock Index Futures," Chap. 6 in Frank J. Fabozzi and Gregory M. Kipnis, eds., *Stock Index Futures* (Homewood, IL: Dow Jones-Irwin, 1984).

[6]Cox, Ingersoll, and Ross have argued in "The Relationship Between Forward and Futures Prices," that this will result in a futures price that is lower than forward prices.

r_B = borrowing rate
r_L = lending rate

For the following strategy:

Sell the futures contract at F
Purchase the bond for P
Borrow P until the settlement date at r_B

the futures price that would produce no arbitrage profit is:

(11.2) $F = P + P\,(r_B - y)$

For the following strategy:

Buy the futures contract at F
Sell (short) the bond for P
Invest (lend) P at r_L until the settlement date

the futures price that would produce no profit is:

(11.3) $F = P + P\,(r_L - y)$

Equations (11.2) and (11.3) together provide boundaries in which the futures price will be in equilibrium. Equation (11.2) provides the upper boundary and equation (11.3) the lower boundary. For example, assume that the borrowing rate is 8% per year, or 2% for 3 months, while the lending rate is 6% per year, or 1.5% for 3 months. Then, using equation (11.2), the upper boundary is:

F (upper boundary) = $100 + $100 (.02 − .03)
          = $99

The lower boundary using equation (11.3) is:

F (lower boundary) = $100 + $100 (.015 − .03)
          = $98.50

In calculating these boundaries, we assumed no transactions costs were involved in taking the position. In actuality, the transactions costs of entering into and closing the cash position as well as the round-trip transaction costs for the futures contract must be considered and do affect the boundaries for the futures contract.

Proceeds from Short Selling.   In the strategy involving short selling of the bond, it is assumed that the proceeds from the short sale are received and reinvested. In practice, for individual investors, the proceeds are not received; in fact, the individual investor is required to put up margin (securities margin, in addition to futures margin) to short-sell. For institutional investors, the bond may be borrowed, but only at a cost. This cost of borrowing can be incorporated into the model by reducing the yield on the bond.

Deliverable Bond and Settlement Date Unknown.   In our example we assume that (1) only one bond is deliverable and (2) the settlement date occurs 3 months from now. As explained earlier in this chapter, futures contracts on Treasury bonds and Treasury notes are designed to allow the short the choice of delivering one of a number of deliverable issues. (We referred to this as the swap option.) Also, because of the timing and wildcard options, the delivery date is not known.

Because there may be more than one deliverable, market participants track the price of each deliverable bond and determine which is the cheapest to deliver. The futures price will then trade in relation to the bond that is cheapest to deliver. As we explained earlier in this chapter, the cheapest to deliver is the bond or note that will result in the smallest loss or the greatest gain if delivered by the short futures position.[7]

There are several reasons, in addition to the ones we have already discussed, why the actual futures price will diverge from the theoretical futures price based on the arbitrage model. First, there is the risk that while an issue may be the cheapest to deliver at the time a position in the futures contract is taken, it may not be the cheapest to deliver after that time. For example, 31 Treasury bond issues were deliverable against the June 1985 bond futures contract. For most of 1985 the 7 5/8s Treasury maturing on February 15, 2007, was the cheapest to deliver. On January 23, 1985, however, the 10 3/8 Treasury maturing on November 15, 2012, was the cheapest to deliver. To see the impact on the futures price, consider the following. On May 9, 1985, the futures price was 91.4063, since the 7 5/8 Treasury was the cheapest to deliver; had the 10 3/8 Treasury been the cheapest to deliver, it has been

---

[7]An alternative procedure is to compute the implied (break-even) repo rate. This rate is the yield that would produce no profit or loss if the bond were purchased and a futures contract were sold against the bond. The cheapest-to-deliver bond is the one with the largest implied repo rate.

estimated that the futures price would have been 92.51595 on that date.[8] The difference in the futures price based on the deliverable is 24/32. Thus a change in the cheapest to deliver can dramatically alter the futures price. Because of this, there will be a divergence between the theoretical futures price and the actual futures price. The second reason for this divergence is the other delivery options granted the short. Finally, there are biases in the CBT conversion factors.[9]

Deliverable Is a Basket of Securities. The municipal index futures contract is a cash settlement contract based on a basket of securities. The difficulty in arbitraging this futures contracts is that it is too expensive to buy or sell every bond included in the index. Instead, a portfolio containing a smaller number of bonds may be constructed to "track" the index.[10] The arbitrage, however, is no longer risk-free because there is the risk that the portfolio will not track the index exactly.[11] This is referred to as *tracking error risk.* A problem in constructing the portfolio so that the arbitrage can be performed is that the composition of the index is revised periodically. Therefore, anyone using this arbitrage trade must constantly monitor the index and periodically rebalance the constructed portfolio.

APPLICATIONS TO PORTFOLIO MANAGEMENT

This section describes various ways in which a money manager can utilize interest rate futures contracts.

[8]See Marcelle Arak, Laurie S. Goodman, and Susan Ross, "The Cheapest to Deliver on the Treasury Bond Futures Contract," *Advances in Futures and Options Research,* Vol. 1, Part B (1986), pp. 49–74.

[9]For a further discussion, see Arak, Goodman, and Ross, "The Cheapest to Deliver on the Treasury Bond Futures Contract"; James F. Meisner and John W. Labuszewski, "Treasury Bond Futures Delivery Bias," *Journal of Futures Market,* Winter 1984, pp. 569–572, and Laura F. Kodres, "Biases Toward the Cheapest to Deliver Bond," unpublished working paper, Northwestern University, 1984.

[10]There are several techniques that can be used to construct this tracking portfolio. These techniques are described in Chapter 13.

[11]The boundaries for the municipal index futures contract are presented in Marcelle Arak, Philip Fischer, Laurie Goodman, and Raj Daryanani, "The MOB: Pricing and Arbitrage," in Frank J. Fabozzi and T. Dessa Garlicki, eds., *Advances in Bond Analysis and Portfolio Strategies* (Chicago, IL: Probus Publishing, 1987).

Changing the Duration of the Portfolio

Money managers who have strong expectations about the direction of the future course of interest rates will adjust the duration of their portfolio to capitalize on their expectations. Specifically, if they expect interest rates to increase, they will shorten the duration of the portfolio; if they expect interest rates to decrease, they will lengthen the duration of the portfolio. Also, anyone using the structured portfolio strategies that we will describe in Chapters 13 and 14 must periodically adjust the portfolio duration to match the duration of some benchmark.

While money managers can alter the duration of their portfolios with cash market instruments, a quick and less expensive means for doing so (on either a temporary or a permanent basis) is to use futures contracts. By buying futures contracts on Treasury bonds or notes, they can increase the duration of the portfolio. Conversely, they can shorten the duration of the portfolio by selling futures contracts on Treasury bonds or notes.

The formula that can be used to approximate the number of futures contracts necessary to adjust the portfolio duration to a new level is:[12]

$$(11.4) \quad \text{Approximate number of contracts} = \frac{(D_T - D_I)P_I}{D_F P_F}$$

where

D_T = target modified duration for the portfolio
D_I = initial modified duration for the portfolio
D_F = modified duration for the futures contract
P_I = initial market value of the portfolio
P_F = market value of the futures contract

Notice that if the money manager wishes to increase the duration, then D_T will be greater than D_I and equation (11.4) will have a positive sign. This means that futures contracts will be purchased. The opposite is true if the objective is to shorten the portfolio duration.

---

[12]This is derived in Frank J. Jones and Beth Krumholz, "Duration Adjustment and Asset Allocation with Treasury Bond and Note Futures Contracts," in *Advances in Bond Analysis and Portfolio Strategies*.

Asset Allocation

A pension sponsor may wish to alter the composition of the pension's funds assets between stocks and bonds. An efficient means of changing asset allocation is to use financial futures contracts—interest rate futures and stock index futures.[13]

To determine the approximate number of interest rate futures contracts needed to change the market value of the portfolio allocated to bonds, assuming that the duration of the portfolio is to remain constant, the following formula can be used:[14]

$$(11.5) \quad \frac{\text{Approximate number}}{\text{of contracts}} = \frac{(P_T - P_I)D_I}{D_F P_F}$$

where P_T = target market value allocated to bonds

Notice that if the market value of the portfolio allocated to bonds is to be increased, the numerator of equation (11.5) will be positive. This means that futures contracts will be purchased. If funds are to be reallocated to stocks and withdrawn from bonds, then the numerator of equation (11.5) will be negative, which means that interest rate futures contracts will be sold.

Creating Synthetic Securities for Yield Enhancement

A cash market security that is the deliverable for a futures contract can be synthetically created by using a position in the futures contract. The yield on the synthetic security should be the same as the yield on the cash market security. If there is a difference between the two yields, it can be exploited so as to enhance the yield on the portfolio.

To see how, consider an investor who owns a 20-year Treasury bond and sells Treasury futures that call for the delivery of that particular bond 3 months from now. While the maturity of the Treasury bond owned is 20 years, the investor has effectively shortened the maturity of the bond to 3 months because it will be delivered then.

[13]See Roger Clarke, "Asset Allocation Using Futures," Chap. 16 in Robert Arnott and Frank J. Fabozzi, eds., *Asset Allocation* (Chicago, IL: Probus Publishing, 1988); and Mark Zurack and Ravi Dattatreya, "Asset Allocation Using Futures Contracts" Chap. 20 in Frank J. Fabozzi and Gregory Kipnis, eds., *The Handbook of Stock Index Futures and Options* (Homewood, IL: Dow Jones-Irwin, 1988).

[14]See Jones and Krumholz, "Duration Adjustment and Asset Allocation with Treasury Bond and Note Futures Contracts."

Consequently, the long position in the 20-year bond and the short futures position are equivalent to a long position in a 3-month riskless security. It is riskless since the investor is locking in the price that he will receive 3 months from now—the futures price. By being long the bond and short the futures, the investor has synthetically created a 3-month Treasury bill. What return should the investor expect to earn from this synthetic position? It should be the yield on a 3-month Treasury bill. If the yield on the synthetic 3-month Treasury bill is greater than the yield on the cash market Treasury bill, the investor will realize an enhanced yield by creating the synthetic short-term security described.

The fundamental relationship for creating synthetic securities is as follows:

(11.6) $RSP = CBP - FBP$

    where
    CBP = cash bond position
    FBP = bond futures position
    RSP = riskless security position

A negative sign before a position means a short position. In terms of our previous example, CBP is the long cash bond position, the negative sign before FBP refers to the short futures position, and RSP is the riskless 3-month security or Treasury bill.

Equation (11.6) states that an investor who is long the cash market security and short the futures contract should expect to earn the rate of return on a risk-free security with the same maturity as the futures contract. Solving equation (11.6) for the long bond position, we have:

(11.7) $CBP = RSP + FBP$

Equation (11.7) states that a cash bond position equals a riskless security position plus a long bond futures position. Thus a cash market bond can be synthetically created by buying a futures contract and investing in a Treasury bill.

Solving equation (11.7) for the bond futures position, we have:

(11.8) $FBP = CBP - RSP$

Equation (11.8) tells us that a long position in the futures contract can be synthetically created by taking a long position in the cash market bond and shorting the short-term riskless security. But shorting the short-term riskless security is equivalent to borrowing money. Notice that it was equation (11.8), that we used in deriving the theoretical futures price when the futures was underpriced. Recall that when the futures price was 92, the strategy to obtain an arbitrage profit was to buy the futures contract and buy the bond with borrowed funds. This is precisely what equation (11.8) states. In this case, instead of creating a synthetic cash market instrument as we did with equations (11.6) and (11.7), we have created a synthetic futures contract. The fact that the synthetic long futures position offered a higher profit than the long futures position provided an arbitrage opportunity.

If we multiply both sides of equations (11.6), (11.7), and (11.8) by a negative sign, we can see how a short futures position can be synthetically created.

In an efficient market these opportunities for yield enhancement should not exist very long. But even in the absence of yield enhancement, synthetic securities can be used by money managers to hedge a portfolio position that they find difficult to hedge in the cash market either because of lack of liquidity or because of other imposed constraints.[15]

Hedging

Hedging with futures involves employing a futures position as a temporary substitute for transactions to be made in the cash market at a later date. Hedging attempts to eliminate price risk by trying to fix the price of a transaction to be made at a later date. If cash and futures prices move together, any loss realized by the hedger from one position (whether cash or futures) will be offset by a profit on the other position. When the profit and loss from each position are equal, the hedge is referred to as a *perfect* hedge.

In practice, hedging is not that simple. The amount of the loss and profit from each position will not necessarily be identical. The outcome of a hedge will depend on the relationship between the cash price and

---

[15]For a more detailed discussion of synthetic securities, see Robert W. Kopprasch, Cal Johnson, and Armand H. Tatevossian, "Strategies for the Asset Manager: Hedging and the Creation of Synthetic Assets," in *Advanced in Bond Analysis and Portfolio Strategies*, and Robert P. Lecky, "Synthetic Asset Strategies," in Frank J. Fabozzi,ed., *Fixed Income Portfolio Strategies* (Chicago, IL: Probus Publishing, 1989).

the futures price when a hedge is placed and when it is lifted. The difference between the cash price and the futures price is called the *basis*. The risk that the basis will change in a way that adversely impacts the hedge is called *basis risk*.

In most hedging applications the bond to be hedged is not identical to the bond underlying the futures contract. This kind of hedging is referred to as *cross hedging*. There may be substantial basis risk in cross hedging. An unhedged position is exposed to price risk, the risk that the cash market price will move adversely. A hedged position substitutes basis risk for price risk.

A *short* (or *sell*) *hedge* is used to protect against a decline in the cash price of a fixed-income security resulting from an increase in interest rates. To execute a short hedge, futures contracts are sold. By establishing a short hedge, the hedger has fixed the future cash price and transferred the price risk of ownership to the buyer of the futures contract. As an example of why a short hedge would be executed, suppose that a pension fund manager knows that bonds must be liquidated in 40 days to make a $5 million payment to the beneficiaries of the pension fund. If interest rates rise during the 40-day period, more bonds will have to be liquidated to realize $5 million. To guard against this possibility, the hedger will sell bonds in the futures market at the exercise price to lock in a selling price.

A *long* (or *buy*) *hedge* is undertaken to protect against an increase in the cash price of a fixed-income security resulting from a decline in interest rates. In a long hedge the hedger buys a futures contract to lock in a purchase price. A pension fund manager may use a long hedge when substantial cash contributions are expected and the manager is concerned that interest rates will fall. Also, a money manager who knows that bonds are maturing in the near future and expects that interest rates will fall can employ a long hedge to lock in a rate. In both cases, a fall in interest rates means that when the proceeds are received, they must be invested at a lower interest rate.

What is the yield that should be earned on a hedged portfolio? Equation (11.6) tells us that taking a long position in the bonds and a short position in the futures is equivalent to taking a long position in a short-term security. Therefore the short-term rate should be realized.

In hedging a bond position, a money manager wants to take a futures position such that any loss in the cash market position will be offset by the gain in the futures position. To do so, the *dollar* price volatility of the futures position must equal the *dollar* price volatility of the position to be hedged. The objective of the hedge can be stated as follows:

Dollar price change of the security to be hedged
= − Dollar price change of futures position

The dollar price change of the futures position will depend on the dollar price change of the deliverable security. In the case of futures on Treasury bond and notes, the deliverable security is the cheapest to deliver.

There are four problems that the money manager encounters:

1. For a given change in yield, the dollar price volatility of the security to be hedged will not necessarily be equal to the dollar price volatility for the deliverable security. For example, if yields change by 50 basis points, the price of the cash market position may change by X, while the price of the deliverable security may change by more or less than X.

2. The factors that result in a change in the yield of a given number of basis points for the security to be hedged may not result in a change of the same number of basis points for the deliverable security. That is, if yields change by x basis points for the security to be hedged, the yield for the deliverable security may change by more or less than x basis points.

3. When the hedge is placed, the basis between the deliverable security and the futures price is known. When the hedge is lifted, the basis may change in such a way as to adversely impact the hedge.

4. In the case of Treasury bond and note futures, the cheapest to deliver may differ from the cheapest to deliver at time the hedge was placed.

Constructing the Hedge.   The objective in hedging can be restated as follows:

Dollar price change of the security to be hedged =
− Dollar price change of the futures contract ×

$$\frac{\text{Dollar price volatility of the security to be hedged}}{\text{Dollar price volatility of the futures contract}}$$

The last ratio is commonly referred to as the *hedge ratio*.

Three approaches can be used to compute the hedge ratio—the price value of a basis point, the yield value of a price change, and dollar duration. If properly applied, all three approaches give the same hedge ratio.

The hedge ratio can be computed using the price value of a basis point, as computed by the following formula:

$$\dfrac{\text{Price value of a basis point for the security to be hedged}}{\text{Price value of a basis point for the futures contract}} \times$$

$$\dfrac{\text{Change in yield for the security to be hedged}}{\text{Change in yield for the futures contract}}$$

The first ratio shows the price change for the security to be hedged relative to the price change for the deliverable security, both based on a yield change of 1 basis point. This corrects for the first problem we cited. The second ratio indicates the relative change in the yield of the fixed-income security and the futures contract (i.e., the cheapest to deliver in the case of Treasury bond and note futures). This ratio is commonly referred to as the *yield beta*. This adjustment is to correct for the second problem we cited, spread risk. We will discuss the yield beta later.

The hedge ratio can be rewritten as:

$$\dfrac{\text{Price value of a basis point for the security to be hedged}}{\text{Price value of a basis point for the futures contract}} \times \text{Yield beta}$$

The hedge ratio can be computed, using the yield value of a price change, from the following formula:

$$\dfrac{\text{Yield value of a price change for the futures contract}}{\text{Yield value of a price change for the security to be hedged}} \times \text{Yield beta}$$

Recall that modified duration indicates the percentage price volatility. In hedging, we are interested in *dollar* price changes. Consequently, to compute the hedge ratio using duration, dollar duration (which is modified duration times the price) must be used. The hedge ratio using dollar duration is computed as follows:

$$\frac{\text{Dollar duration of the security to be hedged}}{\text{Dollar duration of the futures contract}} \times \text{Yield beta}$$

When the first ratio is computed, consideration must be given to any embedded option in the security to be hedged that will affect the price movement of the security. In Chapter 8 we referred to this as *negative convexity*. For example, callable corporates and mortgage-backed securities have embedded call options that may result in negative convexity depending on the relationship between the coupon rate and market yields. Naively applying the price volatility measures without considering the impact of negative convexity may not only make the hedge ineffective, but could actually result in a loss that is considerably greater than would occur with an unhedged position.

Estimating the Yield Beta

The yield beta can be obtained from the following relationship:

Change in yield on security to be hedged =

$a + b$ (Change in yield on deliverable security) + error

The coefficient b is the yield beta. The above relationship is estimated using regression analysis based on historical observations on the yield changes in the security to be hedged and the deliverable security.

How effective this adjustment will be depends on the strength of the relationship. This can be measured by the coefficient of determination (R^2), a value that can range between 0 and 1. The stronger the relationship, the closer the coefficient of determination is to 1. If the coefficient of determination is low, then the security to be hedged and the deliverable security are not strongly related, and therefore the futures position will not do a good job of tracking the cash market position. Even if the two securities are highly correlated the relationship may not hold due to peculiarities affecting one but not both of the securities or if the relationship between the two securities changes over time.

SUMMARY

In this chapter we reviewed the current interest rate futures contracts traded and some nuances of these contracts. We then explained how the theoretical futures price can be determined using arbitrage arguments and factors that would cause the theoretical futures price and the actual futures price to diverge. Finally, we reviewed how futures can be employed in investment management to (1) alter a portfolio's duration, (2) change a fund's asset allocation, (3) create synthetic securities that may offer enhanced yields, and (4) hedge a portfolio position against adverse interest rate movements.

12

INTEREST RATE OPTIONS:
Contracts,
Investment Characteristics,
and Strategies

In earlier chapters we reviewed bonds that have embedded call options and discussed how to analyze such bonds. In this chapter we review exchange-traded and over-the-counter interest rate options. We explain risk-reward characteristics of basic naked option strategies and hedged option strategies. Then we discuss the factors that influence the price of an option and introduce the complex topic of option-pricing models.

OPTIONS ON CASH MARKET INSTRUMENTS

An option is a contract in which the writer of the option grants the buyer of the option the right to purchase from or sell to the writer a designated instrument at a specified price within a specified period of time. The writer, also referred to as the seller, grants this right to the buyer in exchange for a certain sum of money called the *option price* or *option premium*. The price at which the instrument may be bought or sold is called the *exercise* or *strike price*. The date after which an option is void is called the *expiration date*. An *American option* may be exercised at any time up to and including the expiration date. A *European option* may only be exercised on the expiration date.

When an option grants the buyer the right to purchase the designated instrument from the writer, it is called a *call option*. When the option buyer has the right to sell the designated instrument to the writer (seller), the option is called a *put option*. The buyer of any option is said to be *long the option;* the writer (seller) is said to be *short the option.*

The maximum amount that an option buyer can lose is the option price. The maximum profit that the option writer (seller) can realize is the option price. The option buyer has substantial upside return potential, while the option writer has substantial downside risk. We will investigate the risk/reward relationship for option positions later in this chapter.

Differences Between an Option and a Futures Contract

Notice that unlike a futures contract, the buyer of an option has the *right* but not the obligation to perform, while the option seller (writer) has the obligation to perform. Both the buyer and the seller are obligated to perform in the case of a futures contract. Also notice that in a futures contract, the buyer does not pay the seller to accept the obligation, whereas in the case of an option the buyer pays the seller the option price.

Consequently, the risk/reward characteristics of the two contracts are also different. In a futures contract the long position realizes a dollar-for-dollar gain when the price of the futures increases and suffers a dollar-for-dollar loss when the price of the futures decreases. The opposite occurs for the short position. In contrast, options do not provide a symmetric risk/reward relationship. The most that a long may lose is the option price; yet the long retains all the upside potential, although the gain is always reduced by the option price. The maximum profit that the short may realize is the option price, but this position has substantial downside risk.

Exchange-Traded Options on Cash Market Instruments

Options can be written on cash market instruments or futures. Let's look first at those on cash market instruments. Exchange-traded options on cash market instruments include: (1) options on individual common stock issues; (2) options on debt instruments; (3) options on stock indexes; (4) options on foreign exchange; and (5) options on commodities.

At one time there were several exchange-traded option contracts in which the underlying instrument was a debt instrument. For the reasons to be explained in the next section, these contracts were not as attractive as options on interest rate futures contracts. The most liquid exchange-traded option on a fixed-income instrument at the time of this writing is an option on Treasury bonds traded on the Chicago Board Options Exchange. For debt instruments, options on futures have been far more popular than options on the cash market instruments themselves.

Over-the-Counter Options on Treasuries and Mortgage-Backed Securities

Certain institutional investors who want to purchase an option on a specific Treasury security or a Ginnie Mae pass-through can do so on an over-the-counter basis. There are government and mortgage-backed securities dealers who make a market in options on specific securities.

Over-the-counter (or dealer) options are typically purchased by institutional investors who want to hedge the risk associated with owing a specific security. For example, a thrift may be interested in hedging its position in a specific mortgage pass-through security. Typically, the maturity of the option coincides with the time period over which the buyer of the option wants to hedge. Thus the buyer of an over-the-counter option is generally not concerned with the liquidity of the option.[1]

FUTURES OPTIONS

An option on a futures contract (commonly referred to as a *futures option*) gives the buyer the right to buy from or sell to the writer a designated futures contract at a designated price at any time during the life of the option. If the futures option is a call option, the buyer has the right to purchase one designated futures contract at the exercise price. That is, the buyer has the right to acquire a long futures position in the designated futures contract. If the call option is exercised by the buyer, the writer (seller) acquires a corresponding short position in the futures contract.

[1]For a further discussion of over-the-counter options, see Mark Pitts and Frank J. Fabozzi, *Interest Rate Options and Futures* (Chicago, IL: Probus Publishing, 1989).

A put option on a futures contract grants the buyer the right to sell one designated futures contract to the writer at the exercise price. That is, the option buyer has the right to acquire a short position in the designated futures contract. If the put option is exercised, the writer acquires a corresponding long position in the designated futures contract.

At the time of this writing, futures options are available on (1) interest rate futures contracts, (2) stock index futures contracts, (3) currency futures contracts, and (4) commodities futures contracts. Futures options are available on all the interest rate futures contracts reviewed in the previous chapter.

Mechanics of Trading

Exercising a Futures Option.   Since the parties to the futures option will realize a position in a futures contract when the option is exercised, the question is: What will the futures price be? That is, at what price will the long be required to pay for the instrument underlying the futures contract and at what price will the short be required to sell the instrument underlying the futures contract?

Upon exercise, the futures price for the futures contract will be set equal to the current futures price. For a call futures option, the option writer must pay the difference between the current futures price and the exercise price to the buyer of the option. In the case of a put futures option, the option writer must pay the option buyer the difference between the exercise price and the current futures price.

For example, suppose an investor buys a call option on some futures contract in which the exercise price is 85. Assume also that the futures price is currently 95 and that the buyer exercises the call option. The buyer will then have a long position in the futures contract with a futures price of 95; the option writer will have a short position in the same futures contract at a price of 95. In addition, the option writer must pay the buyer 10 (95 − 85).

Suppose, instead, that the futures option is a put and the current futures price is 60 rather than 95. If the buyer of this put option exercised it, the buyer would have a short position in the futures contract at 60; the option writer would have a long position in the futures contract at 60. The writer of the option would pay the buyer 25, the difference between the exercise price of 85 and the current futures price of 60.

Notice that unlike an option on a cash market instrument, in which exercise requires the exchange of dollars equal to the exercise price, the only cash that is exchanged upon exercising a futures option is the difference between the exercise and the current futures price.

Margin Requirements. There are no margin requirements for the buyer of a futures option once the option price has been paid in full. There is no need for margin because the option price is the maximum amount that the buyer can lose regardless of how adverse the price movement of the underlying instrument.

Because the writer (seller) of an option has agreed to accept all of the risk (and none of the reward) of the position in the underlying instrument, the writer (seller) is required to deposit not only the margin required on the interest rate futures contract position, if that is the underlying instrument, but also (with certain exceptions) the option price that he received for writing the option. In addition, as prices adversely affect the writer's position, the writer may be required to deposit additional margin as it is marked to market.

Reasons for the Popularity of Futures Options

There are three reasons why futures options on fixed-income securities have replaced options on cash market instruments as the options vehicles used by institutional investors.[2] First, unlike options on fixed-income securities, futures options on Treasury note and bond futures do not require making payments for accrued interest. Consequently, when a futures option is exercised, the call buyer and the put writer need not compensate the other party for accrued interest.

Second, futures options are believed to be "cleaner instruments" because of the reduced likelihood of delivery squeezes. Market participants who must deliver an instrument are concerned that at the time of delivery the instrument to be delivered will be in short supply, resulting in a higher price to acquire it. Since the deliverable supply of futures contracts is more than adequate for futures options currently traded, there is no concern with a delivery squeeze.

---

[2]Laurie Goodman, "Introduction to Debt Options," Chap. 1 in Frank J. Fabozzi, ed., *Winning the Interest Rate Game: A Guide to Debt Options* (Chicago, IL: Probus Publishing, 1985), pp. 13–14.

Finally, for purposes of pricing any option, it is imperative to know at all times the price of the underlying instrument. In the bond market current prices are not as easily available to traders as price information on the futures contract.

THE INTRINSIC VALUE AND TIME VALUE OF AN OPTION

The cost to the buyer of an option is primarily a reflection of the option's *intrinsic value* and any additional amount over that value. The premium over intrinsic value is often referred to as *time value*.

Intrinsic Value of an Option

The intrinsic value of an option is the economic value of the option if it is exercised immediately. Since the buyer of an option need not exercise the option, and, in fact, will not do so if no economic gain will result from exercising it, the intrinsic value cannot be less than zero.

Call Options.   The intrinsic value of a call option on an interest rate futures contract is the difference between the current futures price and the strike price. For example, if the *strike price* for a call option is $100 and the *current futures price* is $105, the intrinsic value is $5. That is, if the option buyer exercised the option and simultaneously sold the futures, the option buyer would realize $105 from the sale of the futures, which would be covered by acquiring the futures from the option writer for $100, thereby netting a $5 gain.

When a call option has intrinsic value, it is said to be "in the money." Our call option with a strike price of $100 is in the money when the price of the underlying futures contract is greater than $100. When the strike price of a call option exceeds the current futures price, the call option is said to be "out of the money" and has no intrinsic value. An option for which the strike price is equal to the current futures price is said to be "at the money." Both at-the-money and out-of-the-money options have an intrinsic value of zero since it is not profitable to exercise the option.

Put Options.   For a put option, the intrinsic value is equal to the amount by which the current futures price is below the strike price. For example, if the strike price of a put option is $100 and the current futures price is $92, the intrinsic value is $8. That is, if the buyer of the put option exercises the put option and simultaneously sells the futures contract, he will net $8 because the futures contract will be sold to the writer for $100 and purchased in the market for $92.

When the put option has intrinsic value, the option is said to be in the money. For our put option with a strike price of $100, the option will be in the money when the futures price is less than $100. A put option is out of the money when the current futures price exceeds the strike price. A put option is at the money when the strike price is equal to the futures price.

Time Value of an Option

The time value of an option is the amount by which the option price exceeds the intrinsic value. The option buyer hopes that at some time prior to expiration, changes in the market yields will increase the value of the rights conveyed by the option. For this prospect, the option buyer is willing to pay a premium above the intrinsic value. For example, if the price of a call option with a strike price of $100 is $9 when the current futures price is $105, the time value of this option is $4 ($9 minus the intrinsic value of $5). If the current futures price is $90 instead of $105, then the time value of this option is $9 since the option has no intrinsic value.

There are two ways in which an option buyer may realize the value of a position taken in the option. First, he may exercise the option. As we explained earlier in this chapter, by exercising he will be assigned a position in the underlying futures contract at the current futures price and be paid by the writer any difference between the current futures price and the strike price. The investor can then sell the futures contract at the current price. For example, for our hypothetical call option with a strike price of $100 and an option price of $9, in which the current futures price is $105, the option buyer can exercise the option. This will give him a long position in the futures contract currently at $105. The call writer will pay the buyer $5 (the difference between the current futures price of $105 and the strike price of $100). By simultaneously selling the underlying futures for $105, the option buyer will realize $5.

The second way of realizing the value of an option position is by selling the call option for $9. Obviously, this is the preferable alternative because the exercise of an option will cause the immediate loss of any time value (in this case, $4).

Whether any option will be exercised prior to the expiration date depends on whether the total proceeds at the expiration date would be greater by holding the option or by exercising and reinvesting any cash proceeds received until the expiration date.

PROFIT AND LOSS PROFILES FOR SIMPLE NAKED OPTION STRATEGIES

To appreciate the opportunities available with interest rate options, the profit and loss profiles for various option strategies must be understood. We begin with simple strategies in only one option on a bond, which are referred to as *naked option strategies*. That is, no other position is taken in another option or bond. *The profit and loss profiles that we present assume that each option position is held to the expiration date and not exercised early.* Also, to simplify the illustrations, we assume that there are no transaction costs to implement the strategies.

The four naked option strategies that we illustrate are: (1) long call strategy (buying call options); (2) short call strategy (selling or writing call options); (3) long put strategy (buying put options); and (4) short put strategy (selling or writing put options).

Long Call Strategy (Buying Call Options)

The most straightforward option strategy for participating in an anticipated decrease in interest rates (increase in the price of bonds) is to buy a call option on a debt instrument. This is called a *long call strategy*.

To illustrate this strategy, assume that there is a call option on a particular 8% coupon bond with a par value of $100 and 20 years and 1 month to maturity. The call option expires in 1 month and the strike price is $100. The option price is $3. While this option is an option on a cash market security, the principles apply equally to futures options.

Suppose that the current price of the bond is $100 (i.e., the bond is selling at par), which means that the yield on this bond is currently 8%. Since the strike price is equal to the current price of the bond, this option is at the money. What would the profit or loss be for the investor who purchased this call option and held it to the expiration date?

The profit and loss from the strategy will depend on the price of the bond at the expiration date. The price, in turn, will depend on the yield on 20-year bonds with an 8% coupon, since in 1 month the bond will have only 20 years to maturity. Exhibit 12.1 shows the price of a 20-year, 8% coupon bond for interest rates ranging from 4% to 12%. The following outcomes are possible:

1. If the price of the bond at the expiration date is less than $100 (which means that the market yield is greater than 8%), then the investor would not exercise the option. (Why bother exercising the option and paying the option writer $100 when the same bond can be purchased in the market at a lower price?) In this case, the option buyer will lose the entire option price of $3. Notice, however, that this is the maximum loss that the option buyer will realize regardless of how far the price of the bond declines.

2. If the price of the bond is equal to $100 (which means that the market yield is unchanged at 8%), no economic value will result from exercising the option. As in the outcome where the price of the bond is less than $100, the buyer of this call option will lose the entire option price, $3.

3. If the price of the bond is greater than $100 but less than $103 (which means that the market yield is less than 8% but greater than 7.70%—see Exhibit 12.1), the option buyer will exercise the option. By exercising, the option buyer purchases the bond for $100 (the strike price) and can sell it in the market for a higher price. Suppose, for example, the market yield is 7.8%, so that the price of the bond is about $102 at the expiration date. The buyer of this call option will realize a $2 gain by exercising the option. However, the cost of purchasing the call option was $3. Hence $1 is the total loss on this strategy. If the investor failed to exercise the option, he would have lost $3.

4. If the price of the bond at the expiration date is equal to $103 (a market yield of about 7.70%), the investor will exercise the option. In this case, the investor breaks even, realizing a gain of $3 on the bond, which offsets the cost of the option, $3. Although he has no net gain, he has recouped the price of the option.

5. If the price of the bond at the expiration date is greater than $103 (a market yield of less than 7.70%), the investor will exercise the option and realize a profit. For example, if the price of the bond is $113 because the market yield has declined from 8% to 6.8%, exercising the option will generate a profit on the bond of $13. Reducing this gain by the cost of the option ($3) means that the investor will realize a net profit from this strategy of $10.

EXHIBIT 12.1   Price/Yield Relationship for a 20-Year, 8% Coupon Bond

Yield	Price	Yield	Price
4.0	154.71	8.1	99.02
4.2	151.08	8.2	98.05
4.4	147.56	8.3	97.10
4.6	144.15	8.4	96.16
4.8	140.85	8.5	95.23
5.0	137.65	8.6	94.32
5.2	134.56	8.7	93.42
5.4	131.56	8.8	92.53
5.6	128.66	8.9	91.66
5.8	125.84	9.0	90.80
6.0	123.11	9.1	89.95
6.1	121.78	9.2	89.11
6.2	120.47	9.3	88.29
6.3	119.18	9.4	87.48
6.4	117.91	9.5	86.68
6.5	116.66	9.6	85.89
6.6	115.42	9.7	85.11
6.7	114.21	9.8	84.34
6.8	113.01	9.9	83.59
6.9	111.84	10.0	82.84
7.0	110.68	10.2	81.38
7.1	109.54	10.4	79.96
7.2	108.41	10.6	78.58
7.3	107.30	10.8	77.24
7.4	106.21	11.0	75.93
7.5	105.14	11.2	74.66
7.6	104.08	11.4	73.42
7.7	103.04	11.6	72.22
7.8	102.01	11.8	71.05
7.9	101.00	12.0	69.91
8.0	100.00		

Exhibit 12.2 shows the profit/loss in tabular form for the buyer of the hypothetical call option, while Exhibit 12.3 graphically portrays the profit and loss profile. While the break-even point and the loss will depend on the option price and the strike price, the shape shown in Exhibit 12.3 will hold for all buyers of call options. That shape indicates that the maximum loss is the option price and yet there is substantial upside potential.

It is worthwhile to compare the profit and loss profile of a call

EXHIBIT 12.2   Profit/Loss Profile for a Long Call Strategy

Assumptions:
Call option price   = 3
Strike price   = 100
Time to expiration = 1 month

| At expiration date: | | | At expiration date: | | |
Market Yield	Price of Bond	Net Profit	Market Yield	Price of Bond	Net Profit
4.0	154.71	51.71	8.1	99.02	−3.00
4.2	151.08	48.08	8.2	98.05	−3.00
4.4	147.56	44.56	8.3	97.10	−3.00
4.6	144.15	41.15	8.4	96.16	−3.00
4.8	140.85	37.85	8.5	95.23	−3.00
5.0	137.65	34.65	8.6	94.32	−3.00
5.2	134.56	31.56	8.7	93.42	−3.00
5.4	131.56	28.56	8.8	92.53	−3.00
5.6	128.66	25.66	8.9	91.66	−3.00
5.8	125.84	22.84	9.0	90.80	−3.00
6.0	123.11	20.11	9.1	89.95	−3.00
6.1	121.78	18.78	9.2	89.11	−3.00
6.2	120.47	17.47	9.3	88.29	−3.00
6.3	119.18	16.18	9.4	87.48	−3.00
6.4	117.91	14.91	9.5	86.68	−3.00
6.5	116.66	13.66	9.6	85.89	−3.00
6.6	115.42	12.42	9.7	85.11	−3.00
6.7	114.21	11.21	9.8	84.34	−3.00
6.8	113.01	10.01	9.9	83.59	−3.00
6.9	111.84	8.84	10.0	82.84	−3.00
7.0	110.68	7.68	10.2	81.38	−3.00
7.1	109.54	6.54	10.4	79.96	−3.00
7.2	108.41	5.41	10.6	78.58	−3.00
7.3	107.30	4.30	10.8	77.24	−3.00
7.4	106.21	3.21	11.0	75.93	−3.00
7.5	105.14	2.14	11.2	74.66	−3.00
7.6	104.08	1.08	11.4	73.42	−3.00
7.7	103.04	0.04	11.6	72.22	−3.00
7.8	102.01	−0.99	11.8	71.05	−3.00
7.9	101.00	−2.00	12.0	69.91	−3.00
8.0	100.00	−3.00			

option buyer to a long bond strategy in the same bond. The payoff from the strategy depends on the price of the bond at the expiration date, which, in turn, depends on the market yield at the expiration date.

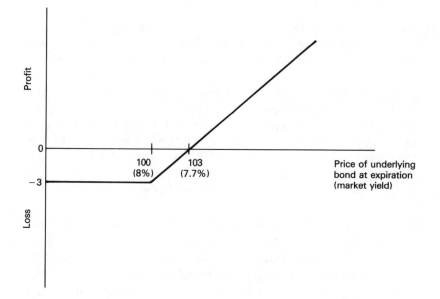

EXHIBIT 12.3   Profit/Loss Diagram for a Long Call Strategy

Consider again the five price outcomes given above:

1. If the price of the bond at the expiration date is less than $100 (market yield rises above 8%), then the investor would lose the entire option price of $3. In contrast, a long bond position will have one of the following three possible outcomes:

    a. If the price of the bond is less than $100 (market yield greater than 8%) but greater than $97 (market yield less than about 8.3%), the loss on the long bond position will be less than $3.

    b. If the price of the bond is $97 (market yield of about 8.3%), the loss on the long bond position will be $3.

    c. If the price of the bond is less than $97, the loss on the long bond position will be greater than $3. For example, if the price at the expiration date is $80 because the market yield has risen to 10.4%, the long bond position will result in a loss of $20.

2. If the price of the bond is equal to $100 because the market yield is unchanged, the buyer of the call option will realize a loss of $3 (the cost of the option). There will be no gain or loss on the long bond position.

3. If the price of the bond is greater than $100 because the market yield has fallen below 8% but less than $103 (market yield above 7.70%), the option buyer will realize a loss of less than $3, while the long bond position will realize a profit.

4.   If the market yield falls to about 7.70% so that the price of the bond at the expiration date is equal to $103, there will be no loss or gain from buying the call option. The long bond position will produce a gain of $3.

5.   If the price of the bond at the expiration date is greater than $103 because the market yield has fallen below 7.7%, both the call option buyer and the long bond position will result in a profit. However, the profit for the buyer of the call option will be $3 less than that on the long bond position. For example, if the market yield falls to 6.8% so that the price of the bond is $113, the profit from the long call position is $10 while the profit from the long bond position is $13.

Exhibit 12.4 compares the long call strategy and the long bond strategy. This comparison clearly demonstrates the way in which an option can change the risk/return profile available to investors. An investor who takes a long position in the bond realizes a profit of $1 for every $1 increase in the price of the bond as the market yield falls. However, as the market yield rises, this investor loses dollar for dollar. So if the price decreases by more than $3, this strategy will result in a loss of more than $3. The long call strategy, in contrast, limits the loss to only the option price of $3, but retains the upside potential, which will be $3 less than for the long bond position.

We can also use this hypothetical call option to see the speculative appeal of options. Suppose an investor has strong expectations that market yields will fall in 3 months. With an option price of $3, the speculator can purchase 33.33 call options for each $100 invested. Thus, if the market yield declines, the investor realizes the price appreciation associated with 33.33 bonds of $100 par each (or $3,333 par). However, with the same $100, the investor could only buy one $100 par value bond and realize the appreciation associated with that one bond if the market yield declines. Now, suppose that in 1 month the market yield declines to 6% so that the price of the bond increases to $123.11. The long call strategy will result in a profit of $670.26 ($23.11 × 33.33 − $100), or a return of 670% on the $100 investment in the call options. The long bond strategy will result in a profit of $23.11, or a 23% return on $100. It is this greater leverage that an option buyer can achieve that attracts investors to options when they wish to speculate on interest rate movements. However, the drawbacks should be highlighted. Suppose that the market yield is unchanged at the expiration date so that the price of the bond is $100. The long call strategy will result in the

EXHIBIT 12.4   Comparison of a Long Call Strategy and Long Bond Strategy

Assumptions:
Current price of bond = 100
Call option price   = 3
Strike price   = 100
Time to expiration   = 1 month

At expiration date:		Profit:	
Market Yield	Price of Bond	Long Call	Long Bond
4.0	154.71	51.71	54.71
4.2	151.08	48.08	51.08
4.4	147.56	44.56	47.56
4.6	144.15	41.15	44.15
4.8	140.85	37.85	40.85
5.0	137.65	34.65	37.65
5.2	134.56	31.56	34.56
5.4	131.56	28.56	31.56
5.6	128.66	25.66	28.66
5.8	125.84	22.84	25.84
6.0	123.11	20.11	23.11
6.1	121.78	18.78	21.78
6.2	120.47	17.47	20.47
6.3	119.18	16.18	19.18
6.4	117.91	14.91	17.91
6.5	116.66	13.66	16.66
6.6	115.42	12.42	15.42
6.7	114.21	11.21	14.21
6.8	113.01	10.01	13.01
6.9	111.84	8.84	11.84
7.0	110.68	7.68	10.68
7.1	109.54	6.54	9.54
7.2	108.41	5.41	8.41
7.3	107.30	4.30	7.30
7.4	106.21	3.21	6.21
7.5	105.14	2.14	5.14
7.6	104.08	1.08	4.08
7.7	103.04	0.04	3.04
7.8	102.01	−0.99	2.01
7.9	101.00	−2.00	1.00
8.0	100.00	−3.00	0.00
8.1	99.02	−3.00	−0.98
8.2	98.05	−3.00	−1.95
8.3	97.10	−3.00	−2.90

EXHIBIT 12.4 (Continued)

At expiration date:		Profit:	
Market Yield	Price of Bond	Long Call	Long Bond
8.4	96.16	−3.00	−3.84
8.5	95.23	−3.00	−4.77
8.6	94.32	−3.00	−5.68
8.7	93.42	−3.00	−6.58
8.8	92.53	−3.00	−7.47
8.9	91.66	−3.00	−8.34
9.0	90.80	−3.00	−9.20
9.1	89.95	−3.00	−10.05
9.2	89.11	−3.00	−10.89
9.3	88.29	−3.00	−11.71
9.4	87.48	−3.00	−12.52
9.5	86.68	−3.00	−13.32
9.6	85.89	−3.00	−14.11
9.7	85.11	−3.00	−14.89
9.8	84.34	−3.00	−15.66
9.9	83.59	−3.00	−16.41
10.0	82.84	−3.00	−17.16
10.2	81.38	−3.00	−18.62
10.4	79.96	−3.00	−20.04
10.6	78.58	−3.00	−21.42
10.8	77.24	−3.00	−22.76
11.0	75.93	−3.00	−24.07
11.2	74.66	−3.00	−25.34
11.4	73.42	−3.00	−26.58
11.6	72.22	−3.00	−27.78
11.8	71.05	−3.00	−28.95
12.0	69.91	−3.00	−30.09

loss of the entire investment of $100, while the long bond strategy will produce neither a gain nor a loss.

Short Call Strategy
(Selling or Writing Call Options)

An investor who believes that interest rates will rise or change very little can, if his expectations prove correct, realize income by writing (selling) a call option. This strategy is called a *short call strategy*.

To illustrate this option strategy we shall use the same call option we used to demonstrate the long call strategy. The profit and loss profile of the short call strategy (the position of the call option writer) is the mirror image of the profit and loss profile of the long call strategy (the position of the call option buyer). That is, the profit (loss) of the short call position for any given price of the bond at the expiration date is the same as the loss (profit) of the long call position. Consequently, the maximum profit that the short call strategy can produce is the option price. But the maximum loss is limited only by how high the price of the bond can increase (i.e., how low the market yield can fall) by the expiration date, less the option price. Exhibit 12.5 diagrams the profit/loss profile for a short call strategy.

Long Put Strategy (Buying Put Options)

The most straightforward option strategy for benefiting from an expected increase in interest rates is to buy a put option. This strategy is called a *long put strategy.*

To illustrate this strategy, we'll assume a hypothetical put option for an 8% coupon bond with a par value of $100, 20 years and 1 month to maturity, and a strike price of $100 that is selling for $2. The current price of the bond is $100 (yield of 8%); hence the put option is at the

EXHIBIT 12.5   Profit/Loss Profile Diagram for a Short Call Strategy

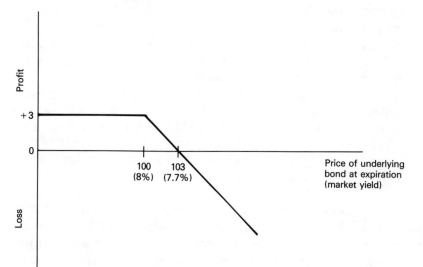

money. The profit or loss for this strategy at the expiration date depends on the market yield at the time. The following outcomes are possible:

1. If the price of the bond is greater than $100 because the market yield has fallen below 8%, the buyer of the put option will not exercise it because exercising would mean selling the bond to the writer for a price that is less than the current market price. Consequently, a loss of $2 (the option price) will result from the long put strategy. Once again, the option price represents the maximum loss to which the buyer of the put option is exposed.

2. If the price of the bond at expiration is equal to $100 because the market yield has remained at 8%, the put will not be exercised, leaving the long put position with a loss equal to the option price of $2.

3. Any price for the bond that is less than $100 because the market yield has risen above 8% but greater than $98 (market yield of approximately 8.2%) will result in a loss; however, by exercising the put option, the loss will be less than the option price of $2. For example, suppose that the market yield rises to 8.6%, resulting in a price of $99.03 for the bond at the expiration date. By exercising the option, the option buyer will realize a loss of $1.03. This is because the buyer of the put option can sell the bond, which he can purchase in the market for $99.03, to the writer for $100, realizing a gain of $0.97. Deducting the $2 cost of the option results in a loss of $1.03.

4. At a $98 price for the bond (a market yield of roughly 8.2%) at the expiration date, the long put strategy will break even: the investor will realize a gain of $2 by selling the bond to the writer of the option for $100, offsetting the cost of the option ($2).

5. If the market yield rises above 8.2% so that the price of the bond is below $98 at the expiration date, the long put position will realize a profit. For example, if the market yield rises 260 basis points (from 8% to 10.6%), the price of the bond at expiration will be $78.58. The long put strategy will produce a profit of $19.42: a gain of $21.42 on the bond less the $2 option price.

The profit and loss profile for the long put strategy is shown in tabular form in Exhibit 12.6 and in graphic form in Exhibit 12.7. As with all long option positions, the loss is limited to the option price. However, the profit potential is substantial: the theoretical maximum profit being generated if the bond price falls to zero.

EXHIBIT 12.6   Profit/Loss Profile for a Long Put Strategy

Assumptions:
Put option price   = 2
Strike price   = 100
Time to expiration = 1 month

| At expiration date: | | | At expiration date: | | |
Market Yield	Price of Bond	Net Profit	Market Yield	Price of Bond	Net Profit
4.0	154.71	−2.00	8.1	99.02	−1.02
4.2	151.08	−2.00	8.2	98.05	−0.05
4.4	147.56	−2.00	8.3	97.10	0.90
4.6	144.15	−2.00	8.4	96.16	1.84
4.8	140.85	−2.00	8.5	95.23	2.77
5.0	137.65	−2.00	8.6	94.32	3.68
5.2	134.56	−2.00	8.7	93.42	4.58
5.4	131.56	−2.00	8.8	92.53	5.47
5.6	128.66	−2.00	8.9	91.66	6.34
5.8	125.84	−2.00	9.0	90.80	7.20
6.0	123.11	−2.00	9.1	89.95	8.05
6.1	121.78	−2.00	9.2	89.11	8.89
6.2	120.47	−2.00	9.3	88.29	9.71
6.3	119.18	−2.00	9.4	87.48	10.52
6.4	117.91	−2.00	9.5	86.68	11.32
6.5	116.66	−2.00	9.6	85.89	12.11
6.6	115.42	−2.00	9.7	85.11	12.89
6.7	114.21	−2.00	9.8	84.34	13.66
6.8	113.01	−2.00	9.9	83.59	14.41
6.9	111.84	−2.00	10.0	82.84	15.16
7.0	110.68	−2.00	10.2	81.38	16.62
7.1	109.54	−2.00	10.4	79.96	18.04
7.2	108.41	−2.00	10.6	78.58	19.42
7.3	107.30	−2.00	10.8	77.24	20.76
7.4	106.21	−2.00	11.0	75.93	22.07
7.5	105.14	−2.00	11.2	74.66	23.34
7.6	104.08	−2.00	11.4	73.42	24.58
7.7	103.04	−2.00	11.6	72.22	25.78
7.8	102.01	−2.00	11.8	71.05	26.95
7.9	101.00	−2.00	12.0	69.91	28.09
8.0	100.00	−2.00			

Once again, we can see how an option alters the risk/return profile for an investor by comparing it to a position in the bond. In the case of a long put position, it would be compared to a short bond position, since both strategies realize profits if market yields rise (price

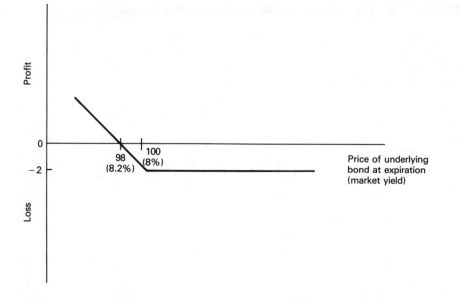

EXHIBIT 12.7 Profit/Loss Profile Diagram for a Long Put Strategy

falls). Suppose that an investor sold the bond short for $100. The short bond position would produce the following profit or loss as compared to the long put position:

1. If the price of the bond increases above $100 because the market yield declines, the long put option will result in a loss of $2, but the short bond position will realize one of the following:
    a. If the price of the bond is less than $102 because the market yield has fallen to below 7.80%, there will be a loss of less than $2.
    b. If the price of the bond is equal to $102, the loss will be $2, the same as for the long put strategy.
    c. If the price of the bond is greater than $102, the loss will be greater than $2. For example, if the price is $125.84 because market yields declined to 5.8%, the short bond position will realize a loss of $25.84, since the short seller must now pay $125.84 for a bond he sold short at $100.
2. If the price of the bond at expiration is equal to $100 because the market yield is unchanged, the long put strategy will realize a $2 loss, while there will be no profit or loss on the short bond strategy.
3. Any price for the bond that is less than $100 but greater than $98 (market yield of about 8.2%) will result in a loss of less than $2 for the

EXHIBIT 12.8   Comparison of a Long Put Strategy and a Short Bond Strategy

Assumptions:
Current price of bond = 100
Put option price   = 2
Strike price   = 100
Time to expiration   = 1 month

| At expiration date: | | Profit: | |
Market Yield	Price of Bond	Long Put	Short Bond
4.0	154.71	−2.00	−54.71
4.2	151.08	−2.00	−51.08
4.4	147.56	−2.00	−47.56
4.6	144.15	−2.00	−44.15
4.8	140.85	−2.00	−40.85
5.0	137.65	−2.00	−37.65
5.2	134.56	−2.00	−34.56
5.4	131.56	−2.00	−31.56
5.6	128.66	−2.00	−28.66
5.8	125.84	−2.00	−25.84
6.0	123.11	−2.00	−23.11
6.1	121.78	−2.00	−21.78
6.2	120.47	−2.00	−20.47
6.3	119.18	−2.00	−19.18
6.4	117.91	−2.00	−17.91
6.5	116.66	−2.00	−16.66
6.6	115.42	−2.00	−15.42
6.7	114.21	−2.00	−14.21
6.8	113.01	−2.00	−13.01
6.9	111.84	−2.00	−11.84
7.0	110.68	−2.00	−10.68
7.1	109.54	−2.00	−9.54
7.2	108.41	−2.00	−8.41
7.3	107.30	−2.00	−7.30
7.4	106.21	−2.00	−6.21
7.5	105.14	−2.00	−5.14
7.6	104.08	−2.00	−4.08
7.7	103.04	−2.00	−3.04
7.8	102.01	-2.00	−2.01
7.9	101.00	−2.00	−1.00
8.0	100.00	−2.00	0.00
8.1	99.02	−1.02	0.98
8.2	98.05	−0.05	1.95
8.3	97.10	0.90	2.90

EXHIBIT 12.8 (Continued)

At expiration date:		Profit:	
Market Yield	Price of Bond	Long Put	Short Bond
8.4	96.16	1.84	3.84
8.5	95.23	2.77	4.77
8.6	94.32	3.68	5.68
8.7	93.42	4.58	6.58
8.8	92.53	5.47	7.47
8.9	91.66	6.34	8.34
9.0	90.80	7.20	9.20
9.1	89.95	8.05	10.05
9.2	89.11	8.89	10.89
9.3	88.29	9.71	11.71
9.4	87.48	10.52	12.52
9.5	86.68	11.32	13.32
9.6	85.89	12.11	14.11
9.7	85.11	12.89	14.89
9.8	84.34	13.66	15.66
9.9	83.59	14.41	16.41
10.0	82.84	15.16	17.16
10.2	81.38	16.62	18.62
10.4	79.96	18.04	20.04
10.6	78.58	19.42	21.42
10.8	77.24	20.76	22.76
11.0	75.93	22.07	24.07
11.2	74.66	23.34	25.34
11.4	73.42	24.58	26.58
11.6	72.22	25.78	27.78
11.8	71.05	26.95	28.95
12.0	69.91	28.09	30.09

long put strategy but a profit for the short bond strategy. For example, a price of $99.02 (market yield of 8.1%) at the expiration date will result in a loss of $1.02 for the long put strategy but a profit of $0.98 for the short bond strategy.

4. At a $98 price for the bond at the expiration date, the long put strategy will break even, but the short bond strategy will generate a $2 profit.

5. At a price below $98 (market yield greater than 8.2%) both strategies will generate a profit. However, the profit will always be $2 less for the long put strategy.

Exhibit 12.8 is a tabular comparison of the profit and loss profile for the long put and short bond strategies. While the investor who pursues a short bond strategy participates in all the upside potential and faces all the downside risk, the long put strategy allows the investor to limit the downside risk to the option price while still maintaining upside potential. However, the upside potential is less than that for a short put position by an amount equal to the option price.

Short Put Strategy (Selling or Writing Put Options)

The last naked option position that we shall consider is the short put strategy. The *short put strategy* involves the selling (writing) of put options. This strategy is employed if the investor expects interest rates to fall or stay flat so that the price of the bond will increase or stay the same. The profit and loss profile for a short put option is the mirror image of that for the long put option. The maximum profit from this strategy is the option price. The maximum loss is limited only by how low the price of the bond can fall by the expiration date less the option price received for writing the option. Exhibit 12.9 graphically depicts this profit and loss profile.

To summarize, long calls and short puts allow the investor to gain if bond prices rise (interest rates fall). Short calls and long puts allow the investor to gain if bond prices fall (interest rates rise). An investor would want to use each strategy under the following circumstances:

Circumstance:	*Strategy:*
Very bullish	Buy call
Slightly bullish	Write put
Slightly bearish	Write call
Very bearish	Buy put

Considering the Time Value of Money

In our illustrations of the four naked option positions, we neglected the time value of money. Specifically, the buyer of an option must pay the seller the option price at the time the option is purchased. Thus the buyer must either finance the purchase price of the option or, if the proceeds do not have to be borrowed, lose the interest that could be earned by investing the option price until the expiration of the option. The seller, in contrast, assuming that he does not have to use the option price as margin for the short position, has the opportunity to invest this option price.

The profit profiles of the naked option positions change when the time value of money is taken into consideration. The break-even price for the buyer and the seller of an option will not be the same as in our illustrations. The break-even price for the underlying instrument at the expiration date is higher for the buyer of the option; for the seller, it is lower.

We also ignored the time value of money in comparing the option strategies with positions in the underlying instrument. In this case, we ignored the fact that when the underlying instrument is a cash market coupon security, coupon payments may be made between the time the option is purchased and the option's expiration date. When these coupon payments are received, they can be reinvested. Thus reinvestment income must be factored into the analysis of an option position. Also, the effects of financing costs and opportunity costs on the long or short bond positions, respectively, must be factored into the analysis. For the sake of simplicity, however, we shall ignore the time value of money throughout the remainder of this chapter.

EXHIBIT 12.9   Profit/Loss Profile Diagram for a Short Put Strategy

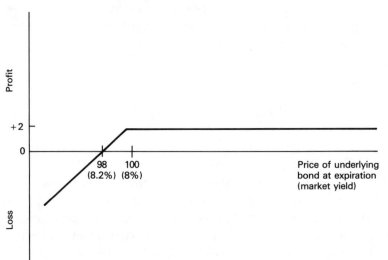

HEDGE STRATEGIES

Hedge strategies involve taking a position in an option and a position in the underlying bond in such a way that changes in the value of one position will offset any unfavorable price (interest rate) movement in the other position. We discuss two popular hedge strategies here: (1) the covered call writing strategy; and (2) the protective put buying strategy.

Covered Call Writing Strategy

A covered call writing strategy involves writing a call option on bonds held in the portfolio. That is, the investor is in a short position in a call option and a long position in the underlying bond. If the price of the bond declines because interest rates rise, there will be a loss on the long bond position. However, the income generated from the sale of the call option will either (1) fully offset the loss in the long bond position, (2) partially offset the loss in the long bond position, or (3) more than offset the loss in the long bond position so that a profit is generated.

To illustrate this strategy, suppose that an investor owns $100 par of an 8%, 20-year and 1-month bond selling at par. Also suppose that a call option on this bond with a $100 strike price that matures in 1 month can be sold for $3. If the investor has decided to hold the bond and write a call option on the same bond, the profit or loss for this strategy will depend on the market yield on the bond at the expiration date. One of the following outcomes will occur:

1. If the price of the bond is greater than $100 as a result of a decline in the market yield, the call option buyer will exercise the option and pay the option writer $100. The value of the portfolio at the expiration date is then $103 ($100 received from the bond plus $3 received from writing the call option). Thus the profit from this strategy if the price of the bond is greater than $100 is $3 (the option price). The chance for upside potential on the long bond position has been forfeited for the guaranteed $3 option price.
2. If the market yield is unchanged at 8%, the price of the bond is equal to $100 at the expiration date; the call option buyer will not exercise the option. The value of the portfolio will still be $103, resulting in a $3 profit.

3. If the market yield rises such that the price of the bond is less than $100 but greater than $97, there will be a profit, but it will be less than $3. For example, suppose that the price of the bond is $98 (market yield of about 8.3%). The long bond position will have a value of $98, while the short call position generates $3. The portfolio value is therefore $101, resulting in a profit of $1. The $3 option price received has cushioned the decline in the value of the long position.

4. At a price of $97 (market yield of roughly 8.3%), the long bond position will have a value of $97, and the short call position generates $3. There is no profit or loss for the portfolio since the portfolio value is unchanged at $100.

5. Should market yields rise more than 70 basis points, the price of the bond will be less than $97 at expiration and the portfolio will realize a loss. For example, suppose that the price of the bond at expiration is $71 because the market yield increased to 11.8%. The portfolio value will be $74. Hence there is a loss of $26.

The profit and loss profile for this covered call writing strategy is graphically portrayed in Exhibit 12.10. There are two important points that you should recognize from this illustration. First, this strategy has allowed the investor to reduce the downside risk for his portfolio. In this example, by selling the at-the-money option, the risk is reduced by an amount equal to the option price. In exchange for this reduction of downside risk, the investor has agreed to cap his potential profit. In our illustration, the maximum profit is the option price.

The second point can be seen by comparing Exhibit 12.9 and Exhibit 12.10. Notice that the shape of the two profit and loss profiles is the same. That is, the covered call writing strategy has the same profit and loss profile as a short put strategy. This is not an accident. There is a relationship between put and call options that we shall discuss later in this chapter.

Protective Put Buying Strategy

An investor may want to protect the value of bonds held in his portfolio. A way of doing this with options is to buy a put option. By doing so, the investor is guaranteed to receive the strike price of the put option for his bonds held less the cost of the option. Should the market yield fall, thereby increasing the price of the bonds, the investor will be able to participate in the price increase; however, the profit will be reduced by the cost of the option. This strategy is called a *protective put*

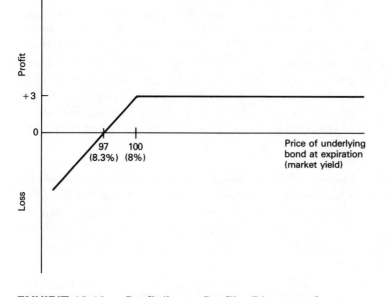

EXHIBIT 12.10   Profit/Loss Profile Diagram for a Covered Call Strategy

buying strategy and consists of taking a long position in a bond held in the portfolio and a long put position (buying a put option) in which the bond held in the portfolio is the underlying bond for the put option.

For example, suppose that an investor has a $100 par value, 8%, 20-year and 1-month bond in his portfolio and that the current market value of the bond is $100. Assume further that a 1-month put option selling for $2 can be purchased with a strike price of $100. One month from now at the expiration date the profit or loss can be summarized as follows:

1. If the price of the bond is greater than $102 (a decline in the market yield to less than 7.80%), the investor will realize a profit from this strategy. For example, suppose the market yield declines to 6% so that the bond price is $123.11. Since the cost of purchasing the put option was $2, the net profit for this position will be $21.11. The investor has given up his $2 profit for downside protection on the bond held in his portfolio.
2. If the price of the bond is equal to $102, no profit or loss will be realized from this strategy.

3. There will be a loss of less than $2 if the price of the bond is less than $102 but greater than $100. For example, a price of $101 (market yield of 7.9%) will result in a loss for this strategy of $1: a $1 gain in the long bond position but a cost of $2 to acquire the long put position.

4. In none of the previous outcomes will the investor exercise the put option. However, if the price of the bond is below $100 because the market yield has increased, the option will be exercised. At any price below $100, the investor will be assured of receiving $100 for the bond. Thus the value of the portfolio will be $100 minus the cost of the option ($2), resulting in a maximum loss of $2.

Exhibit 12.11 is a graphic presentation of the profit and loss profile for this protective put buying strategy. By implementing this strategy, the investor has effectively assured a price of $100 (the strike price of the put option) at a cost of $2. The investor has maintained all the upside potential, though this upside potential is reduced by $2, the cost of the put option.

Suppose that, in addition to the put option with a strike price of $100, there is a put option with a strike price of $96. As we shall see shortly, the price for this put option with the same expiration date but

EXHIBIT 12.11   Profit/Loss Profile Diagram for a Protective Put Strategy

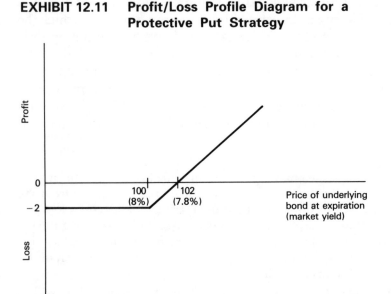

a lower strike price would be less than the put option with a strike price of $100. Suppose that the option price is $1.25. The investor who pursues a protective put option strategy using this put option with a strike price of $96 will have guaranteed a minimum price of $96 at a cost of $1.25. The upside potential will be reduced by $1.25. However, the downside risk will be $4 greater than that with the put whose strike price equals $100.

As can be seen, the strike price determines the minimum price that will be guaranteed by the put option and thus the downside risk of the option. However, the higher the strike price, the greater the cost of guaranteeing the minimum price. This is because the higher the strike price, the more attractive the put option is to an option buyer, resulting in a higher price. Therefore, when implementing a protective put strategy, an investor must evaluate the trade-off between a higher minimum price for the underlying instrument and the associated higher cost of purchasing the put option.

Once again, notice the shape of the payoff pattern for the protective put option in Exhibit 12.11. Note that the profit/loss pattern is the same as that for the long call option strategy shown in Exhibit 12.3.

PUT-CALL PARITY RELATIONSHIP
AND EQUIVALENT POSITIONS

Is there a relationship between the price of a call option and the price of a put option on the same underlying instrument, with the same strike price and the same expiration date? There is. To see this relationship, which is commonly referred to as the *put-call parity relationship*, let's use an example.

In our previous illustrations we used a put and a call option on the same underlying instrument (a bond currently with 20 years and 1 month to maturity), both options having a strike price of $100 and 1 month to expiration. The price of the underlying bond was assumed to be $100. The call price and put price were assumed to be $3 and $2, respectively. Consider the following strategy:

> Buy the bond at a price of $100
> Sell a call option at a price of $3
> Buy a put option at a price of $2

This strategy therefore involves:

Long the bond
Short the call option
Long the put option

Exhibit 12.12 shows the profit and loss profile at the expiration date for this strategy. Notice that no matter what the price of the underlying bond at expiration date, the strategy will produce a profit of $1. Ignoring the cost of financing the long position and the long put position, this situation cannot exist in an efficient market. The actions of market participants in implementing this strategy to capture the $1 profit will result in one or more of the following consequences, which will tend to eliminate the $1 profit: (1) an increase in the price of the bond; (2) a decrease in the call option price; and/or (3) an increase in the put option price.

In our example, assuming the bond price doesn't change, this means that the call price and the put price must be equal. But this is true only when we ignore the time value of money (financing cost, opportunity cost, coupon income, and reinvestment income). Also, in the illustration we did not consider the possibility of early exercise of the options. Thus we have been considering a put-call parity relationship for only European options.

Ignoring the time value of money and considering European options, the outcome from the following position must be one of no arbitrage profits:

(12.1) Long the bond + Short call option + Long put option = 0

In terms of price, it can be shown that there will be no arbitrage profits at *any* time (not just expiration) if:

(12.2) $P_{po} = P_{co} + S - P_b$
   where P_b = current price of the underlying bond
      P_{co} = price of call option
      P_{po} = price of put option
      S = strike (exercise) price of option

and the strike price and expiration date are the same for both options. This relationship is one form of the put-call parity relationship for European options when the time value of money is ignored. It is approximately true for American options. Considering the time value of money, the put-call parity relationship for coupon bonds is:

Exhibit 12.12   Profit/Loss Profile for a Strategy Involving a Long Bond Position, Short Call Option Position, and Long Put Option Position

Assumptions:
Current price of bond = 100
Price of call option   = 3
Call strike price   = 100
Price of put option   = 2
Put strike price   = 100
Time to expiration   = 1 month

At expiration date:

Market Yield	Price of Bond	Profit from Long Bond	Price Received for Call	Price Paid for Put	Overall Profit
4.0	154.71	0*	3	−2	1
4.2	151.08	0*	3	−2	1
4.4	147.56	0*	3	−2	1
4.6	144.15	0*	3	−2	1
4.8	140.85	0*	3	−2	1
5.0	137.65	0*	3	−2	1
5.2	134.56	0*	3	−2	1
5.4	131.56	0*	3	−2	1
5.6	128.66	0*	3	−2	1
5.8	125.84	0*	3	−2	1
6.0	123.11	0*	3	−2	1
6.1	121.78	0*	3	−2	1
6.2	120.47	0*	3	−2	1
6.3	119.18	0*	3	−2	1
6.4	117.91	0*	3	−2	1
6.5	116.66	0*	3	−2	1
6.6	115.42	0*	3	−2	1
6.7	114.21	0*	3	−2	1
6.8	113.01	0*	3	−2	1
6.9	111.84	0*	3	−2	1
7.0	110.68	0*	3	−2	1
7.1	109.54	0*	3	−2	1
7.2	108.41	0*	3	−2	1
7.3	107.30	0*	3	−2	1
7.4	106.21	0*	3	−2	1
7.5	105.14	0*	3	−2	1
7.6	104.08	0*	3	−2	1
7.7	103.04	0*	3	−2	1
7.8	102.01	0*	3	−2	1
7.9	101.00	0*	3	−2	1
8.0	100.00	0	3	−2	1

EXHIBIT 12.12   (Continued)

At expiration date:

Market Yield	Price of Bond	Profit from Long Bond	Price Received for Call	Price Paid for Put	Overall Profit
8.1	99.02	0⁺	3	−2	1
8.2	98.05	0⁺	3	−2	1
8.3	97.10	0⁺	3	−2	1
8.4	96.16	0⁺	3	−2	1
8.5	95.23	0⁺	3	−2	1
8.6	94.32	0⁺	3	−2	1
8.7	93.42	0⁺	3	−2	1
8.8	92.53	0⁺	3	−2	1
8.9	91.66	0⁺	3	−2	1
9.0	90.80	0⁺	3	−2	1
9.1	89.95	0⁺	3	−2	1
9.2	89.11	0⁺	3	−2	1
9.3	88.29	0⁺	3	−2	1
9.4	87.48	0⁺	3	−2	1
9.5	86.68	0⁺	3	−2	1
9.6	85.89	0⁺	3	−2	1
9.7	85.11	0⁺	3	−2	1
9.8	84.34	0⁺	3	−2	1
9.9	83.59	0⁺	3	−2	1
10.0	82.84	0⁺	3	−2	1
10.2	81.38	0⁺	3	−2	1
10.4	79.96	0⁺	3	−2	1
10.6	78.58	0⁺	3	−2	1
10.8	77.24	0⁺	3	−2	1
11.0	75.93	0⁺	3	−2	1
11.2	74.66	0⁺	3	−2	1
11.4	73.42	0⁺	3	−2	1
11.6	72.22	0⁺	3	−2	1
11.8	71.05	0⁺	3	−2	1
12.0	69.91	0⁺	3	−2	1

*If the price of the bond is greater than the strike price, the buyer of the call option will exercise the option.
⁺If the price of the bond is less than the strike price, the investor will exercise the put option.

(12.3) $P_{po} = P_{co} + PV\ (S) + PV\ (\text{coupon}) - P_b$

where $PV\ (S)$ =   present value of the strike price
        $PV\ (\text{coupon})$ =   present value of the coupon payments

Equivalent Positions

Working with equation (12.1), we can identify equivalent positions, that is, positions that will provide the same profit profile. For example, subtracting the long put position from both sides of equation (12.1), we have:

(12.4) Long the bond + Short call option = −Long put option

But the position on the right-hand side of equation (12.4) is the same as a short put position. Therefore:

(12.5) Long the bond + Short call option = Short put option

We've seen equation (12.5) several places throughout this book. Earlier in this chapter we showed that a covered call position, which is a long bond position plus a short call option position on the same bond, has the same profit profile as a short put option position. This is what equation (12.5) states. In our discussion of callable bonds and mortgage-backed securities, we stated that owning such securities is equivalent to a long bond position plus a short call position. Thus, these securities will have a payoff similar to a short put position. But remember, the equivalent position holds only for European options, and a more precise relationship requires that the time value of money be considered.

Manipulating equation (12.1) gives us the following equivalent positions:

Short the bond + Short put = Short call
Long the bond   + Long put   = Long call
Short the bond + Long call = Long put
Long call   + Short put = Long the bond
Long put   + Short call = Short the bond

Thus an investor can synthetically create any of the positions on the right-hand side of these equations by taking the two positions indicated on the left-hand side.

THE OPTION PRICE

Factors That Influence the Option Price

The following six factors will influence the option price:
1. Current price of the underlying instrument
2. Strike price
3. Time to expiration
4. Short-term risk-free interest rate over the life of the option
5. Coupon rate on the bond
6. Expected volatility of yields (or prices) over the life of the option

The impact of each of these factors may depend on whether (1) the option is a call or a put, (2) the option is an American option or a European option, and (3) the underlying instrument is a bond or a futures contract on a bond.[3]

Current Price of the Underlying Instrument.   For a call option, as the current price of the underlying instrument increases (decreases), the option price increases (decreases). For a put option, as the current price of the underlying instrument decreases (increases), the option price increases (decreases).

Strike Price.   All other factors being constant, the higher the strike price, the lower the price of a call option. For a put option, the opposite is true: the higher the strike price, the higher the price of a put option.

Time to Expiration.   For American options (both puts and calls), all other factors held constant, the longer the time to expiration, the higher the option price. No general statement can be made for European options. The impact of the time to expiration on European options will depend on whether the option is a put or a call.

Short-Term Risk-Free Interest Rate over the Life of the Option.   Holding all other factors constant, the price of a call option on a bond will increase as the short-term risk-free interest rate rises. For a put option, the opposite is true: an increase in the short-term risk-free interest rate

---

[3]For a more detailed discussion of the impact of these factors on the price of an option, see Pitts and Fabozzi, *Interest Rate Options and Futures.*

will decrease the price of a put option. In contrast, for a futures option, the price of both a call and a put option will decrease if the short-term risk-free interest rate rises.[4]

Coupon Rate.   For options on bonds, coupons tend to decrease the price of a call option because the coupons make it more attractive to hold the bond than the option. Thus call options on coupon-bearing bonds will tend to be priced lower than similar call options on non–coupon-bearing bonds. Conversely, coupons tend to increase the price of put options.

Expected Volatility of Yields Over the Life of the Option.   As the expected volatility of yields over the life of the option increases, the price of the option will also increase. The reason is that the greater the expected volatility, as measured by the standard deviation or variance of yields, the greater the probability that the price of the underlying bond or futures contract will move in the direction that will benefit the option buyer.

Theoretical Call Option Price

Exhibit 12.13 shows the shape of the theoretical price of a call option based on the price of the underlying instrument. The line from the origin to the strike price along the horizontal axis is the intrinsic value of the call option when the price of the underlying instrument is less than the strike price, since the intrinsic value is zero. The 45-degree line extending from the horizontal axis is the intrinsic value of the call option once the price of the underlying instrument exceeds the strike price. The reason for this is that the intrinsic value of the call option will increase by $1 each time the price of the underlying instrument increases by $1. Thus the slope of the line representing the intrinsic value after the strike price is reached is 1.

The theoretical call option price is shown by the convex line. The difference between the theoretical call option price and the intrinsic value at any given price for the underlying instrument is the time value of the option.

Exhibit 12.14 also shows the theoretical call option price, but with three tangent lines drawn. The slope of the tangent line shows how the theoretical price will change for small changes in the price of the underlying instrument. That is, if we let:

[4]See ibid. for a more detailed explanation.

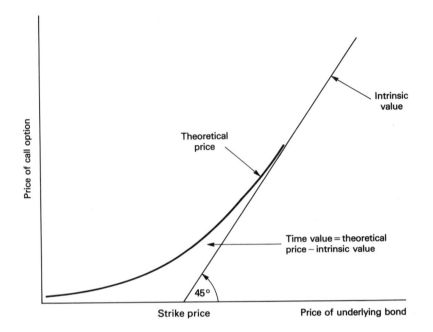

Exhibit 12.13   Theoretical Price of a Call Option

P_{co} = Theoretical price of the call option
P_b = Price of the underlying bond

then:

$$P_{co} = f(P_b)$$

The slope of the convex curve representing the theoretical call option price at any point is then:

$$\frac{dP_b}{dP_u}$$

When we discussed the duration of callable bonds in Chapter 8, we referred to this measure as the *delta* of the option. Delta, also commonly referred to as the *hedge ratio*, plays an important role in: (1) portfolio and trading strategies; (2) option-pricing models (discussed next); and (3) assessing the price volatility of a callable bond, as explained in Chapter 8 in determining the call-adjusted duration.

The steeper the slope of the line, the greater the delta. When an option is deep out of the money (that is, the price of the underlying

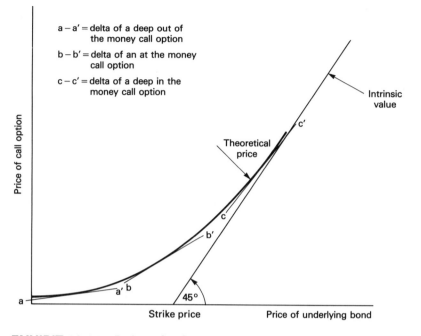

EXHIBIT 12.14   Delta of a Call Option

instrument is substantially below the strike price), the slope of the line is relatively flat (see line a–a' in Exhibit 12.14). This means a delta close to zero. To understand why, consider a call option with a strike price of $100 and 3 months to maturity. If the price of the underlying instrument is $15, how much would you expect the price of the option to increase if the price of the underlying instrument increased by $1, from $15 to $16? Not much, since the price of the underlying instrument is still considerably below the strike price.

For a call option that is deep in the money, the delta will be close to 1. That is, the call option price will increase almost dollar for dollar with an increase in the price of the underlying instrument. In terms of Exhibit 12.14, the slope of the tangent line approaches the slope of the intrinsic value line after the strike price is reached. The slope of that line is 1. Thus the delta for a call option ranges from zero (for deep out-of-the-money options) to 1 (for deep-in-the-money call options). The delta for an at-the-money option is approximately 0.5.

Notice that these properties for delta agree with our statements in Chapter 8 when we analyzed the call-adjusted duration.

When analyzing a trading or investment strategy, traders and money managers look at other properties of an option besides its delta. One consideration is the convexity of the option, which is commonly referred to as its *gamma*.[5]

Option-Pricing Models

To implement portfolio and trading strategies it is necessary to estimate the theoretical price of an option. Several models have been developed to do this. Like the models we used in discussing the pricing of futures contracts in the previous chapter, options-pricing models are based on an arbitrage or riskless hedge argument. The expected price of the underlying instrument is not an input. Option-pricing models differ from futures-pricing models in that a key factor in the valuation of an option is the expected price or yield volatility over the life of the option.

The most popular option-pricing model for American call options on common stock is the Black-Scholes option-pricing model.[6] The key insight of this model is that a synthetic option can be created by taking an appropriate position in the underlying common stock and borrowing or lending funds at the riskless interest rate.

To create a synthetic option, the delta of an option must be computed. As we just explained, the delta indicates how the price of the option will change when the price of the underlying common stock changes. For example, suppose that on the basis of the current price of the underlying common stock, a call option has a delta of 0.5. This means that two call options will have the same price movement as one share of the common stock. The profit/loss profile of an option can be created by taking a position in the underlying common stock based on the delta of the option and by borrowing or lending at the riskless

---

[5]The gamma of an option is the change in its delta for a change in the price of the underlying instrument. There are other measures of the price sensitivity of an option to changes in the factors that impact the option price. For example, *kappa* is a measure of the change in the price of an option with a change in the volatility of the underlying instrument. *Theta* is the change in the price of an option with a change in the time to expiration. For a discussion of the role of these measures in options strategies, see Richard M. Bookstaber, *Option Pricing and Investment Strategies* (Chicago, IL: Probus Publishing, 1987), Chap. 4; and James F. Meisner and John A. Richards, "Option Premium Dynamics: With Applications to Fixed Income Portfolio Analysis," in Frank J. Fabozzi and T. Dessa Garlicki, eds., *Advances in Bond Analysis and Portfolio Strategies* (Chicago, IL: Probus Publishing, 1987).

[6]Fischer Black and Myron Scholes, "The Pricing of Corporate Liabilities," *Journal of Political Economy*, May–June 1973, pp. 637–659.

interest rate.[7] Since the synthetic option and the option have the same payoff under all possible prices for the underlying common stock at the expiration date, the synthetic option and the option must sell at the same price. From this relationship, the price of the option can be determined.

Several assumptions underlie the Black-Scholes option-pricing model. While some of these assumptions have been relaxed in modified versions of the model, a still-critical assumption is that the variance (volatility) of the price of the underlying instrument is constant over the life of the option. In the case of options on bonds and interest rate futures, we know that this is not true. As a bond approaches its maturity date, we know from Chapter 4 that its price volatility will decline.

An alternative option-pricing model that is more adaptable to options on bonds and interest rate futures is the *binomial option-pricing model*.[8] Specifically, different assumptions about the process driving interest rates, and therefore bond prices, can be incorporated into a binomial option-pricing model.[9] Several models assume that bond prices are affected by movements in the short-term risk-free interest rate, and that a change in this rate not only affects the price of short-term bonds, but is also a signal that interest rates will change in the future. As a result, bonds of all maturities will be affected. There are also models

---

[7]This same insight is the basis for a strategy popularly known as *portfolio insurance*. A portfolio insurance strategy attempts to ensure a minimum value for a portfolio. We know from our earlier discussion that a protective put buying strategy can be used. A portfolio insurance strategy synthetically creates a put option. Since the delta of an option changes as the price of the underlying instrument changes, a portfolio insurance strategy requires rebalancing the portfolio to adjust to the new delta. For this reason, a portfolio insurance strategy is referred to as a *dynamic hedging strategy*.

For a discussion of portfolio insurance as applied to bond portfolios, see Bookstaber, *Option Pricing and Investment Strategies*, Chap. 7; William J. Marshall, "Portfolio Insurance: Limiting the Exposure of Actively Managed Pension Funds Under Statement of Financial Accounting Standards No. 87," in *Advances in Bond Analysis and Portfolio Strategies;* and Robert B. Platt and Gary D. Latainer, "The Use of Synthetic Option Strategies in Fixed Income Portfolios," Chap. 9 in Frank J. Fabozzi, ed., *Winning the Interest Rate Game: A Guide to Debt Options* (Chicago, IL: Probus Publishing, 1985).

[8]John Cox, Stephen Ross, and Mark Rubinstein, "Option Pricing: A Simplified Approach," *Journal of Financial Economics,* September 1979, pp. 229–263; Richard Rendleman and Brit Bartter, "Two-State Option Pricing," *Journal of Finance,* December 1979, pp. 1093–1110; and William Sharpe, *Investments* (Englewood Cliffs, NJ: Prentice Hall, 1981), Chap. 16.

[9]For a more technical discussion, see Peter Ritchken, *Options: Theory, Strategy, and Applications* (Glenview, IL: Scott, Foresman, 1987), Chap. 13.

that assume that bond prices are affected by more than one interest rate. [10]

A recent development in options pricing are models based on a yield diffusion process, as opposed to a price diffusion process, used in the binominal model.[11] In the yield diffusion process, the *yield* volatility is an important input.

Implied Volatility

Option-pricing models provide a theoretical option price based on the six factors that we discussed at the beginning of this section. The only one of these factors that is not known and must be estimated is the expected volatility of yield or price over the life of the option. A popular methodology to assess whether an option is fairly priced is to assume that the option is priced correctly and then, using an option-pricing model, estimate the volatility that is implied by that model, given the observed option price, and the other five factors that determine the price of an option. The estimated volatility computed in this manner is called the *implied volatility.*

For example, suppose that a money manager using some option-pricing model, the current price of the option, and the five other factors that determine the price of an option computes an implied yield volatility of 12%. If the money manager expects that the volatility of yields over the life of the option will be greater than the implied volatility of 12%, the option is considered to be undervalued. In contrast, if the money manager's expected volatility of yields over the life of the option is less than the implied volatility, the option is considered to be overvalued.

---

[10]For example, the Brennan-Schwartz model assumes there are two interest rates that determine the price of a bond: (1) the short-term risk-free interest rate: and (2) the long-term interest rate. (See Michael Brennan and Eduardo Schwartz, "Alternative Methods for Valuing Debt Options," Working Paper 888, University of British Columbia, Vancouver, BC, 1982.) The Cox-Ingersoll-Ross model assumes the second variable is the market portfolio, and therefore changes in the market portfolio will influence bond prices. (See John Cox, John Ingersoll, and Stephen Ross, "A Reexamination of Traditional Hypotheses About the Term Structure of Interest Rates," *Journal of Finance,* September 1981, pp. 769–799.) In Richard's two-state variable model, the second variable is the inflation rate. (See Scott Richard, "An Arbitrage Model of the Term Structure of Interest Rates," *Journal of Financial Economics,* March 1978, pp. 33–58.)

[11]For a discussion of one of the models, see Yu Zhu and Farshid Jamshidian, "Call-Adjusted Duration Model and Its Application in Bond Portfolio Management," Chap. 6 in Frank J. Fabozzi, (ed.), *The Handbook of Fixed Income Options* (Chicago, IL: Probus Publishing, 1988); and Farshid Jamshidian and Yu Zhu, "Analysis of Bonds with Imbedded Options," *Advances in Futures and Options Research,* vol. 3, 1988.

While we have focused on the option price, the key to understanding the options market is knowing that trading and investment strategies in this market involve buying and selling volatility. Estimating the implied volatility and comparing it to the trader's or money manager's expectations of future volatility is just another way of evaluating options. If an investor uses expected volatility to compute the fair value of the option, the option will appear cheap or expensive in exactly the same cases.

SUMMARY

In this chapter we reviewed interest rate options contracts that are currently traded. Options on interest rate futures contracts (futures options) have replaced options on cash market instruments as the primary vehicle for implementing option-based strategies. In addition to exchange-traded options, there are over-the-counter (or dealer) options. The risk/reward profiles for four naked option strategies (buy call options, sell call options, buy put options, and sell put options) were each explained and compared to similar positions in the underlying instrument. The maximum profit that an option writer (seller) can realize is the option price; however, the option writer is exposed to substantial downside risk. For an option buyer, the maximum possible loss is the option price; moreover, the option buyer retains all the upside potential (reduced by the option price). Two basic hedge strategies, covered call writing and protective put buying, were also explained.

The put-call parity relationship defines the relationship between the price of a put option, a call option, and the underlying instrument. This relationship can be used to identify portfolio positions that offer a similar profit profile.

There are six factors that influence an option's price: current price of the underlying instrument; strike price; time to expiration; short-term risk-free interest rate over the life of the option; coupon rate; and expected volatility of yields or prices over the life of the option. Option-pricing models attempt to estimate the theoretical price of an option on the basis of arbitrage or riskless-hedge arguments. Modifications to the binomial option-pricing model have been used to price options on bonds and interest rate futures contracts. Since the trading in the options market involves buying and selling volatility, an alternative methodology for evaluating options is to determine an option's implied volatility and compare it to expected volatility. If expected volatility is greater (less) than implied volatility, the option is undervalued (overvalued).

13

STRUCTURED
PORTFOLIO STRATEGIES I:
Indexing

In this chapter and the next, we describe several structured portfolio strategies. These strategies generally do not rely on expectations of interest rate movements or changes in yield spread relationships. Instead, the objective is to design a portfolio that will achieve the performance of some predetermined benchmark. The performance to be achieved may be: (1) the return on a specific benchmark index; (2) sufficient dollars to satisfy a future single liability; or (3) sufficient dollars to satisfy each liability of a future liability stream. The structured bond portfolio strategy used when the performance to be achieved is the replication of a predetermined benchmark index is called an *indexing strategy*. When the performance objective is to generate sufficient funds to pay off predetermined future liabilities, the strategy is called a *liability funding strategy*. Indexing is discussed in this chapter; liability funding is discussed in Chapter 14.

OBJECTIVE, GROWTH, AND MOTIVATION
FOR BOND INDEXING

Indexing a portfolio means designing it so that its performance will match that of some predetermined index. Performance is measured in terms of total rate of return realized (or simply, total return) over some investment horizon. Total return over some investment horizon incorporates all three sources of return from holding a portfolio of bonds, that is

$$\text{Total return} = \frac{\begin{array}{c}\text{Coupon interest}\\\text{received}\end{array} + \begin{array}{c}\text{Change in}\\\text{portfolio value}\end{array} + \begin{array}{c}\text{Interest-on-}\\\text{interest}\end{array}}{\text{Portfolio value at beginning of period}}$$

Indexing an equity portfolio is commonplace. On the bond side, indexing is a relatively recent phenomenon. In 1980, for example, only $40 million of assets was managed under bond indexing strategies. By late 1986, the amount had grown to over $40 billion.[1]

Two major factors explain the recent popularity and phenomenal rate of growth of bond indexing. First, the empirical evidence seems to suggest that historically the overall performance of bond investment advisors has been poor. SEI Corporation found that for the 5-year period 1981 to 1985 only 29% of active bond managers were able to outperform a popular bond index, the Shearson Lehman Index.[2] Over an 8-year period, SEI Corporation found that 58% of surveyed managers did not perform as well as this same index.[3] Almost three quarters of the money managers surveyed by Trust Universe Comparison Services underperformed the Merrill Lynch/Government Master Index over the 3-year period ending December 31, 1985.[4]

The second factor explaining the popularity of bond indexing is the lower advisory management fees charged for an indexed portfolio compared to active management fees. Advisory fees charged by active managers typically range from 15 to 50 basis points. In contrast, the range for indexed portfolios is 1 to 20 basis points, with the upper range representing the fees for enhanced and customized benchmark funds discussed later in this chapter.[5] Some pension funds have decided to

[1]Sharmine Mossavar-Rahmani, "Understanding and Evaluating Index Fund Management," in Frank J. Fabozzi and T. Dessa Garlicki, eds., *Advances in Bond Analysis and Portfolio Strategies* (Chicago, IL: Probus Publishing, 1987), p. 433.

[2]As reported in George Anders, "Returns Seesaw for Managers Seeking to Top Index on Bonds," *The Wall Street Journal,* April 21, 1986, p. 37.

[3]As reported in Tom Herman, "Bond-Index Funds Pick Up Appeal by Outperforming Many Managers," *The Wall Street Journal,* January 3, 1986, p. 15.

[4]Philip H. Galdi, "Indexing Fixed Income Portfolios," in *Advances in Bond Analysis and Portfolio Strategies,* pp. 453–454.

[5]Mossavar-Rahmani, "Understanding and Evaluating Index Fund Management," p. 434.

avoid advisory fees and manage some or all of their funds in-house employing an indexing strategy.[6]

Critics of bond indexing have been quick to point out, however, that while an indexing strategy matches the performance of some index, the performance of that index does not necessarily represent optimal performance. For the 5-year period ending September 1981, for example, 50% of active managers outperformed a popular index.[7] Moreover, matching an index does not mean that the money manager will satisfy a client's return requirement objective. For example, if the objective of a life insurance or a pension fund is to have sufficient funds to satisfy a predetermined liability, indexing only reduces the likelihood that the performance will not be materially lower than the index. Indexing does not ensure that there will be sufficient funds to satisfy the predetermined liability. Finally, matching an index means that the money manager is restricted to the sectors of the bond market that are in the index, even though there may be attactive opportunities in market sectors excluded from the index. For example, in Chapter 10 we discussed a wide range of mortgage-backed securities. While the broad-based bond market indexes typically include agency pass-through securities, other mortgage-backed securities such as conventional pass-throughs, stripped mortgage-backed securities, and collateralized mortgage obligations are generally not included. Yet it is in these fairly new markets that attractive returns to enhance performance may be available.

At the theoretical level, the index fund approach is supported both by the work of Markowitz[8] on the construction of efficient portfolios and by capital market theory as developed by Sharpe,[9] Lintner,[10] and Mossin.[11] Markowitz demonstrated how portfolios can

---

[6]The United Mine Workers Health & Retirement Funds, for example, runs a $200 million bond index fund in-house. (Fran Hawthorne, "The Battle of the Bond Indexes," *Institutional Investor,* April 1986, p. 118.)

[7]As reported in Mossavar-Rahmani, "Understanding and Evaluating Index Fund Management," pp. 436–437.

[8]Harry M. Markowitz, "Portfolio Selection," *Journal of Finance,* March 1952, pp. 71–91; and *Portfolio Selection: Efficient Diversification of Investment* (New York: John Wiley & Sons, 1959).

[9]William F. Sharpe, "Capital Asset Prices: A Theory of Market Equilibrium Under Conditions of Risk," *Journal of Finance,* September 1964, pp. 425–442.

[10]John Lintner, "Security Prices, Risk, and Maximal Gains from Diversification," *Journal of Finance,* December 1965, pp. 587–616.

[11]Jan Mossin, "Equilibrium in a Capital Asset Market," *Econometrica,* October 1966, pp. 76–83.

be constructed so as to maximize return for a given level of risk. Such portfolios are referred to as *efficient portfolios.*

The Sharpe-Lintner-Mossin analysis demonstrated that a "market" portfolio offers the highest level of return per unit of risk in an *efficient* market. An efficient market is one in which market participants cannot consistently earn abnormal risk-adjusted returns after transaction costs and management advisory fees are taken into account. The efficiency of the market can be captured by combining securities in a portfolio with characteristics similar to those of the market. The theoretical market portfolio consists of all risky assets. The weight of each risky asset in the market portfolio, then, is equal to the ratio of its market value to the aggregate market value of all risky assets. That is, the market portfolio is a capitalization-weighted (value-weighted) portfolio of all risky assets.[12]

STUDIES OF MARKET EFFICIENCY

The theoretical arguments for indexing are based on the assumption that the bond market is efficient.[13] In an efficient market, the market price fully reflects all information that is relevant to the valuation of an issue. As a result, it is not possible for investors to consistently "outperform" the market. Outperforming the market means realizing a return that exceeds the market return after adjusting for (1) the risk accepted by the investor, (2) transaction costs, and (3) management advisory fees. Therefore in an efficient market, active strategies that depend on expectations of interest rate changes, yield spread changes, or credit rating changes will, on average, not outperform the market.

There are three forms of market efficiency—weak, semistrong, and strong.[14] These three forms are distinguished by the information set that is believed to be reflected in the price of the security at any given

[12]Granito argues that while the theoretical arguments are appropriate for indexing a common stock portfolio, they are inappropriate for justifying indexing of a bond portfolio. See Michael R. Granito, "The Problem with Bond Index Funds," *The Journal of Portfolio Management,* Summer 1987, pp. 41–48.

[13]The term *market efficiency* has been used in several contexts to describe the characteristics of a capital market. In an *operationally* efficient capital market, market participants can obtain transaction services as cheaply as possible given the costs dealers and brokers incur in providing those services. *Pricing efficiency* refers to a market in which prices at any given point in time fully reflect all available information that is relevant to the value of the securities. When we use the term *market efficiency* in this chapter, we mean the pricing efficiency of the market.

[14]Eugene F. Fama, "Efficient Capital Markets: A Review of Theory and Empirical Work," *Journal of Finance,* May 1970, pp. 384–417.

point in time. *Weak efficiency* means that the price of the security fully reflects the price and trading history of the security. *Semistrong efficiency* means that the price of the security fully reflects all publicly available information (which, of course, includes price and trading history). *Strong efficiency* exists in a market in which the price of a security fully reflects all information whether or not it is publicly available.

Studies that focus on the efficiency of the bond market examine one of the following questions: (1) Are there market participants who have superior interest rate forecasting ability? (2) Do active money managers consistently outperform popular indexes? (3) Are bonds priced so that there are arbitrage trading opportunities? (4) Does the market use all publicly available information to value an issue?

Studies examining the first question are tests of the weak form of the efficiency of the bond market. The overwhelming evidence suggests that interest rate movements cannot be predicted with enough consistency and accuracy to generate superior investment performance.[15] As for the second question, we cited earlier in this chapter several studies that suggest that, on average, money managers have not done better than some popular indexes. However, these studies are deficient because they do not properly reflect the risk accepted by the money managers surveyed.

Only a few studies have focused on the third question, and they have been limited to the government bond market for three reasons: (1) the price data are more readily available than for other sectors of the

---

[15]The following studies support this view: Thomas J. Sargent, "Rational Expectations and the Term Structure of Interest Rates," *Journal of Money, Credit and Banking*, February 1972, pp. 74–97; Michael J. Prell, "How Well Do the Experts Forecast Interest Rates?" *Federal Reserve Bank of Kansas Monthly Review*, September-October 1973, pp. 3–13; Oswald D. Bowlin and John D. Martin, "Extrapolations of Yields over the Short Run: Forecast or Folly?" *Journal of Monetary Economics* (1975), pp. 275–288; J. Walter Elliott and Jerome R. Baier, "Econometric Models and Current Interest Rates: How Well Do They Predict Future Rates?" *Journal of Finance*, September 1979, pp. 975–986; Richard Roll, *The Behavior of Interest Rates* (New York: Basic Books, 1970); Michael J. Hamburger and Elliott N. Platt, "The Expectations Hypothesis and the Efficiency of the Treasury Bill Market," *Review of Economics and Statistics*, May 1975, pp. 190–199.

However, a study by Brennan and Schwartz does not support the position that the market is efficient. They formulated a model to detect underpriced and overpriced bonds. For the government bond market, they found a strong relationship between the price-prediction errors generated from their model and subsequent bond returns. They conclude: "Whether or not this is interpreted as evidence of market inefficiency and profit opportunity will depend upon one's belief in the adequacy of the underlying equilibrium model and the accuracy of the price data." (See Michael J. Brennan and Eduardo Schwartz, "An Equilibrium Model of Bond Pricing and Tests of Market Efficiency," *Journal of Financial and Quantitative Analysis*, September 1982, pp. 301–330.)

bond market; (2) the price data are more reliable than for other sectors of the bond market; and (3) tests can be conducted without concern about the impact of credit risk.

To illustrate the problem with obtaining reliable prices for empirical testing even in the highly liquid government bond market, consider the following actual price quotes from five government dealers who were requested to provide quotes at the same point in time for the same Treasury issue (10.75%, maturing August 15, 2005):[16]

Dealer	Bid Price	Ask Price
A	128-2/32	128-6/32
B	128-3/32	128-5/32
C	128-4/32	128-8/32
D	128-5/32	128-9/32
E	128-6/32	128-8/32

The difference between the high bid price and low bid price is 4/32; it is also 4/32 for the ask prices. The results of any empirical tests on the efficiency of the government bond market will be materially impacted by the database used by the researcher. In most empirical studies of the efficiency of the government bond market, the prices used are those reported to the Federal Reserve by the reporting dealers. These prices are typically "indicator" prices, not execution prices, and they are only closing prices. Thus they are not necessarily the prices at which the dealer would buy or sell an issue. The prices are then averaged. Thus the prices are only the average of closing indicator prices. Subject to these price data limitations, studies of the government bond market suggest that this market is efficient, yet trading opportunities to enhance returns do occur.[17]

Studies examining whether all publicly available information is quickly embodied into the price of an issue (a test of the semistrong form of market efficiency) have been limited to the impact of corporate bond rating changes on bond yields. In an efficient market, rating changes should be anticipated by market participants since the data used by the commercial rating agencies, as well as their systems for rating issues, are generally known to market participants. Consequently, there should be no reaction to any change in bond rating. But

---

[16]Mossavar-Rahmani, "Understanding and Evaluating Index Fund Management."

[17]Robert M. Conroy and Richard J. Rendleman, "A Test of Market Efficiency in Government Bonds," *The Journal of Portfolio Management*, Summer 1987, pp. 57–64.

for a sample of public utility bonds, Katz found that there was no anticipation of a rating change.[18] In fact, his results suggest that there may be a 6- to 10-week lag between the rating change and a complete adjustment to the new rating. A study by Hettenhouse and Sartoris, also based on a sample of public utility bonds, found that while the upgrading of an issue was anticipated, the downgrading of an issue was not.[19] Focusing only on the downgrading of issues, Grier and Katz found that the anticipation of rating reclassifications differs for public utility and industrial issues.[20] For public utility issues, rating downgrades were not anticipated—just as was found in the earlier study by Katz. However, for the industrial bond issues in Grier and Katz's sample, a downgrading of the issuer's rating was anticipated.

Assuming that the ratings by commercial rating agencies are good indicators of the creditworthiness of issuers, these three studies suggest that the corporate bond market is inefficient and that the degree of inefficiency varies with the sector of the corporate bond market—the Grier and Katz study suggests that the public utility bond market may be less efficient than the industrial bond market. In contrast, a study by Weinstein of a sample of public utility and industrial bonds found that bond prices reflected rating changes 6 to 18 months prior to a change, with no adjustment in the 5 months before a change.[21] His findings suggest that the corporate bond market is efficient in the sense that public information about the issuer's credit worthiness is embodied into the price of the issue.

A fair conclusion is that there is no overwhelming evidence about the efficiency of the corporate bond market. Moreover, there is no evidence on another major sector of the bond market—the mortgage-backed securities market.

[18]Steven Katz, "The Price Adjustment Process of Bonds to Rating Reclassifications: A Test of Bond Market Efficiency," *Journal of Finance*, May 1974, pp. 551–559.

[19]George W. Hettenhouse and William L. Sartoris, "An Analysis of the Informational Value of Bond Rating Changes," *Quarterly Review of Economics and Business*, Summer 1976, pp. 65–78.

[20]Paul Grier and Steven Katz, "The Differential Effects of Bond Rating Changes Among Industrial and Public Utility Bonds by Maturity," *Journal of Business*, April 1976, pp. 226–239.

[21]Mark I. Weinstein, "The Effect of a Rating Change Announcement on Bond Prices," *Journal of Financial Economics* (1977), pp. 329–350.

SELECTING AN INDEX

A money manager who wishes to pursue an indexing strategy must determine which bond index to replicate. There are a number of bond indexes from which to select.[22] The most popular broad-based bond indexes are the Shearson Lehman Government/Corporate Index, the Merrill Lynch Domestic Master Index, and the Salomon Brothers Broad Investment-Grade Bond Index. There are also subindexes of the broad-based bond indexes that focus on a particular sector of the bond market. The major sectors are the Treasury market, the agency market, the corporate market, and the mortgage-backed securities market.

In recent years money managers, in consultation with their clients, have been moving in the direction of "customized benchmarks." A customized benchmark is one that has been designed to meet a client's specific requirements and long-term objectives.[23] For example, in December 1986 Salomon Brothers introduced its Large Pension Fund Baseline Bond Index as a standardized customized benchmark tailor-made for large pension funds "seeking to establish long-term core portfolios that more closely match the longer durations of their nominal dollar liabilities."[24]

Why have broker/dealer firms developed and aggressively marketed their bond indexes? Enhancing the firm's image is only a minor reason. The key motivation is the potential profit that the firm will generate by executing trades to set up an indexed portfolio and rebalance it. Typically, a broker/dealer charges a money manager who wants to set up or rebalance an index only a nominal amount for providing the necessary data, but then expects that the bulk of the trades will be executed through its own trading desks. Also, by keeping the make-up of the index proprietary (unlike the Dow Jones or S&P stock indexes), those firms attempt to lock customers in to using their index.

---

[22]For a listing of popular bond indexes, see Arthur Williams III and Noreen M. Conwell, "Fixed Income Indexes," in Frank J. Fabozzi and Irving M. Pollack, eds., *The Handbook of Fixed Income Securities*, 2nd ed. (Homewood, IL: Dow Jones-Irwin, 1987).

[23]For a discussion of customized benchmarks and the reasons for the growing interest in them, see Sharmine Mossavar-Rahmani, "Customized Benchmarks in Structured Management," *The Journal of Portfolio Management*, Summer 1987, pp. 65–68.

[24]Martin L. Leibowitz, Thomas Klaffky, and Steven Mandel, "Introducing the Salomon Brothers Large Pension Fund Baseline Bond Index" (New York: Salomon Brothers Inc, December 1986), p. 1.

INDEXING METHODOLOGIES

Once a money manager has decided to pursue an indexing strategy and has selected an index (broad-based bond index, subindex, or customized benchmark), the next step is to construct a portfolio that will track the index. Any discrepancy between the performance of the indexed portfolio and the index (whether positive or negative) is referred to as *tracking error.* Tracking errors have three sources: (1) transaction costs in constructing the indexed portfolio; (2) differences in the composition of the indexed portfolio and the index itself; and (3) discrepancies between prices used by the organization constructing the index and transaction prices paid by the indexer.

One approach in constructing the indexed portfolio is for the money manager to purchase all the issues in the index according to their weight in the benchmark index. While the indexed portfolio will obviously mirror the performance of the index before transaction costs, tracking error will result from the transaction costs associated with purchasing all the issues and reinvesting cash flow (maturing principal and coupon interest). Since a broad-based bond index may include over 5,000 issues, large transaction costs may make this approach impractical. In addition, some issues in the index may not be available at the prices used in constructing the index.

Instead of purchasing all issues in the index, the money manager may purchase just a sample of issues. While this approach reduces tracking error resulting from high transaction costs, it increases tracking error resulting from the mismatch of the indexed portfolio and the index.

Generally speaking, the fewer the number of issues used to replicate the index, the smaller is the tracking error due to transaction costs but the greater is the tracking error risk due to the mismatch of the characteristics of the indexed portfolio and the index. In contrast, the greater the number of issues purchased to replicate the index, the greater is the tracking error due to transaction costs and the smaller is the tracking error risk due to the mismatch of the index portfolio and the index. Obviously, then, there is a trade-off between tracking error and the number of issues used to construct the indexed portfolio.

There are three popular methodologies for designing a portfolio to replicate an index: (1) the stratified sampling or cell approach; (2) the optimization approach; and (3) the variance minimization approach. For each of these approaches, the initial question that the indexer must ask is: What are the factors that affect a bond index's performance? Each approach assumes that the performance of an individual bond depends on a number of systematic factors that affect the performance of all bonds and a factor unique to the individual issue. The objective of the three approaches is to construct an indexed portfolio that eliminates the performance attributed to the factors unique to all the issues in the indexed portfolio.

Stratified Sampling or Cell Approach

Under this approach the index is divided into cells, each cell representing a different characteristic of the index. The most common characteristics used to break down an index are: (1) duration; (2) coupon; (3) maturity; (4) market sectors (Treasury, corporate, mortgage-backed); (5) credit rating; (6) call factors; and (7) sinking-fund features. The last two factors are particularly important since the call and refunding features of an issue will impact its performance.[25]

For example, suppose that the following characteristics are selected to partition a Treasury/agency/corporate bond index:

Characteristic 1—call-adjusted duration range:
1. Less than or equal to 5
2. Greater than 5

Characteristic 2—maturity range:
1. Less than 5 years
2. Between 5 and 15 years
3. Greater than 15 years

Characteristic 3—market sectors:
1. Treasury
2. Agencies
3. Corporates

Characteristic 4—credit rating:
1. Triple A
2. Double A
3. Single A
4. Triple B

The total number of cells would be equal to:

---

[25]For a discussion of the importance of call and sinking-fund features on performance, see Chris P. Dialynas, "The Active Decisions in the Selection of Passive Management and Performance Bogeys," in *Advances in Bond Analysis and Portfolio Strategies*.

$2 \times 3 \times 3 \times 4 = 72$

The objective is then to select from all of the issues in the index one or more issues in each cell that can be used to represent that entire cell. The total dollar amount purchased of the issues from each cell will be based on the percentage of the index's total market value that the cell represents. For example, if 40% of the total market value of all the issues in the index are corporate bonds, then 40% of the market value of the indexed portfolio should be composed of corporate bond issues.

The number of cells that the indexer uses will depend on the dollar amount of the portfolio to be indexed. In indexing a portfolio of less than $50 million, for example, using a large number of cells would require purchasing odd lots of issues. This increases the cost of buying the issues to represent a cell, and thus would increase the tracking error. Reducing the number of cells to overcome this problem increases tracking error risk of index mismatch because the characteristics of the indexed portfolio may differ materially from those of the index.

Optimization Approach[26]

In this approach the money manager seeks to design an indexed portfolio that will match the cell breakdown just described and satisfy other constraints but also optimize some objective. An objective may be to maximize the yield to maturity or some other yield measure, to maximize convexity, or to maximize expected total returns.[27] Constraints other than matching the cell breakdown might include not purchasing more than a specified amount of one issuer or group of issuers and overweighting certain sectors for enhanced indexing (discussed later in this chapter).

The computational technique used to derive the optimal solution to the indexing problem in this approach is mathematical programming. When the objective function that the indexer seeks to optimize is a linear function, linear programming (a specific form of mathematical programming) is used. If the objective function is quadratic, then the particular mathematical programming technique used is quadratic programming. This form lends itself easily to sensitivity analysis.

---

[26]For an illustration of this technique, see Galdi, "Indexing Fixed Income Portfolios."

[27]For a mathematical presentation of this approach as well as the variance minimization approach, see Christina Seix and Ravi Akoury, "Bond Indexation: The Optimal Quantitative Approach," *The Journal of Portfolio Management*, Spring 1986, pp. 50–53.

Variance Minimization Approach

The variance minimization approach is by far the most complex. With this approach it is necessary to use historical data to estimate the variance of the tracking error. This is done by estimating a price function for every issue in the index. The price function is estimated on the basis of two sets of factors: (1) the cash flows from the issue discounted at the theoretical spot rates;[28] and (2) other characteristics such as those discussed earlier. Using a large universe of issues and elaborate econometric techniques, the price function is estimated from historical data. Once the price function for each issue is obtained, a variance equation for the tracking error can be constructed. The objective then is to minimize the variance of the tracking error in constructing the indexed portfolio. Since the variance is a quadratic function (the difference between the benchmark return and the indexed portfolio's return, squared), quadratic programming is used to find the optimal indexed portfolio in terms of minimized tracking error. The biggest problem with this approach is that estimating the price function from historical data is very difficult in the Treasury market, let alone the corporate market or the new issue market. Also the price function may not be stable.

Although the stratified sampling (or cell) approach seems to be the easiest to use, it is extremely difficult to implement when large, diversified portfolios are utilized as the benchmark. In this case, many cells are required and the problem becomes complex. Also, since the hand-picking of issues to match each cell is subjective, tracking error may result. Mathematical programming reduces the complexity of the problem when well-defined constraints are employed and allows the indexer to optimally analyze large quantities of data. In practice, most indexers use either the optimization or variance minimization approach for tracking the benchmark.

TRACKING ERROR

How well do indexed portfolios constructed using an optimization approach track benchmark indexes? Exhibit 13.1 presents the results of a study by Salomon Brothers on the tracking error for the Salomon Brothers Broad Based Investment-Grade Bond Index and

---

[28]See Chapter 6.

three subindexes using an optimal indexed portfolio methodology devised by Salomon Brothers. The tracking error was computed each month between January 1985 and November 1986 as the difference between the monthly return on the indexed portfolio and the monthly return on the benchmark index. A positive (negative) tracking error indicates that the monthly return on the indexed portfolio outperformed (underperformed) the monthly return on the index. Summary statistics (standard deviation, mean, high, and low) for the monthly tracking errors and the cumulative tracking error over the entire 2-year period are shown in Exhibit 13.1.

As can be seen from the exhibit, tracking error varies according to the benchmark. The smallest tracking error resulted when the index benchmark comprised only government securities. This is expected since most government securities have similar features, no credit risk, and minimal call risk if any. By far the more difficult sector to track was the corporate bond market. This was probably because of the difference between the call and sinking-fund characteristics of the indexed portfolio and those of the index, as well as the smaller diversification (higher unique risk) for the indexed portfolio relative to the index. For the broad market index, the tracking performance was similar to that of the government index. This is understandable because the government index makes up 60% of the broad market index.

EXHIBIT 13.1   Tracking Error of Monthly Returns in Basis Points (1984–1985)

Sector	Standard Deviation	Mean	High	Low	Total Return Cumulative	Total Return Annualized
Broad market	54	2	13	−6	69	34
Governments	2	2	5	−1	63	31
Corporates*	17	9	40	−26	301	156
Mortgages	3	0	6	−7	6	3
Broad market (Including transaction costs)	5	0	11	−8	−12	−6

*Analysis between January 1985 and November 1986.
Source: Sharmine Mossavar-Rahmani, "Understanding and Evaluating Index Fund Management," in Frank J. Fabozzi and T. Dessa Garlicki, eds., *Advances in Bond Analysis and Portfolio Strategies* (Chicago, IL: Probus Publishing, 1987). Based on Salomon Brothers Broad Investment-Grade Bond Index and its components.

LOGISTICAL PROBLEMS IN IMPLEMENTING
AN INDEXING STRATEGY[29]

An indexer faces several logistical problems in constructing an indexed portfolio. First of all, the prices for each issue used by the organization that publishes the index may be not be execution prices available to the indexer. In fact, they may be materially different from the prices offered by some dealers, as we demonstrated earlier in this chapter when we listed five bid-ask prices for the same U.S. Treasury bond. The differences between prices offered by various dealers are even greater in the corporate bond market

In addition, the prices used by organizations reporting the value of indexes are based on bid prices. However, dealer ask prices are the ones that the money manager would have to transact at when constructing or rebalancing the indexed portfolio. Thus there will be a bias between the performance of the index and the indexed portfolio equal to the bid-ask spread.

Furthermore, there are logistical problems unique to certain sectors in the bond market. Consider first the corporate bond market. There are typically about 3,500 issues in the corporate bond sector of a broad-based index. Because of the illiquidity of this sector of the bond market, not only may the prices used by the organization that publishes the index be unreliable, but many of the issues may not even be available. Next, consider the mortgage-backed securities market. There are over 300,000 agency pass-through issues. The organizations that publish indexes lump all these issues into a few hundred generic issues. The indexer is then faced with the difficult task of finding pass-through securities with the same risk/return profiles of these hypothetical issues.[30]

Finally, recall that the total return depends on the reinvestment rate earned on coupon interest. If the organization publishing the index regularly overestimates the reinvestment rate, then the indexed portfolio could underperform the index by 10 to 15 basis points a year.[31]

---

[29]For a more detailed discussion, see Mossavar-Rahmani, "Understanding and Evaluating Index Fund Management," pp. 438–440.

[30]For an explanation of how to deal with the unique problems associated with tracking a mortgage-backed securities index, see Llewellyn Miller, Edward P. Krawitt, and Michael P. Wands, "Mortgage Index Portfolios," Chap. 39 in Frank J. Fabozzi, ed., *The Handbook Mortgage-Backed Securities*, 2nd ed. (Chicago, IL: Probus Publishing, 1988).

[31]Hawthorne, "The Battle of the Bond Indexes," p. 122.

ENHANCED INDEXING

So far we have discussed straight or "plain vanilla" indexing. The objective of this strategy is to replicate the total return performance of some predetermined index. In *enhanced indexing* (also called *"indexing plus"*), the objective is to consistently exceed the total return performance of the index by an amount sufficient to justify a higher management advisory fee and a higher level of risk of underperforming the index. The total return on the index becomes the minimum total return objective rather the target total return. Thus enhanced indexing brings active strategies back into the portfolio management process. However, the active strategies employed to generate an enhanced return above the index should be low-risk strategies.

What are some of the strategies employed in enhanced indexing? We discussed most of them earlier in this book. For example, in Chapter 6 we described strategies for synthetically creating an issue out of two or more issues so that the synthetic issue will have the same duration but better convexity. Thus the overall risk of the portfolio will not be increased. Any of the swap strategies employed would involve only those issues in the index. Another strategy for enhancing total return is to use securities not included in the index. For example, the broad-based indexes do not include derivative mortgage-backed securities (collateralized mortgage obligations and stripped mortgage-backed securities). If the money manager pursuing an enhanced index strategy believes that derivative mortgage-backed securities will outperform the agency pass-through securities in the index, he will substitute the former securities for the latter. Or the money manager may be able to synthetically create agency pass-through securities by using stripped mortgage-backed securities (interest-only and principal-only securities) that would exhibit better performance in certain interest rate environments.[32]

SUMMARY

Active portfolio management strategies rely on expectations of interest rate changes and/or changes in yield relationships. In contrast, this

---

[32]For a further discussion of strategies to outperform an index, see Mark L. Dunetz and James M. Mahoney, "Indexation and Optimal Strategies in Portfolio Management," in Frank J. Fabozzi, ed., *Fixed Income Portfolio Strategies*. (Chicago, IL: Probus Publishing, 1989).

chapter explained that structured portfolio strategies are designed to satisfy a predetermined objective—either matching the performance of a specific bond index (or outperforming it by enough to offset the strategy's higher costs and risk, as in the case of enhanced indexing) or generating sufficient funds to satisfy a single or multiple liability.

We saw that the indexing approach requires selecting a bond index (broad-based index, subindex, or customized index) and constructing an indexed portfolio so as to minimize tracking error. The methodologies used to construct an indexed portfolio include the sampling or cell approach, the optimization approach, and the variance minimization approach. In an enhanced indexing strategy the performance of the index becomes the minimum return objective that the indexer attempts to achieve.

14

STRUCTURED PORTFOLIO STRATEGIES II:
Liability Funding (Immunization and Cash Flow Matching)

In the previous chapter we explained that the objective of a structured portfolio strategy is to design a portfolio that will achieve the performance of some predetermined benchmark. When the predetermined benchmark is either a single liability or multiple liabilities, the strategy is referred to as *liability funding*. Specifically, when the liability is a single liability, an immunuization strategy is employed. When there are multiple liabilities, there are two strategies to choose from: multi-period immunization and cash flow matching. This chapter describes liability funding strategies. We begin with the immunization of a single liability.

IMMUNIZATION OF A PORTFOLIO TO SATISFY A SINGLE LIABILITY[1]

To comprehend the basic principles underlying the immunization of a portfolio against interest rate changes so as to satisfy a single liability, consider the situation faced by a life insurance company that sells a guaranteed investment contract (GIC). Under this policy, for a

---

[1] The theory of immunization was first set forth in F. M. Reddington, "Review of the Principle of Life Office Valuations," *Journal of the Institute of Actuaries* (1952), pp. 286–340.

lump sum payment a life insurance company guarantees that specified dollars will be paid to the policyholder at a specified future date. Or, equivalently, the life insurance company guarantees a specified rate of return on the payment. For example, suppose that a life insurance company sells a GIC that guarantees an interest rate of 6.25% every 6 months (12.5% on a bond-equivalent yield basis) for 5.5 years (11 6-month periods). Also suppose that the payment made by the policy-holder is $8,820,262. Then the value that the life insurance company has guaranteed the policyholder 5.5 years from now is:[2]

$$\$8,820,262 \ (1.0625)^{11} = \$17,183,033$$

When investing the $8,820,262, the target accumulated value for the portfolio manager of the life insurance company is $17,183,033 after 5.5 years, which is the same as a target yield of 12.5% on a bond-equivalent basis.

Suppose the portfolio manager buys $8,820,262 par value of a bond selling at par with a 12.5% yield to maturity that matures in 5.5 years. Will the portfolio manager be assured of realizing the target yield of 12.5% or, equivalently, a target accumulated value of $17,183,033? As we explained in Chapter 3, the portfolio manager will only realize a 12.5% yield if the coupon interest payments can be reinvested at 6.25% every 6 months. That is, the accumulated value will depend on the reinvestment rate.

To demonstrate this we will suppose that immediately after investing the $8,820,262 in the 12.5% coupon, 5.5-year maturity bond, yields in the market change and stay at the new level for the remainder of the 5.5 years. Exhibit 14.1 illustrates what happens at the end of 5.5 years. The first column shows the new yield level. The second column shows the total coupon interest payments. The third column gives the interest-on-interest over the entire 5.5 years if the coupon interest payments are reinvested at the new yield level shown in the first column.[3] The price of the bond at the end of 5.5 years shown in the fourth column is the par value. The fifth column is the accumulated value from all three sources: coupon interest, interest-on-interest, and bond price. The realized compound yield is shown in the last column,

---

[2]Actually, the life insurance company will not guarantee the interest rate that it expects to earn, but a lower rate. The spread between the interest rate that the life insurance company can earn and the interest rate it guarantees is the return for the risk of not achieving the target rate.

[3]The formula for computing the interest-on-interest is given in Chapter 3.

EXHIBIT 14.1   Accumulated Value and Realized Compound Yield After 5.5 Years: 5.5-Year, 12.5% Bond Selling to Yield 12.5%

Investment horizon (years)	= 5.5
Coupon rate	= 0.125
Maturity (years)	= 5.5
Yield to maturity	= 0.125
Price	= 100
Par value purchased	= $8,820,262
Purchase price	= $8,820,262
Target accumulated value	= $17,183,033

			After 5.5 Years:		
New Yield*	Coupon Interest	Interest-on-Interest	Price of Bond⁺	Accumulated Value	Realized Compound Yield
0.160	$6,063,930	$3,112,167	$8,820,262	$17,996,360	0.1340
0.155	6,063,930	2,990,716	8,820,262	17,874,908	0.1326
0.145	6,063,930	2,753,177	8,820,262	17,637,369	0.1300
0.140	6,063,930	2,637,037	8,820,262	17,521,230	0.1288
0.135	6,063,930	2,522,618	8,820,262	17,406,810	0.1275
0.130	6,063,930	2,409,984	8,820,262	17,294,086	0.1262
0.125	6,063,930	2,298,840	8,820,262	17,183,033	0.1250
0.120	6,063,930	2,189,433	8,820,262	17,073,625	0.1238
0.115	6,063,930	2,081,648	8,820,262	16,965,840	0.1225
0.110	6,063,930	1,975,462	8,820,262	16,859,654	0.1213
0.105	6,063,930	1,870,852	8,820,262	16,755,044	0.1201
0.100	6,063,930	1,767,794	8,820,262	16,651,986	0.1189
0.095	6,063,930	1,666,266	8,820,262	16,550,458	0.1178
0.090	6,063,930	1,566,246	8,820,262	16,450,438	0.1166
0.085	6,063,930	1,467,712	8,820,262	16,351,904	0.1154
0.080	6,063,930	1,370,642	8,820,262	16,254,834	0.1143
0.075	6,063,930	1,275,014	8,820,262	16,159,206	0.1132
0.070	6,063,930	1,180,808	8,820,262	16,065,000	0.1120
0.065	6,063,930	1,088,003	8,820,262	15,972,195	0.1109
0.060	6,063,930	996,577	8,820,262	15,880,769	0.1098
0.055	6,063,930	906,511	8,820,262	15,790,703	0.1087
0.050	6,063,930	817,785	8,820,262	15,701,977	0.1077

*Immediate change in yield.
⁺Maturity value.

using the following formula:[4]

$$2\left[\left(\frac{\text{Accumulated value}}{\$8,820,262}\right)^{1/11} - 1\right]$$

[4] The formula for finding the realized compound yield is given in Chapter 3.

If yields do not change, so that the coupon payments can be reinvested at 12.5% (6.25% every 6 months), the target accumulated value will be achieved by the portfolio manager. If market yields rise, an accumulated value (realized compound yield) higher than the target accumulated value (target yield) will be achieved. This is because the coupon interest payments can be reinvested at a higher rate than the initial yield to maturity. Contrast this with what happens when the yield declines. The accumulated value (realized compound yield) will be less than the target accumulated value (target yield). *Therefore investing in a coupon bond with a yield to maturity equal to the target yield and a maturity equal to the investment horizon does not assure that the target accumulated value will be achieved.*

Suppose that instead of investing in a bond maturing in 5.5 years the portfolio manager invests in a 15-year bond with a coupon rate of 12.5% that is selling at par to yield 12.5%. Exhibit 14.2 presents the accumulated value and realized compound yield if the market yield changes immediately after the bond is purchased and remains at the new yield level. The fourth column of the exhibit is the market price of a 12.5% coupon, 9.5-year bond (since 5.5 years have passed), assuming the market yields shown in the first column. If the market yield increases, the portfolio will fail to achieve the target accumulated value; the opposite will be true if the market yield decreases—the accumulated value (realized compound yield) will exceed the target accumulated value (target yield).

The reason for this result can be seen in Exhibit 14.3 which summarizes the change in interest-on-interest and the change in price resulting from a change in the market yield. For example, if the market yield rises instantaneously by 200 basis points, from 12.5% to 14.5%, interest-on-interest will be $454,336 greater; however, the market price of the bond will decrease by $894,781. The net effect is that the accumulated value will be $440,445 less than the target accumulated value. The reverse will be true if the market yield decreases. The change in price of the bond will more than offset the decline in the interest-on-interest, resulting in an accumulated value that exceeds the target accumulated value.

Now we can see what is happening to the accumulated value. There is a trade-off between interest rate (or price) risk and reinvestment risk. For this 15-year bond, the target accumulated value will be realized only if the market yield does not increase.

EXHIBIT 14.2 Accumulated Value and Realized Compound Yield After 5.5 Years: 15-Year, 12.5% Bond Selling to Yield 12.5%

Investment horizon (years)	= 5.5
Coupon rate	= .1250
Maturity (years)	= 15
Yield to maturity	= .1250
Price	= 100
Par value purchased	= $8,820,262
Purchase price	= $8,820,262
Target accumulated value	= $17,183,033

			After 5.5 Years		
New Yield*	Coupon Interest	Interest-on-Interest	Price of Bond	Accumulated Value	Realized Compound Yield
0.160	$6,063,930	$3,112,167	$7,337,902	$16,514,000	0.1173
0.155	6,063,930	2,990,716	7,526,488	16,581,134	0.1181
0.145	6,063,930	2,753,117	7,925,481	16,742,587	0.1200
0.140	6,063,930	2,637,037	8,136,542	16,837,510	0.1211
0.135	6,063,930	2,522,618	8,355,777	16,942,325	0.1223
0.130	6,063,930	2,409,894	8,583,555	17,057,379	0.1236
0.125	6,063,930	2,298,840	8,820,262	17,183,033	0.1250
0.120	6,063,930	2,189,433	9,066,306	17,319,669	0.1265
0.115	6,063,930	2,081,648	9,322,113	17,467,691	0.1282
0.110	6,063,930	1,975,462	9,588,131	17,627,523	0.1299
0.105	6,063,930	1,870,852	9,864,831	17,799,613	0.1318
0.100	6,063,930	1,767,794	10,152,708	17,984,432	0.1338
0.095	6,063,930	1,666,266	10,452,281	18,182,477	0.1359
0.090	6,063,930	1,566,246	10,764,095	18,394,271	0.1382
0.085	6,063,930	1,467,712	11,088,723	18,620,366	0.1406
0.080	6,063,930	1,370,642	11,462,770	18,861,342	0.1431
0.075	6,063,930	1,275,014	11,778,867	19,117,812	0.1457
0.070	6,063,930	1,180,808	12,145,682	19,390,420	0.1485
0.065	6,063,930	1,088,003	12,527,914	19,679,847	0.1514
0.060	6,063,930	996,577	12,926,301	19,986,808	0.1544
0.055	6,063,930	906,511	13,341,617	20,312,058	0.1576
0.050	6,063,930	817,785	13,774,677	20,656,393	0.1609

*Immediate change in yield.

Since neither a coupon bond with the same maturity nor a bond with a longer maturity ensures realization of the target accumulated value, maybe a bond with a maturity shorter than 5.5 years will. Consider a 12.5% bond with 6 months remaining to maturity selling at par. Exhibit 14.4 shows the accumulated value and realized compound

EXHIBIT 14.3   Change in Interest-on-Interest and Price Due to Interest Rate Change After 5.5 Years: 15-Year, 12.5% Bond Selling to Yield 12.5%

New Yield	Change in Interest-on-Interest	Change in Price	Total Change in Accumulated Value
0.160	$813,327	-$1,482,360	-$669,033
0.155	692,875	-1,293,774	-601,898
0.145	454,336	-894,781	-440,445
0.140	338,197	-683,720	-345,523
0.135	223,778	-464,485	-240,707
0.130	111,054	-236,707	-125,654
0.125	0	0	0
0.120	-109,407	246,044	136,636
0.115	-217,192	501,851	284,659
0.110	-323,378	767,869	444,491
0.105	-427,989	1,044,569	616,581
0.100	-531,046	1,332,446	801,400
0.095	-632,574	1,632,019	999,445
0.090	-732,594	1,943,833	1,211,239
0.085	-831,128	2,268,461	1,437,333
0.080	-928,198	2,606,508	1,678,309
0.075	-1,023,826	2,958,605	1,934,779
0.070	-1,118,032	3,325,420	2,207,388
0.065	-1,210,838	3,707,652	2,496,814
0.060	-1,302,263	4,106,039	2,803,776
0.055	-1,392,329	4,521,355	3,129,026
0.050	-1,481,055	4,954,415	3,473,360

yield over the 5.5-year investment horizon. The second column shows the accumulated value after 6 months. The third column shows the value that is accumulated after 5.5 years by reinvesting the value accumulated after 6 months at the yield shown in the first column. That is:

$$\$9,371,528\left(1 + \frac{\text{New yield}}{2}\right)^{10}$$

By investing in this 6-month bond, the portfolio manager incurs no interest rate risk, though there is reinvestment risk. The target accumulated value will be achieved only if the market yield remains at 12.5% or rises. Once again, the portfolio manager is not assured of achieving the target accumulated value.

EXHIBIT 14.4   **Accumulated Value and Realized Compound Yield: 6-Month, 12.5% Bond Selling to Yield 12.5%**

Investment horizon (years)   = 5.5
Coupon Rate   = 0.125
Maturity (years)   = 0.5
Yield to maturity   = 0.125
Price   = 100
Par value purchased   = $8,820,262
Purchase price   = $8,820,262
Target accumulated value   = $17,183,033

| New Yield* | After 6 Months | After 5.5 Years | |
		Accumulated Value	Realized Compound Yield
0.160	$9,371,528	$20,232,427	0.1568
0.155	$9,371,528	$19,768,932	0.1523
0.145	$9,371,528	$18,870,501	0.1432
0.140	$9,371,528	$18,435,215	0.1386
0.135	$9,371,528	$18,008,986	0.1341
0.130	$9,371,528	$17,591,647	0.1295
0.125	$9,371,528	$17,183,033	0.1250
0.120	$9,371,528	$16,782,980	0.1205
0.115	$9,371,528	$16,391,330	0.1159
0.110	$9,371,528	$16,007,924	0.1114
0.105	$9,371,528	$15,632,609	0.1068
0.100	$9,371,528	$15,265,232	0.1023
0.095	$9,371,528	$14,905,644	0.0977
0.090	$9,371,528	$14,553,697	0.0932
0.085	$9,371,528	$14,209,247	0.0886
0.080	$9,371,528	$13,872,151	0.0841
0.075	$9,371,528	$13,542,270	0.0795
0.070	$9,371,528	$13,219,466	0.0749
0.065	$9,371,528	$12,903,604	0.0704
0.060	$9,371,528	$12,594,550	0.0658
0.055	$9,371,528	$12,292,175	0.0613
0.050	$9,371,528	$11,996,349	0.0567

*Immediate change in yield.

If we assume there is a one-time instantaneous change in the market yield, is there a coupon bond that the portfolio manager can purchase to assure the target accumulated value regardless of whether the market yield rises or falls? The portfolio manager should look for a coupon bond such that regardless of how the market yield changes, the change in the interest-on-interest will be offset by the change in the price.

Consider, for example, an 8-year, 10.125% coupon bond selling at 88.20262 to yield 12.5%. Suppose $10,000,000 of par value of this bond is purchased for $8,820,262. Exhibit 14.5 provides the same

EXHIBIT 14.5   Accumulated Value and Realized Compound Yield: 8-Year, 10.125% Bond Selling to Yield 12.5%

Investment horizon (years) = 5.5
Coupon rate   = 0.10125
Maturity (years)   = 8
Yield to maturity   = 0.125
Price   = 88.20262
Par value purchased   = $10,000,000
Purchase price   = $8,820,262
Target accumulated value   = $17,183,033

| | | | After 5.5 Years | | |
New Yield*	Coupon Interest	Interest-on-Interest	Price of Bond	Accumulated Value	Realized Compound Yield
0.160	$5,568,750	$2,858,028	$8,827,141	$17,253,919	0.1258
0.155	5,568,750	2,746,494	8,919,852	17,235,096	0.1256
0.145	5,568,750	2,528,352	9,109,054	17,206,156	0.1253
0.140	5,568,750	2,421,697	9,205,587	17,196,034	0.1251
0.135	5,568,750	2,316,621	9,303,435	17,188,807	0.1251
0.130	5,568,750	2,213,102	9,402,621	17,184,473	0.1250
0.125	5,568,750	2,111,117	9,503,166	17,183,033	0.1250
0.120	5,568,750	2,010,644	9,605,091	17,184,485	0.1250
0.115	5,568,750	1,911,661	9,708,420	17,188,831	0.1251
0.110	5,568,750	1,814,146	9,813,175	17,196,071	0.1251
0.105	5,568,750	1,718,078	9,919,380	17,206,208	0.1253
0.100	5,568,750	1,623,436	10,027,059	17,219,245	0.1254
0.095	5,568,750	1,530,199	10,136,236	17,235,185	0.1256
0.090	5,568,750	1,438,347	10,246,936	17,254,033	0.1258
0.085	5,568,750	1,347,859	10,359,184	17,275,793	0.1260
0.080	5,568,750	1,258,715	10,473,006	17,300,472	0.1263
0.075	5,568,750	1,170,897	10,588,428	17,328,075	0.1266
0.070	5,568,750	1,084,383	10,705,477	17,358,610	0.1270
0.065	5,568,750	999,156	10,824,180	17,392,086	0.1273
0.060	5,568,750	915,197	10,944,565	17,428,511	0.1277
0.055	5,568,750	832,486	11,066,660	17,467,895	0.1282
0.050	5,568,750	751,005	11,190,494	17,510,248	0.1286

*Immediate change in yield.

EXHIBIT 14.6   Change in Interest-on-Interest and Price Due to Interest Rate Change After 5.5 Years: 8-Year, 10.125% Bond Selling to Yield 12.5%

New Yield	Change in Interest-on-Interest	Change in Price	Total Change in Accumulated Value
0.160	$746,911	−$676,024	$70,887
0.155	635,377	−583,314	52,063
0.145	417,235	−394,112	23,123
0.140	310,580	−297,579	13,001
0.135	205,504	−199,730	5,774
0.130	101,985	−100,544	1,441
0.125	0	0	0
0.120	−100,473	101,925	1,452
0.115	−199,456	205,254	5,798
0.110	−296,971	310,010	13,038
0.105	−393,039	416,215	23,176
0.100	−487,681	523,894	36,212
0.095	−580,918	633,071	52,153
0.090	−672,770	743,771	71,000
0.085	−763,258	856,019	92,760
0.080	−852,402	969,841	117,439
0.075	−940,221	1,085,263	145,042
0.070	−1,026,734	1,202,311	175,578
0.065	−1,111,961	1,321,014	209,053
0.060	−1,195,921	1,441,399	245,478
0.055	−1,278,632	1,563,494	284,862
0.050	−1,360,112	1,687,328	327,216

information for this bond as Exhibits 14.1 and 14.2 did for our previous examples. Looking at the last two columns, we see that the accumulated value and the realized compound yield are never less than the target accumulated value and the target yield. Thus the target accumulated value is assured regardless of what happens to the market yield. Exhibit 14.6 shows why. When the market yield rises, the change in the interest-on-interest more than offsets the decline in price. When the market yield declines, the increase in price exceeds the decline in interest-on-interest.

What characteristic of this bond assures that the target accumulated value will be realized regardless of how the market yield changes? The Macaulay duration for each of the four bonds that we considered is:

Bond	Macaulay Duration
5.5-year, 12.5% coupon, selling at par	4.14 years
15-year, 12.5% coupon, selling at par	7.12 years
6-month, 12.5% coupon, selling at par	0.50 years
8-year, 10.125% coupon, selling for 88.20262	5.50 years

Notice that the last bond, which assures that the target accumulated value will be achieved regardless of what happens to the market yield, has a Macaulay duration equal to the length of the investment horizon. This is the key. *To immunize a portfolio's target accumulated value (target yield) against a change in the market yield, a portfolio manager must invest in a bond (or a bond portfolio) such that (1) the Macaulay duration is equal to the investment horizon and (2) the initial present value of the cash flow from the bond (or bond portfolio) equals the present value of the future liability.*

Rebalancing an Immunized Portfolio

In our illustrations of the principles underlying immunization, we assumed a one-time instantaneous change in the market yield. In practice, the market yield will fluctuate over the investment horizon. As a result, the Macaulay duration of the portfolio will change as the market yield changes. In addition, the Macaulay duration will change simply because of the passage of time.

Even in the face of changing market yields a portfolio can be immunized if it is rebalanced so that its Macaulay duration is equal to the remaining time of the investment horizon. For example, if the investment horizon is initially 5.5 years, the initial portfolio should have a Macaulay duration of 5.5 years. After 6 months the investment horizon will be 5 years, but the Macaulay duration of the portfolio will probably be different from 5 years. Thus the portfolio must be rebalanced so that its Macaulay duration is equal to 5. Six months later the portfolio must be rebalanced again so that its Macaulay duration will equal 4.5 years. And so on.

How often should the portfolio be rebalanced to adjust its Macaulay duration? On the one hand, more frequent rebalancing increases transaction costs, thereby reducing the likelihood of achieving the target yield. On the other hand, less frequent rebalancing will result in the Macaulay duration wandering from the target Macaulay duration, which will also reduce the likelihood of achieving the target yield. Thus the portfolio manager faces a trade-off: some transaction costs must be accepted to prevent the Macaulay duration from wandering too far from its target; but some maladjustment in the Macaulay duration must be lived with or transaction costs will become prohibitively high.

Immunization Risk

The sufficient condition for the immunization of a single liability is that the Macaulay duration of the portfolio be equal to the length of the investment horizon. However, a portfolio will only be immunized against interest rate changes if the yield curve is flat and any changes in the yield curve are parallel changes (that is, interest rates move either up or down by the same number of basis points for all maturities). Recall from Chapter 4 that Macaulay duration is a measure of price volatility for parallel shifts in the yield curve. If there is a change in interest rates that does not correspond to this shape-preserving shift, matching the Macaulay duration to the investment horizon will not assure immunization. That is, the target yield will no longer be the minimum realized yield for the portfolio.

Empirical studies of the effectiveness of immunization strategies based on Macaulay duration clearly demonstrate that immunization does not work perfectly in the real world. In the first study of immunization, Fisher and Weil found that the duration-based immunization strategy would have come closer to the target yield or exceeded it more often than a strategy based on matching the maturity of the portfolio to the investment horizon for the period 1925 through 1968, even after considering transaction costs.[5] When Ingersoll critically evaluated the Fisher-Weil study, using actual prices rather than the indices utilized by their study, he did not find support for the claim that a duration-matching strategy outperformed a maturity strategy.[6] However, studies by Bierwag, Kaufman, Schweitzer, and Toevs,[7] Hackett,[8]

---

[5]Lawrence Fisher and Roman L. Weil, "Coping with the Risk of Interest Rate Fluctuations: Returns to Bondholders from Naive and Optimal Strategies," *Journal of Business*, October 1971, pp. 408–431.

[6]Jonathan E. Ingersoll, "Is Immunization Feasible? Evidence from the CRSP Data," in George K. Kaufman, G. O. Bierwag, and Alden Toevs, eds., *Innovations of Bond Portfolio Management: Duration Analysis and Immunization* (Greenwich, CT: JAI Press, 1983).

[7]G. O. Bierwag, George C. Kaufman, Robert Schweitzer, and Alden Toevs, "The Art of Risk Management in Bond Portfolios," *The Journal of Portfolio Management*, Spring 1981, pp. 27–36.

[8]T. Hackett, "A Simulation Analysis of Immunization Strategies Applied to Bond Portfolios," unpublished doctoral dissertation, University of Oregon, 1981.

Lau,[9] and Leibowitz and Weinberger[10] all support the theory that a duration-matched portfolio will outperform a maturity-matched portfolio. Yet, contrary to what immunization theory would lead us to expect, a common finding was that when a duration-matched strategy was employed, the realized yield was frequently below the target yield. As for the magnitude of the divergence, Leibowitz and Weinberger found that for 5-year investment horizons from January 1958 to January 1975, the realized yield did not fall below the target yield by more than 25 basis points.

The divergence of the realized yield from the target yield is due to the assumption that the yield curve is flat and changes only in a parallel fashion. Several researchers have relaxed this assumption and developed measures of duration based on a yield curve that is not flat and does not shift in a parallel fashion. Exhibit 14.7 shows the different shifts that are possible. Panel A is the yield curve and yield curve shift assumed in Macaulay duration. Panel B assumes that the yield curve is not flat, but that any changes are parallel changes. Panels C and D show two examples of when changes in interest rates do not preserve the shape of the yield curve.

Bierwag, Kaufman, Schweitzer, and Toevs empirically examined how duration strategies based on more complex duration measures assuming different yield curve shifts would perform compared to Macaulay duration. They concluded that Macaulay duration "immunized almost as well as the more complex [duration] strategies and appear to be the most cost effective."[11] Lau reached the same conclusion—Macaulay duration is just about as effective as the more complex duration measures.

Since there are many Macaulay duration–matched portfolios that can be constructed to immunize a liability, is it possible to construct one that has the lowest risk of not realizing the target yield? That is, in light of the uncertain way in which the yield curve may shift, is it possible to develop a criterion for minimizing the risk that a Macaulay duration–matched portfolio will not be immunized? Fong

---

[9]Patrick W. Lau, "An Empirical Examination of Alternative Interest Rate Immunization Strategies," unpublished doctoral dissertation, University of Wisconsin at Madison, 1983.

[10]Martin L. Leibowitz and Alfred Weinberger, "Contingent Immunization—Part II: Problem Areas," *Financial Analysts Journal*, January-February 1983, pp. 35–50.

[11]Bierwag, Kaufman, Schweitzer, and Toevs, "The Art of Risk Management in Bond Portfolios," p. 33.

and Vasicek[12] and Bierwag, Kaufman, and Toevs[13] have explored this question. Exhibit 14.8 graphically illustrates how to minimize immunization risk.

EXHIBIT 14.7   Yield Curve Shifts

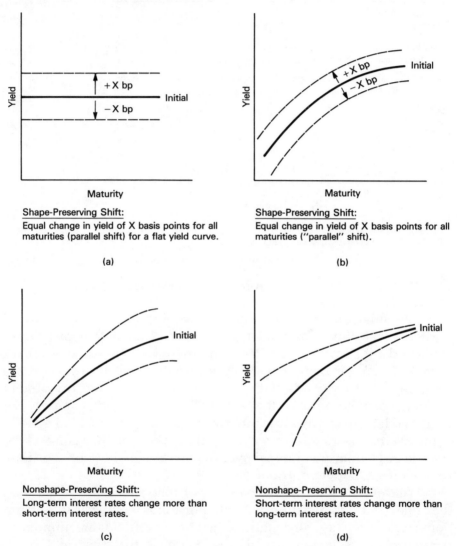

Shape-Preserving Shift:
Equal change in yield of X basis points for all maturities (parallel shift) for a flat yield curve.

(a)

Shape-Preserving Shift:
Equal change in yield of X basis points for all maturities ("parallel" shift).

(b)

Nonshape-Preserving Shift:
Long-term interest rates change more than short-term interest rates.

(c)

Nonshape-Preserving Shift:
Short-term interest rates change more than long-term interest rates.

(d)

[12]H. Gifford Fong and Oldrich Vasicek, "A Risk Minimizing Strategy for Multiple Liability Immunization," *Journal of Finance,* December 1984, pp. 1541–1546.

[13]G. O. Bierwag, George K. Kaufman, and Alden Toevs, "Bond Immunization and Stochastic Process Risk," working paper, Center for Capital Market Research, University of Oregon, July 1981.

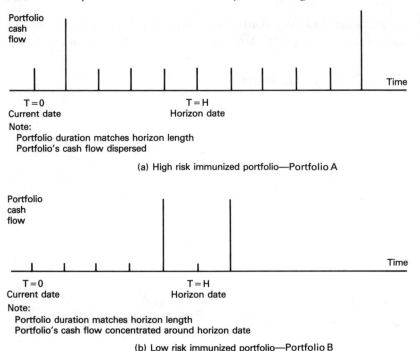

(a) High risk immunized portfolio—Portfolio A

(b) Low risk immunized portfolio—Portfolio B

EXHIBIT 14.8   Illustration of Immunization Risk Measure

The spikes in the two panels of Exhibit 14.8 represent actual portfolio cash flows. The taller spikes depict the actual cash flows generated by securities that have matured, and the smaller spikes represent coupon payments. Both Portfolio A and Portfolio B are composed of two bonds with a duration equal to the investment horizon. Portfolio A is, in effect, a barbell portfolio—one composed of short and long maturities and interim coupon payments. For Portfolio B, the two bonds mature very close to the investment horizon and the coupon payments are nominal over the investment horizon. Portfolio B is, in effect, a bullet portfolio.

We can now see why the barbell portfolio should be riskier than the bullet portfolio. Assume that both portfolios have Macaulay durations equal to the horizon length, so that both portfolios are immune to parallel changes in the yield curve. Suppose that the yield curve changes in a nonparallel way so that short-term interest rates decline while long-term interest rates increase. Both portfolios would then produce an accumulated value at the end of the investment horizon that is below the target accumulated value, since they would experience a capital loss owing to the higher long-term interest rate and a lower interest-on-interest resulting from a lower reinvestment rate when the short-term interest rate declines. The accumulated value for the barbell portfolio at the end of the investment horizon, however, would miss the target accumulated value by more than the bullet portfolio. There are two reasons for this. First, the lower reinvestment rates are experienced on the barbell portfolio for larger interim cash flows over a longer time period than on the bullet portfolio. Second, the portion of the barbell portfolio still outstanding at the end of the investment horizon is much longer than the maturity of the bullet portfolio, resulting in a greater capital loss for the barbell compared to the bullet. Thus the bullet portfolio has less risk exposure than the barbell portfolio to any changes in the interest rate structure that might occur.

What should be evident from this analysis is that immunization risk is the risk of reinvestment. The portfolio that has the least reinvestment risk will have the least immunization risk. When there is a high dispersion of cash flows around the investment horizon date, the portfolio is exposed to high reinvestment risk. When the cash flows are concentrated around the investment horizon date, as in the case of the bullet portfolio, the portfolio is subject to low reinvestment risk.

Fong and Vasicek have developed a measure of immunization risk. They have demonstrated that if the yield curve shifts in any arbitrary way, the relative change in the portfolio value will depend on the product of two terms. The first term depends solely on the characteristics of the investment portfolio. The second term is a function of interest rate movement only. The second term characterizes the nature of the change in the shape of the yield curve. Since that change will be impossible to predict *a priori*, it is not possible to control for it. However, the first term can be controlled for when constructing the immunized portfolio since it depends solely on the composition of the portfolio. This first term is, then, a measure of risk for immunized portfolios, and is:

$$\frac{\dfrac{CF_1(1-H)^2}{(1+y)^1} + \dfrac{CF_2(2-H)^2}{(1+y)^2} + \ldots + \dfrac{CF_n(n-H)^n}{(1+y)^n}}{\text{Initial investment value of the portfolio}}$$

where

CF_t = the cash flow of the portfolio at time period t
y = yield for the portfolio
H = length of the investment horizon
n = the time to receipt of the last cash flow

The immunization risk measure agrees with our earlier graphic analysis of the relative risk associated with a barbell and a bullet portfolio. For the barbell portfolio (Portfolio A in Exhibit 14.8), the portfolio's cash flow payments are widely dispersed in time and the immunization risk measure would be high. The portfolio cash flow payments for the bullet portfolio (Portfolio B in Exhibit 14.8) are close to the investment horizon so the immunization risk measure is low. Notice that if all the cash flows are received at the investment horizon, the immunization risk measure is zero. In such a case, the portfolio is equivalent to a pure discount security (zero-coupon security) that matures on the investment horizon date. If a portfolio can be constructed that replicates a pure discount security maturing on the investment horizon date, that portfolio will be the one with the lowest immunization risk. Typically, however, it is not possible to construct such an ideal portfolio.

The objective in constructing an immunized portfolio, then, is to match the Macaulay duration of the portfolio to the investment horizon and select the portfolio that minimizes the immunization risk. The immunization risk measure can be used to construct approximate confidence intervals for the target yield and the target accumulated value.

Zero-Coupon Bonds and Immunization

So far we have dealt with coupon bonds. An alternative approach to immunizing a portfolio against changes in the market yield is to invest in zero-coupon bonds with a maturity equal to the investment horizon. This is consistent with the basic principle of immunization since the Macaulay duration of a zero-coupon bond is its maturity. However, in practice, the yield on zero-coupon bonds is typically lower than the yield on coupon bonds. Thus using zero-coupon bonds to fund a bullet liability requires more funds since a lower target yield (equal to the yield on the zero-coupon bond) is being locked in.

Suppose, for example, that a portfolio manager must invest funds to satisfy a known liability of $20 million 5 years from now. If a target yield of 10% on a bond-equivalent basis (5% every 6 months) can be locked in using zero-coupon Treasury bonds, the funds necessary to satisfy the $20 million liability will be the present value of $20 million using a discount rate of 10%:

$$\frac{\$20,000,000}{(1.05)^{10}} = \$12,278,260$$

Suppose, instead, that by using coupon Treasury securities, a target yield of 10.3% on a bond-equivalent basis (5.15% every 6 months) is possible. Then the funds needed to satisfy the $20 million liability will be:

$$\frac{\$20,000,000}{(1.0515)^{10}} = \$12,104,240$$

Thus a target yield higher by 30 basis points would reduce the cost of funding the $20 million by $174,020 ($12,278,260 – $12,104,240). But the reduced cost comes at a price—the risk that the target yield will not be achieved.

Credit Risk and the Target Yield

The target yield may not be achieved if any of the bonds in the portfolio default or decrease in value due to credit quality deterioration. Restricting the universe of bonds that may be used in constructing an immunized portfolio to Treasury securities eliminates default risk. However, the target yield that can be achieved will be lower than that for bonds with credit risk, so that the cost of funding a liability would be increased.

In most immunization applications the client specifies an acceptable level of credit risk. Issues selected for the immunized portfolio are then restricted to those with that quality rating or higher. The greater the credit risk the client is willing to accept, the higher is the achievable target yield, but the greater is the risk that the immunized portfolio will fail to meet that target yield because of defaulted or downgraded issues.

Once the minimum credit risk is specified and the immunized portfolio is constructed, the portfolio manager must then monitor the individual issues for possible decreases in credit quality. Should an issue be downgraded below the minimum quality rating, that issue must be sold or the acceptable level of risk changed.

Call Risk

When the universe of acceptable issues includes corporate bonds, the target yield may be jeopardized if a callable issue is included and is subsequently called. Call risk can be avoided by restricting the universe of acceptable bonds to noncallable bonds and deep-discount callable bonds. This strategy does not come without a cost. Because noncallable and deep-discount bonds offer lower yields in a low-interest-rate environment, restricting the universe to these securities reduces the achievable target yield and therefore increases the cost of funding a liability. Also, it may be difficult to find acceptable noncallable bonds.

An immunized portfolio that includes callable bond issues must be carefully monitored so that issues likely to be called are sold and replaced with bond issues that have a lower probability of being called.

Constructing the Immunized Portfolio

Once the universe of acceptable issues is established and any constraints are imposed, the portfolio manager has a large number of possible portfolios out of which to construct an initial immunized portfolio and from which to select to rebalance an immunized portfolio. An objective function can be specified, and a portfolio that optimizes the objective function using mathematical programming tools can be determined. A common objective function, given the risk of immunization discussed earlier, is to miminize the immunization risk measure.[14]

---

[14]For a discussion of alternative objective functions, see H. Gifford Fong and Frank J. Fabozzi, *Fixed Income Portfolio Management* (Homewood, IL: Dow Jones-Irwin, 1985), Chap. 6; Peter C. Christensen and Frank J. Fabozzi, "Bond Immunization: An Asset Liability Optimization Strategy," Chap. 31 in Frank J. Fabozzi and Irving M. Pollack, eds., *The Handbook of Fixed Income Securities* (Homewood, IL: Dow Jones-Irwin, 1987); and Peter C. Christensen and Frank J. Fabozzi, "Dedicated Bond Portfolios," Chap. 32 in *The Handbook of Fixed Income Securities*.

Contingent Immunization

Contingent immunization is a strategy that consists of identifying both the available immunization target rate and a lower safety net level return with which the investor would be minimally satisfied. The money manager pursues an active portfolio strategy until an adverse investment experience drives the then-available potential return—the combined active return from actual past experience and immunized return from expected future experience—down to the safety net level. When that point is reached, the money manager is obligated to completely immunize the portfolio and lock in the safety net level return.

To illustrate this strategy, suppose that a client investing $50 million is willing to accept a 10% rate of return over a 4-year planning horizon at a time when a possible immunized rate of return is 12%. The 10% return is called the *safety net return*. The difference between the immunized return and the safety net return is called the *safety cushion*. In our example, the safety cushion is 200 basis points (12% minus 10%).

Since the initial portfolio value is $50 million, the *minimum* target value at the end of 4 years, based on semiannual compounding is:

$$\$50,000,000 \ (1.05)^8 = \$73,872,772$$

Since the rate of return at the time is 12%, the assets required at this time to achieve the minimum target value of $73,872,772 is the present value discounted at 12% on a semiannual basis; that is:

$$\frac{\$73,872,772}{(1.06)^8} = \$43,348,691$$

Therefore the safety cushion of 200 basis points translates into an initial *dollar safety margin* of $6,651,309 ($50,000,000 − $43,348,691). Had the safety net rate of return been 11% instead of 10%, the safety cushion would have been 100 basis points and the initial dollar safety margin $1,855,935. As can be seen, the smaller the safety cushion, the smaller the dollar safety margin.

The money manager initially pursues an active portfolio strategy within the contingent immunization strategy. Suppose that the money manager placed all of the funds into a 20-year, 12% coupon bond selling at par to yield 12%. Let's look at what happens if the market yield falls to 9% at the end of 6 months. The value of the portfolio at the end of 6 months would consist of:

Price of the 19.5-year, 12% coupon bonds at a 9% market yield
6 months' coupon interest

The price of the bond would increase from 100 to 127.34, so that the price of $50 million of these bonds would rise to $63.67 million. Coupon interest is $3 million (.50×.12×$50 million). Thus the portfolio value at the end of 6 months is $66.67 million. How much would be necessary to achieve the minimum target return of $73,872,772 if a portfolio can be immunized at the current interest rate of 9%? The required dollar value is found by computing the present value of the minimum target return at 9% for 3.5 years. The required dollar amount is:

$$\frac{\$73,872,772}{(1.045)^7} = \$54,283,888$$

The portfolio value of $66.67 million is greater than the required portfolio value of $54,283,888. The money manager can therefore continue to actively manage the portfolio. The dollar safety margin is now $12,386,112 ($66,670,000 − $54,283,888). As long as the dollar safety margin is positive (that is, the portfolio value is greater than the required portfolio value to achieve the minimum target value at the prevailing interest rate), the portfolio is actively managed.

Suppose that instead of declining to 9% in 6 months, interest rates rose to 14.26%. The market value of the bonds would decline to $42,615,776. The portfolio value would then equal $45,615,776 (the market value of the bonds plus $3 million of coupon interest). The required dollar amount to achieve the minimum target value of $73,872,772 at the current interest rate (14.26%) would be:

$$\frac{\$73,872,772}{(1.0713)^7} = \$45,614,893$$

The required dollar amount is approximately equal to the portfolio value (that is, the dollar safety margin is almost zero). Thus the money manager would be required to immunize the portfolio in order to achieve the minimum target value (safety net return) over the investment horizon.

The three key factors in implementing a contingent immunization strategy are: (1) establishing accurate immunized initial and ongoing available target returns; (2) identifying a suitable and immunizable safety net return; and (3) designing an effective monitoring procedure to ensure that the safety net return is not violated.

STRUCTURING A PORTFOLIO TO SATISFY MULTIPLE LIABILITIES

Thus far we have discussed immunizing a single liability. For pension funds, there are multiple liabilities that must be satisfied—payments to the beneficiaries of the pension fund. A stream of liabilities must also be satisfied for a life insurance company that sells an insurance policy requiring multiple payments to policyholders, such as an annuity policy. There are two strategies that can be used to satisfy a liability stream: (1) multiperiod immunization; and (2) cash flow matching.

Multiperiod Immunization

A portfolio is immunized if there is sufficient cash flow to satisfy all liabilities even if interest rates change. Even if there is a parallel shift in the yield curve, Bierwag, Kaufman, and Toevs demonstrate that matching the duration of the portfolio to the duration of the liabilities is not a sufficient condition to immunize a portfolio seeking to satisfy a liability stream.[15] Instead, it is necessary to decompose the portfolio payment stream in such a way that each liability is immunized by one of the component streams. The key to understanding their approach is recognizing that the payment stream on the portfolio, not the portfolio itself, must be decomposed in this manner. There may be no actual bonds that would give the component payment stream.

In the special case of a parallel shift of the yield curve, Fong and Vasicek demonstrate the conditions that must be satisfied to assure the immunization of multiple liabilities.[16] The necessary and sufficient

---

[15]G. O. Bierwag, George K. Kaufman, and Alden Toevs, "Immunization Strategies for Funding Multiple Liabilities," *Journal of Financial and Quantitative Analysis*, March 1983, pp. 113–124.

[16]Fong and Vasicek, "A Risk Minimizing Strategy for Multiple Liability Immunization."

conditions are: (1) the portfolio's duration must equal the duration of the liabilities; (2) the distribution of durations of individual portfolio assets must have a wider range than the distribution of the liabilities;[17] and (3) the present value of the cash flow from the bond portfolio must equal the present value of the liability stream.

However, these conditions will immunize only in the case of a parallel shift in the yield curve. To cope with the problem of failure to immunize because of nonparallel shifts in the yield curve, Fong and Vasicek generalize the immunization risk measure for a single liability discussed earlier in this chapter to the multiple liability case. An optimal immunization strategy is to minimize this immunization risk measure subject to the three constraints discussed (duration, dispersion of assets and liabilities, and equality of present value of asset cash flow and liability stream), as well as any other constraints that a client may impose.

Cash Flow Matching

An alternative to multiperiod immunization is cash flow matching. The approach, also referred to as *dedicating a portfolio,* can be summarized as follows. A bond is selected with a maturity that matches the last liability stream. An amount of principal equal to the amount of the last liability is then invested in this bond. The remaining elements of the liability stream are then reduced by the coupon payments on this bond, and another bond is chosen for the new, reduced amount of the next-to-last liability. Going backward in time, this cash flow matching process is continued until all liabilities have been matched by the payment of the securities in the portfolio.

Exhibit 14.9 provides a simple illustration of this process for a 5-year liability stream. Linear programming techniques can be employed to construct a least-cost cash flow matching portfolio from an acceptable universe of bonds.

The differences between the cash flow matching and multiperiod immunization strategies should be understood. First, unlike the

---

[17]The reason for the second condition can be illustrated with the following example. Suppose that a liability stream with 10 payments of $5 million each year is funded with a zero-coupon bond with a maturity (duration) equal to the duration of the liability stream. Suppose also that when the first $5 million payment is due, interest rates rise so that the value of the zero-coupon bond falls. Even though interest rates have increased, there is no offset to reinvestment income because the bond is a zero-coupon bond. Thus there is no assurance that the portfolio will generate sufficient cash flow to satisfy the remaining liabilities. In the case of a single liability, the second condition is automatically satisfied.

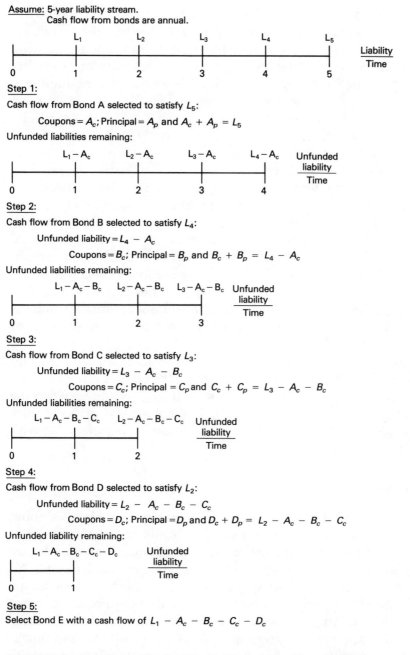

Assume: 5-year liability stream.
Cash flow from bonds are annual.

Step 1:

Cash flow from Bond A selected to satisfy L_5:

Coupons $= A_c$; Principal $= A_p$ and $A_c + A_p = L_5$

Unfunded liabilities remaining:

Step 2:

Cash flow from Bond B selected to satisfy L_4:

Unfunded liability $= L_4 - A_c$

Coupons $= B_c$; Principal $= B_p$ and $B_c + B_p = L_4 - A_c$

Unfunded liabilities remaining:

Step 3:

Cash flow from Bond C selected to satisfy L_3:

Unfunded liability $= L_3 - A_c - B_c$

Coupons $= C_c$; Principal $= C_p$ and $C_c + C_p = L_3 - A_c - B_c$

Unfunded liabilities remaining:

Step 4:

Cash flow from Bond D selected to satisfy L_2:

Unfunded liability $= L_2 - A_c - B_c - C_c$

Coupons $= D_c$; Principal $= D_p$ and $D_c + D_p = L_2 - A_c - B_c - C_c$

Unfunded liability remaining:

Step 5:

Select Bond E with a cash flow of $L_1 - A_c - B_c - C_c - D_c$

EXHIBIT 14.9   Illustration of Cash Flow Matching Process

immunization approach, the cash flow matching approach has no duration requirements. Second, with immunization, rebalancing is required even if interest rates do not change. In contrast, no rebalancing is necessary for cash flow matching except to delete and replace any issue whose quality rating has declined below an acceptable level. Third, there is no risk that the liabilities will not be satisfied (barring any defaults) with a cash-flow-matched portfolio. For a portfolio constructed using multiperiod immunization, there is immunization risk due to reinvestment risk.

The differences just cited may seem to favor the use of cash flow matching. However, what we have ignored is the relative cost of the two strategies. Using the cost of the initial portfolio as an evaluation measure, Gifford Fong Associates has found that cash-flow-matched portfolios, using a universe of corporate bonds rated at least double A, cost from 3% to 7% more in dollar terms than multiperiod immunized portfolios. The reason cash flow matching is more expensive is that, typically, the matching of cash flows to liabilities is not perfect. This means that more funds than necessary must be set aside to match the liabilities. Optimization techniques used to design cash-flow-matched portfolios assume that excess funds are reinvested at a conservative reinvestment rate. With multiperiod immunization, all reinvestment returns are assumed to be locked in at a higher target rate of return. Therefore money managers face a trade-off in deciding between the two strategies: the avoidance of the risk of not satisfying the liability stream under cash flow matching versus the lower cost attainable with multiperiod immunization.

SUMMARY

This chapter showed that liability funding strategies involve designing a portfolio that will produce sufficient funds to satisfy liabilities whether or not interest rates change. When there is only one future liability to be funded, an immunization strategy can be used. An immunization strategy is designed so that as interest rates change, interest rate risk and reinvestment risk will offset each other in such a way that the minimum cumulative value (or minimum rate of return) becomes the target cumulative value (or target yield). An immunization strategy requires that a money manager create a bond portfolio with a duration equal to the investment horizon. Because immunization theory is based on parallel shifts in the yield curve, the risk is that a portfolio will not be immunized even if the duration-matching condition is satisfied. Immunization risk can be quantified so that a portfolio that minimizes this risk can be constructed.

One form of immunization is contingent immunization. This strategy allows the money manager who is willing to accept a return lower than the prevailing return to actively manage the portfolio. The money manager can continue to actively manage the portfolio until the current value of the portfolio is just sufficient to generate the minimum target cumulative value when immunized at the prevailing market yield. At that point the money manager will immunize the portfolio.

When there are multiple liabilities to be satisfied, either multiperiod immunization or cash-flow-matching can be used. Multiperiod immunization is a duration-matching strategy that exposes the portfolio to immunization risk. The cash flow matching strategy does not impose any duration requirement. While the only risk that the liabilities will not be satisfied is that issues will be called or will default, the dollar cost of a cash-flow-matched portfolio may be higher than that of a portfolio constructed using a multiperiod immunization strategy.

INDEX